LEARNING UNLIMITED

TRANSFORMING LEARNING
IN THE WORKPLACE

2ND EDITION

ALASTAIR RYLATT

First edition published in Australia by Business + Publishing in 1994
Second edition 2001

First published in Great Britain by Kogan Page in 2001

Kogan Page Limited
120 Pentonville Road
London N1 9JN
N1 9JN

Stylus Publishing Inc.
22883 Quicksilver Drive
Sterling
VA 20166-2012

British Library Cataloguing in Publication Data
A CIP record for this book is available from the British Library.
ISBN 0 7494 3544 5

Typeset by Saxon Graphics Ltd, Derby
Printed and bound in Great Britain by Clays Ltd, St Ives plc

Contents

Contents

Contents

Preface

WHY I WROTE THIS BOOK

The priceless value of learning is just as important at the beginning of the 21st century as it was thousands of years ago when humankind first walked our planet. Learning is fundamental to life and living. The ability to learn gives all living creatures the confidence, choices and skills that no other experience can provide. Furthermore, the opportunity to learn is a precious gift that gives us the chance to expand our capabilities, so that we can live a better existence and achieve our dreams.

In the modern digital society, learning plays a fundamental role in helping us to deal with the challenges we face. We need only look at the expansion in knowledge work and the pressures of doing business to understand that keeping up to date and employable is vital if we are to survive and thrive in our daily work. Whether we work in a corporate enterprise, a community group, a government body, or a small business, our ability to retain our talent and capture wisdom is integral to our survival.

For individuals, the message is the same. Whether you are a full-time employee, subcontractor, self-employed or are seeking a new career, a desire to learn is the life force that helps us to maintain a meaningful and rewarding working life.

This leads me to the fundamental purpose of *Learning Unlimited* – to provide individuals and business organisations of all persuasions with timeless and universal advice on how to meet these learning challenges in a smart and effective way – in a way that increases the chances of helping people achieve greater meaning, joy and enlightenment in what they are doing.

For *Learning Unlimited* to meet this challenge, there needs to be a major rethink of how the learning process is viewed and interpreted. The word 'transformation' has been deliberately chosen to highlight that better learning will occur only when workplaces and their people are committed to implementing strategies and techniques that support discovery, innovation and renewal. In essence, for better learning to occur, workplaces need to be able to transform from a culture that sponsors isolated and fragmented learning to one that radiates empowered and never-ending discovery and inquiry in every aspect of organisational activity. It is only then that workplaces will have the flexibility and know-how to meet their challenges successfully. This, of course, takes imagination, knowledge and resilience.

Since becoming interested in workplace learning in the early 1980s, I have come to realise that general advice on transforming it is very fragmented and disjointed. Different schools of thought often seek to push their own jargon and understanding of the world without first understanding each other. As a result, we end up with a mismatch of strategies, terminology and ideals – and line managers, employees or team leaders are given the task of improving workplace learning without having access to the right information and advice to help them confront their challenges. *Learning Unlimited* aims to bring some form of reunification to how best practice learning can be successfully implemented in a wider range of business situations.

Since publishing the first edition in 1994, the response to *Learning Unlimited* has given me enormous pleasure and satisfaction. Students and professionals worldwide have enjoyed its practicality and its timelessness. It is my wish that this second edition will continue this well into the future.

In the past decade so much has changed in how and what we learn. We only need to spend 10 minutes on the World Wide Web to understand that we have entered a totally new time zone of human evolution. Advances in technology and the better use of knowledge-based systems have meant a fundamental change in how learning and discovery occur. What could have taken weeks to discover in the past can now be found in just minutes. In practice, this means that the individual has far more resources at his or her fingertips than just six months ago. Counterbalancing the power of the digital age is the constant realisation that all the technology in the world will not make a scrap of difference if people do not have the time or desire to acquire, share and reflect on their knowledge. As has been clearly demonstrated for thousands of years, people need to connect and build on each others' ideas for any real transformation to occur.

SCOPE OF THIS BOOK

The goal of *Learning Unlimited* is to provide individuals with the tools, perspectives and strategies to improve learning within their workplace. Hence my practical and 'hands on' approach, which enables the reader to access a range of advice and insights. I have steered clear of listing case study after case study and have preferred to bring the lessons learnt to the surface rather than name-dropping organisation after organisation. However, when discussing high technology, some branding and links to the World Wide Web were necessary to fast-track quick and thoughtful implementation.

Similarly, it would be only right to mention a number of organisations and stories about them that have directly or indirectly influenced my thinking in recent years. These are Baxter World Trade Corporation, Center for Creative Leadership (US), BP, Andersen Consulting, Merck Sharp and Dohme, Penrith City Council, Lend Lease, Australian Quality Awards Ltd, City of Sydney, Centrelink, Hink Street School, Roche Products, Zurich Insurance and Vodafone.

FOR WHOM IS THIS BOOK WRITTEN?

The inclusive and expansive nature of *Learning Unlimited* means that the material should appeal to a broad range of people, including senior managers, team leaders, line managers, trainers, project managers, human resource professionals, total quality managers, change agents, trade union officials, students, academics, knowledge workers, information technology specialists and the self-employed – in other words, everyone!

STRUCTURE OF THIS BOOK

Learning Unlimited has been designed to assist the reader to select areas of relevance and to act on that advice. The book begins with an introduction that defines the term 'workplace learning' while also exploring the basic principles of the 'learning organisation' and how wisdom and knowledge can better be generated. Thereafter the material is structured in three distinct parts:

- **Part 1: Developing a true commitment to change** provides a necessary conceptual overview to transforming workplace learning within today's rapidly changing environment.
- **Part 2: Proven implementation strategies** contains 14 chapters of practical advice on how to transform learning in the workplace.
- **Part 3: Moving to action** offers a range of action-planning and review exercises to consolidate your thoughts and priorities and to help you to develop and implement a worthwhile and integrated strategy.

HOW TO USE THIS BOOK

Some of you may read *Learning Unlimited* from cover to cover, while others will focus on the main points, opting to read it like a newspaper. To assist readers with either reading style, the 20 chapters are each of approximately the same length. Each chapter opens with a quote significant to the material and a listing of five key principles arising out of the discussion, and finishes with a summary. Most chapters include diagrams and exercises to aid understanding. The style used is conversational, contemporary and relaxed and, where possible, stories, metaphors and analogies have been used to add clarity.

The structure of the material has attempted to follow a logical order but, given the interactive and synergistic nature of the topic, the sequencing is not that important. What is important is that the material is readily accessible to the reader.

ACKNOWLEDGEMENTS

Writing a book of this magnitude cannot be done unless you have intellectual and emotional support from a number of people. Covering such a wide range of topics has required me to seek advice from many people, without whom *Learning Unlimited* would not have been completed. I particularly would like to thank the following people for their invaluable contributions in the revised edition: Tim Noonan, Simon Boddy, Robert Coco from Business + Publishing, Norbert Vogel from Australian Quality Council, Kris Varma from Sydney Port Corporation, David Williams from Zurich Insurance and John Davies from TRAININGpoint.net.

Finally, I would like to thank the many hundreds of people who have supported my writing over the last five years. Also special thanks to my wonderful wife Elaine, my brother Andrew, and Hilda, Christopher, Mum, Peter Jenkyns, John Lizzio, and Berne Carrigan for their never-ending and unconditional love.

ABOUT THE AUTHOR

Alastair Rylatt, BBus, Grad Dip Employment Relations, FAITD, Associate Fellow of AHRI, AIMM and MASTD, is Director of Excel Human Resource Development, a consulting operation based in Sydney, Australia. He is acknowledged internationally as an inspiring presenter, expert strategist, career coach and award-winning author in workplace learning and change management.

Since the 1970s, Alastair has overseen and implemented many initiatives that have improved the adaptability of people to the frenzy of the modern workplace. He has completed more than 250 projects, which have involved 2,000 organisations of all shapes and sizes, including: Australian

Institute of Management, Coca Cola, General Sekiyu K K (Japan), Harlequin Mills & Boon, NSW Office of State Revenue, University of Sydney, Vodafone and Wagga Wagga Council.

The first edition of *Learning Unlimited*, published in 1994, has become a best seller. Alastair's other books are: *Navigating the Frenzied World of Work: The complete survival guide* (1997) and *Creating Training Miracles* (Prentice Hall Australia, 1995), which won best business book for Asia Pacific in the 1995 Financial Times/Booz Allen & Hamilton Awards.

Alastair would like to hear your reflections on this book. He can be contacted at:

e-mail: arylatt@ozemail.com.au
Workplace Learning Help Desk: http://www.excelhrd.aust.com/

*May you continue a journey of learning
that helps you to discover true meaning,
build a world of greater promise and hope,
have a good laugh, and live your dreams.*

Introduction

LEARNING: TOWARDS A BETTER FUTURE

Whatever your walk of life, the fast and chaotic pace of change is never too far away. It has become central to everything we do. There are certainly times when we need to step back and reflect on our achievements, but at some point we must take action to move ourselves and our businesses forward. To do this, we must take the lead and assume active responsibility for advancing our learning. (In a practical sense, this means shaping a strategy that helps us to work towards our goals, and taking action to achieve these goals.)

A commitment to learning requires a commitment to other things, including a desire to make a difference, being open to the discovery of new options, taking risks and being tolerant of the uncertainty of modern times. The days of predicability are gone. However, the journey need not be a difficult and constant struggle – modern change provides wonderful and exciting opportunities to make a difference and build a better future.

We are now living in a time where learning provides so much choice and promise in what we can do – at no time in human history has there been so much freedom to develop our skills and capabilities. The vast growth of the Internet has dramatically changed people's access to information and knowledge. Irrespective of economic or cultural circumstances, people are increasingly getting their rightful chance to learn and join in with communities of common interest, regardless of where they live and what they do. For those people who are employed within the more empowered companies and communities, the option of sharing knowledge is beginning to be seen as the smartest way of stimulating a higher level of awareness, empathy and mutual understanding. In this world, there is a greater chance that everyone wins through stronger partnership and co-operation.

Six months can be a lifetime in modern chaotic change. We can no longer rely on our current knowledge to keep us employed and marketable. If we are to contribute effectively and cope with new challenges, we must be constantly upgrading our skills and reinventing ourselves. Within the workplace, this means providing service with zeal, optimism and confidence.

Despite the pressure to develop solutions to cope with the demands of modern business, personal and professional growth must cover much more than just 'pure' survival skills. Learning must generate enthusiasm and vigour rather than fear and helplessness. Ultimately, the conviction that 'learning is for all' must be embraced if unlimited learning is to occur.

So what of 'transformed workplace learning'? Is it possible? Does it happen? Is there a set formula for substantially improving the level and quality of learning in all aspects of business? Or is this book subject to the same rhetoric and potential disappointments that often occur when individuals try to act on someone else's advice? To address these concerns, four questions need to be explored:

- What is a 'learning organisation'?
- What is 'workplace learning'?
- How does a process of transformation work?
- What strategies can be implemented that will drive the required change?

WHAT IS A LEARNING ORGANISATION?

A question that I am often asked is: 'Can you please define a learning organisation?' Many authors and professionals have tried to answer this question. Some notable examples include:

- Karen Watkins and Victoria Marsick (1993) in *Sculpting the Learning Organization* describe a learning organisation as a place that:

   ...empowers its people, integrates quality initiatives with quality of worklife, creates free space for learning, encourages collaboration and sharing the gains, promotes inquiry and creates continuous learning opportunities...Learning in learning organizations changes perceptions, behaviours, beliefs, mental models, strategies, policies and procedures in people and organizations.

- Michael Beck (1992) in an article, 'Learning Organisations: How to create them', defines a learning organisation as one that:

   ...facilitates learning and personal development for all its employees, while continually transforming itself.

However, it is my personal belief that the learning organisation has become too limited for today's approach to business. The term 'learning organisation' does not generate the imagery required to drive modern business growth and enlightenment. In practice, contemporary business strategy is about extending networks of co-operation and commitment between people who work within the operational centre of an organisation and those who work elsewhere. Whether they are in other workplaces, or are customers, trade unions, suppliers or the community at large, it is important to recognise that organisations are becoming increasingly seamless and global in nature. The modern workplace must now attract and engage a wider pool of talent within its core business operations in order to survive.

So, in considering the term 'learning organisation', *see it as a living and adaptive system that embraces change by building a community of understanding across multiple networks and realities, rather than relying on one corporate viewpoint or answer.*

What other qualities must a learning organisation have? According to Senge(1990, 1994), Marquardt and Reynolds (1994), McGill, Slocum Jr and Lei (1992), Slocum and Pitts (1999) and Argyris (1982), a learning organisation must demonstrate a commitment to each of the following principles in the workplace.

Building systems that output learning

Workplaces should actively modify their policies, structures and procedures to support discovery. Senge (1990) in his pathfinding book, *The Fifth Discipline,* sees 'systems thinking' as the main foundation stone for creating a learning organisation. Senge also makes the important acknowledgment that people need to recognise that systems often cause their own crises (that is, crises are not only caused by external forces or individual mistakes).

Sponsoring personal excellence

The learning organisation should encourage best practice innovation and self-management. The organisation and its employees work in partnership to support continuous improvement. Employees are actively encouraged to continually seek out and review their goals and visions in line with organisational priorities.

Creating new mental models

Learning organisations constantly question the assumptions and mindsets of their employees to ensure that truth, openness and innovation are championed at the expense of secrecy and politics. Improved performance and potential are achieved by people's willingness to share their mindsets and to state the assumptions and values on which they base their behaviour. This generates a spirit and love for learning that touches the heart and soul of every employee.

Moulding a shared vision

People within learning organisations learn and excel by being open and frank about the purpose and agendas of the organisation. This commitment to the core values of learning is displayed as an integral part of all vision, mission and planning processes. The employee-organisational relationship is seen as a synergistic partnership where all parties are listened to, consulted with, and have some freedom of choice. The power of this partnership is based on the principles of commitment, respect, integrity and the rapid transfer of knowledge.

Promoting teamwork

Learning organisations use teamwork as a high leverage strategy to stimulate growth and achievement. To achieve this, teams work hard to stamp out destructive behaviour that inhibits learning. The transition to greater team maturity and responsibility is an underlying behaviour of a learning organisation.

Perfecting 'dialogue'

One of the best indicators of a learning organisation is the way in which people resolve challenges. Instead of just solving short-term challenges and problems, the workforce focuses its energy on developing the skills and behaviours that help build a shared view of what is happening in a broader context. This is achieved by championing openness, systematic thinking, creativity, self-awareness and empathy. Sometimes called 'double loop' or action learning, it is also about helping people explore not only what they are doing, but why.

Considering, therefore, all the qualities of a learning organisation, it is apparent why the dream of the learning organisation has captured the imagination of so many people. Yet for many, the dream of the learning organisation has become a nightmare of false promises and unfulfilled action. In dealing with this frustration it is important to recognise that the real benefit is the discovery and knowledge that is created along the way.

Reading and hearing about testimonials of so-called best practice makes it easy to fall into the trap of believing that it is an easy or painless journey. If we concentrated more on getting the basics right (such as better communication, celebrating what you are doing right and treating people with respect), we would be far better placed to make a smooth transition to becoming a learning organisation. To undertake this transition, there needs to be an understanding of the three other key issues referred to earlier:

- What is meant by the term 'workplace learning'?
- How does the process of transformation take place?
- What strategies can be implemented that will drive the required change?

WHAT IS WORKPLACE LEARNING?

Workplace learning can be defined as *a sustained and high leverage development of people in line with organisational outcomes*. This definition has five implicit assumptions:

1. Organisations, of all forms, need to work towards achieving business improvement, and an improved capacity to accept and generate change. In saying this, business issues could include a wide range of issues such as customer service, total quality, reducing costs, better community consultation, better environmental controls and gain sharing.
2. It is no longer acceptable to see workplace learning as for full-time employees only. The process of building the learning capability of a business includes many fellow-travellers – subcontractors, joint venture partners, community representatives, customers, trade unions, suppliers and casual and part-time employees.
3. Workplace learning processes must seek and obtain a mutual understanding and acceptance of two sets of needs: the need of individuals to discover and achieve their own goals and meaning in life, combined with the need of the organisation to achieve better performance and potential. In saying this, it is anticipated that the worlds of the individual and the organisation may not see 'eye to eye' at times, but eventually the relationship must be a win-win one for the workplace learning process to succeed.
4. In using the term 'workplace learning' it is recognised that different jargon is often used to mean similar or dissimilar outcomes. For example, the phrases 'career development', 'training and development', and 'human resource development' are often substituted. The definition is not that important. What is important is the outcome: that best practice

learning and knowledge creation occurs in order to enhance employee and business capability. If that outcome occurs under another name, then that is fine.

5. Finally, workplace learning is much more than a training course or a single on-the-job activity. In its essence, workplace learning is an ongoing, never-ending, lifelong process that occurs in every aspect of organisational activity – from planning through to customer delivery.

HOW DOES A PROCESS OF TRANSFORMATION WORK?

Given this definition of workplace learning, how does an organisation, team or individual go about initiating the necessary transformation to become a learning organisation? The first step is to understand the process of transformation. The second is to install a mechanism that will allow the workplace learning process to operate at an optimum level.

To explain how the transformation process takes place, I will share a framework that I have used and adapted over the past decade. The origin of this framework was a group discussion at university in the early 1980s. For me, the principles of this transformation framework are as applicable today as they were then.

The process of transformation can be seen to involve four main variables, each seeking to *empower*, rather than impose change. The variables are:

- Dissatisfaction with the status quo (D).
- Clear vision of the future (V).
- Knowledge and self-awareness (K).
- Belief in one's ability to change (B).

To use this framework successfully it is useful to apply the following formula:

Transformation $(T) = (D + V + K) \times B$

Explaining transformation as a mathematical formula allows us to see the interconnected and flexible nature of the process. For me, it has been useful to picture the formula as if it were four pulleys on a window blind facing the sunny side of a house. Depending on the time of the day, you will need to adjust the light by lengthening and shortening the four pulleys on the blind. There is no 'set adjustment' to the blind. You will need to constantly review and update the light intensity. Like the analogy of a window blind, the four variables of the transformation formula will need to be adjusted and used as needed. For example, there are times when only one pulley will be used, while on other occasions all four variables may be required in symphony. You will notice, however, that one variable (B) has a bigger influence and this will be explained as the discussion unfolds.

Each of the variables is now examined, followed by a number of prompting questions that may assist in using the framework within any workplace.

Dissatisfaction with the status quo (D)

The desire to change can often originate from a desire to change an undesirable situation. Having people express their displeasure at the status quo can be enough to bring about a change. Questions that can assist this process include:

- How would you 'sum up' the current situation?
- What would be the advantages and disadvantages of changing the current situation?
- What impact is the current situation having on you personally, the team or the organisation and your relationships?
- How long do you wish to continue in the current situation before you take action?
- What knowledge or evidence do you need of the change?

Clear vision of the future (V)

While focusing your energy on dissatisfaction with the status quo may help bring about transformation, it may not be sufficient. It may be necessary to move the agenda or discussion to one where new possibilities of a different and better situation of the future are explored. People need to create a clearer picture of the future before they can initiate a transformation process. The clearer and more tangible a future vision and core values, the better the chance that a transition will take place. Questions that can help create a clearer vision include:

- What would your perfect scenario be like?
- What would you see? What would you feel? What would you hear if you were successful in managing the change?
- What knowledge do you need to create your goal or vision?
- If you were successful in reaching your vision, what strategies and changes would you have made to get there?

Knowledge and self-awareness (K)

There may be a lack of knowledge about how, what and why a change is happening. This can include such issues as the nature, duration and rationale of the change, and the skills required to manage the period of transition. Examples of prompting questions include:

- What are the benefits of the change?
- Describe how you see this change affecting you.
- What role do you see yourself playing in this change?
- What skills, attitudes or behaviours may need to be developed or modified?
- What skills, attitudes or behaviours will not be required?

Belief in one's ability to change (B)

This final variable is particularly important. A person, a team or an organisation must firmly believe that they can change for a transformation to occur. This process of gaining self-confidence requires the clearing of 'wounded beliefs' and replacing them with more 'positive' and 'supportive' thoughts for concrete action. From experience, if this transformation does not occur, all the benefits achieved from other discussion may lead to no change. Belief in one's ability to change (B) is the multiplying factor that will most help someone take action. This means the role of assisting people to gain strength and resilience by supplying adequate resources, plus an opportunity to practise and use the new desired skills as quickly as possible, cannot be underestimated, particularly when people are often torn between accepting or resisting the change. Questions that can restore a positive belief are:

- Describe a past successful example of where you have changed.
- How did you go about changing?
- How did the successful completion of the change make you feel?
- What lessons can be learnt from this experience?
- What strengths do you have that can help you cope with and manage the change?
- What obstacles or issues are affecting your ability to change now?
- The fact that you explore what you need to do indicates that some part of you wants to take action. What are your reasons?
- What added support and resources do you need to help the change process?
- How and when did you arrive at the thought that you can't change?
- What evidence are you using to say that this thought is true?

WHAT STRATEGIES CAN BE IMPLEMENTED THAT WILL DRIVE THE REQUIRED CHANGE?

Having described some of the background and terminology to transforming workplace learning, the machinery required to make that change needs to be explored. For workplace learning to be transformed to a level that enhances business performance, three essential steps need to occur:

- true commitment to change;
- a quality consideration of a number of implementation strategies;
- a high-quality measurable action plan using the principles of best practice project management.

As represented in Figure 0.1, *Learning Unlimited* provides guidance and practical tips on all three parts of the workplace learning transformation process.

Part 1, 'Developing a true commitment to change', signatures the five basic concepts that enable an individual, a team or an organisation to begin the process of workplace learning transformation. These five concepts are:

- People must first understand and communicate the new mindsets to leverage learning in today's rapidly changing environment (Chapter 1).
- People need to provide the leadership and the sustainability to be a successful change agent (Chapter 2).
- All workplace and career trends must be respected and acknowledged (Chapter 3).
- Championing knowledge work and the creation of wisdom (Chapter 4).
- Adequate time and resources need to be invested to help people overcome learning challenges (Chapter 5).

Part 2 specifies how an organisation, team or individual can meet business challenges through effective implementation of the strategies listed in Figure 0.1. This listing represents best practices research and observation. To achieve a successful outcome there needs to be an understanding of the range, benefit and use of each strategy. No strategy in itself is superior to any other; each has its own advantages and disadvantages based on the need at the end. It is quite likely that any action will involve a combination of strategies. There are certainly no instant cures.

The primary aims of each chapter within Part 2 are:

- Chapter 6, 'Identifying and evaluating business requirements', provides ways to assist workplace learning. It also offers methods to

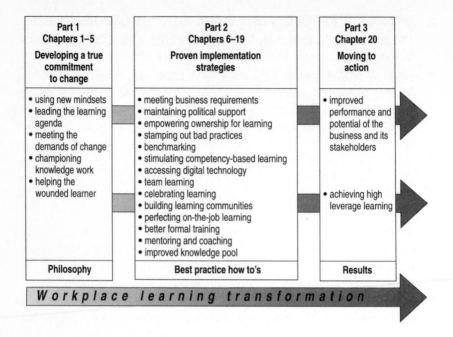

Figure 0.1 An overview of the strategies and techniques for transforming learning in the workplace

evaluate and quantify business improvement, and general strategies to stay wiser and more innovative.

■ Chapter 7, 'Gaining and maintaining political support', tackles the important issue of gaining and maintaining the endorsement of decision makers. This process is central to the success of workplace reform.

■ Chapter 8, 'Empowering ownership for learning', explores avenues to stimulate involvement of people in workplace learning. A number of practical options is included (for example, consultation mechanisms, developing a plan, performance management and redefinition of the training role).

■ Chapter 9, 'Stamping out practices that alienate learning', looks at how to improve the mix and quality of systems and behaviour that are at the 'nerve centre' of workplace discovery. This chapter contains a range of methods to stimulate higher levels of knowledge creation in your business practice.

■ Chapter 10, 'Benchmarking best practices', specifies a number of 'tried and true' methods of getting the best value out of this process. Great care is taken to provide an honest and practical overview of how to link benchmarking to workplace learning while exploring essential areas of integrity and ethics.

- Chapter 11, 'Stimulating competency-based learning', traverses this often misunderstood discipline by describing how competencies are best designed, assessed and linked to business activity.
- Chapter 12, 'Accessing digital technology for learning', gives an up-to-date picture of what is happening. Predictions for the future are made, while providing a checklist from which you can get the best value out of the advances of technology to foster better learning, knowledge management and innovation.
- Chapter 13, 'Embracing team learning', cements the view that teamwork is a very high leverage activity of workplace learning. The discussion focuses on how to promote better learning in all forms of teams. This will also enhance project-driven teamwork, where people are expected to support multiple challenges simultaneously.
- Chapter 14, 'Celebrating learning', details how the spirit that drives human energy can be activated. Central to this discussion of celebration is the skill of sharing the lessons learnt through story and metaphor.
- Chapter 15, 'Building a learning community', provides tips on how partnerships and fellow-travellers can first be found and then sustained to manage your business and thinking. Apart from exercises assisting your capacity to locate key people to assist your business, much of the discussion centres on how to sustain universal commitment and enthusiasm for learning.
- Chapter 16, 'Perfecting on-the-job learning', begins with an important examination of how the motivation of the learner can be identified. A series of models is then disclosed that increase on-the-job personal growth, effectiveness and action learning.
- Chapter 17, 'Getting results from training', explores a number of practical ideas on how to identify, design, deliver and assess high-quality off-the-job learning. This will encompass trends such as distance education and self-directed learning.
- Chapter 18, 'Promoting mentoring and coaching', highlights the critical role that mentoring and coaching play in the quality of workplace learning. A number of strategies are shared on how to get the most impact from both of these endemic processes.
- Chapter 19, 'Revitalising and expanding your knowledge pool', takes a strategic look at the management of people who make up an 'organisational business brain'. Key areas of opportunity include telecommuting, skill retention, implementing flexible working practices and virtual teams.

Having completed Part 2, Part 3, 'Moving to action', offers 'a smorgasbord of action-planning activities' to assist with the implementation of ideas and strategies.

11

PART I

Developing A True Commitment To Change

Many hours can be spent designing, delivering and evaluating workplace learning activities. However, this time can be wasted if key decision makers are not interested in, curious about and supportive of the process.

Developing true commitment to reform is the 'fuel' that drives the combustion of the workplace learning engine. Without this 'fuel', the engine will slow down and eventually stop.

The ongoing challenge confronting all industries is securing a true commitment to change by convincing individuals, teams and organisations that workplace learning is important to their future. To do this requires an excellent understanding of a number of diverse and important issues.

The finesse of developing true commitment lies in the capacity to ask the right questions, and identify and share powerful knowledge so that people are constantly engaged and interested in change. It is only then that a new beginning or a resurgence of workplace learning can occur.

The next five chapters provide an overview of the key areas that are part and parcel of gaining commitment to change.

1

New Mindsets For Workplace Learning

> *You cannot be a learning organisation unless you are an unlearning organisation.*
>
> Jay Kulkarni

KEY PRINCIPLES

- Business requires lateral thinking, intense co-operation and sharing of knowledge.
- Learning requires well-integrated design, delivery and assessment.
- Modern change requires a trusting and boundaryless attitude to learning.
- Identifying meaningful competencies is a vital business strategy.
- Workplace learning must focus on the 'whole person'.

UNLEASHING OUR TRUE POTENTIAL

There comes a time in the life of any workplace when it must come clean, and decide whether it is genuinely interested in developing the true capacity of its people. In many organisations this decision has already been resolved, either in the affirmative or in the negative.

If the answer is in the affirmative, the organisation then must determine whether existing policies, systems and activities are supporting or inhibiting workplace learning. If, on the other hand, the organisation has avoided workplace learning, the question then becomes: Is it time to change? This question is best determined by asking: Is the absence of support for workplace learning hurting the business?

Curiously, given this pendulum of possible affirmative and negative replies, I have yet to meet one manager or team leader who would say, outright, that they do not want their people to learn. However, many of them have done just that, going out of their way to frustrate the workplace learning process.

The rationale for such destructive behaviour has never been clearly explained to me, but my guess is that the answer lies within the words 'power' and 'control', manifesting itself in people hoarding or withholding vital information for personal gain. Many organisations have built-in incentives and systems that fail to support better sharing and accountability for learning in the workplace. Many people have developed their skills on the premise that knowledge is to be protected rather than shared. This leads to the creation of decision-making, corporate communication and digital technology systems that are (at best) sluggish in meeting the new demands and pressures being faced.

Such paternalistic behaviour is particularly evident when people feel under some personal form of threat or change. As a consequence, these people deliberately avoid investing time and energy in the development of others. In time their people become so repressed and alienated that, like their 'leaders', they suffer from being 'prisoners' to their own thinking. This is best characterised by people who see each new problem or challenge as another 'brick wall' rather than seeing it as a chance to learn something new. The folly of such an attitude becomes increasingly apparent in a modern business environment where lateral thinking, intense co-operation and scenario thinking are the behaviours that provide the 'kiss of life' of improved business performance.

Sadly, behaviour that stifles workplace learning has become so entrenched in some organisations that any form of enlightenment is out of the question.

NEW DOCTRINES TO INSPIRE TRANSFORMATION

Making the transition towards the acceptance of workplace learning is a challenging road and requires continuous injections of energy and resources to build capability, create interesting work and stimulate personal growth. If your organisation desires workplace learning that adds value it must follow a set of principles that helps make that happen. These doctrines or mindsets have the capacity to transform the growth and performance of the workforce by providing much-needed clarity and a sense of purpose to all actions, plans and strategies. The importance of clarity can be highlighted by pausing to consider the daily pressures that are placed on us during our normal working lives.

As I lay in bed this morning, I spent 20 minutes mapping out my day, including which bills I am going to pay and which credit cards I am going to use; how to transport myself across town to meet a friend for an appointment at 11 am; how I am going to schedule in my daily walk; the sort of breakfast I will have; which work assignment I will start first and when I will complete it; and which television programme I wish to videotape today. All this was considered before 6 am. After breakfast and a 30-minute walk, I sorted my mail, cleared my e-mail and answered telephone messages in my office. This activated a whole new set of decisions and priorities.

Coping with such pressures in modern society is a very demanding and yet necessary part of living. When we reflect on the pressures placed on us, it is easy to understand how people can become overwhelmed and try to escape wherever possible. As a close colleague once said, 'Do you realise that you make more decisions in one month than your great-grandparents made in their lifetime?'. Working in the area of transforming workplaces also generates its own added pressures. While we try to resolve our own life challenges we are also trying to cope with the enormity of the latest technological, environmental and societal trends.

Clearly, with all this happening we need a strategy to deal with the complexity of our lives. Principles can help guide us. Clear principles or mindsets allow us to firm up our actions while being 100 per cent clear about our intentions, our values and our assumptions. This is particularly critical in modern chaotic systems, where questioning and unfreezing the status quo and seeking connections of thought and strategy are central to sustaining a business advantage. Only then will we have the clarity and purpose to bring about positive change that is adaptive and self-generating.

Here are eight mindsets that are fundamental to the process of workplace learning transformation.

1: *Workplace learning must be greater than change*
In a world of such uncertainty the only safeguard is that learning must be greater than change. To meet this challenge, high leverage workplace learning processes must be selected and maintained. These processes must capture the right wisdom, muster the right resources and put ideas into action as quickly as possible. Leading strategies include: team learning; celebrating learning; harnessing the power of high technology; benchmarking best practices; championing resourceful learning; articulating workplace desire and stimulating formal and informal networking.

2: *Workplace learning must be systematic and interactive*

Figure 1.1 shows that the design, delivery and assessment of workplace learning must consider a wide number of inputs before business results, competency improvement and highly satisfied people can be achieved. If workplace learning inputs are not well planned and integrated, it is quite likely that undesired, avoidable and unplanned chaos will result.

Workplace learning is not only systematic but also highly interactive, as demonstrated by Figure 1.2, which uses the 'orange tree' as a metaphor to show why workplace learning needs constant nurturing and care if it is to bear healthy fruit. In the modern workplace this means having a careful blend of strategies, policies, programmes and resources. All workplaces will face their fair share of chaos, but having a systematic and interactive approach to workplace learning will certainly increase the capacity of the business to respond in a positive and enlightened fashion.

3: *Workplace learning must be geared to business outcomes*

Workplace learning outcomes must be linked to both the short-term and long-term business needs of the organisation. For this linkage to be strong and robust, all planning processes must totally understand and reflect vital social, economic, environmental and community issues. As the business activity is implemented, ongoing funding and sponsorship of workplace learning should only be guaranteed after demonstrable measurement of results.

The goal of workplace learning should be to bring about measurable improvements in performance, productivity, quality and

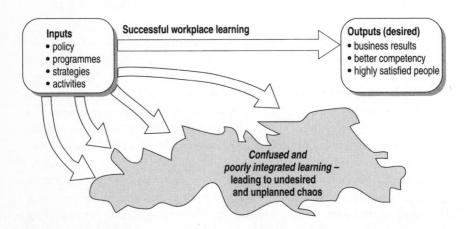

Figure 1.1 A systematic view of workplace learning

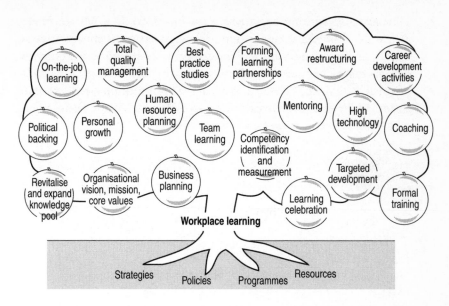

Figure 1.2 An interactive view of workplace learning

potential. Good workplace learning can only be achieved by the daily commitment of continuous improvement and innovation. It requires people who are not only interested in improving business performance but are also prepared to coach and inspire confidence in the ways the work is undertaken. Performance management systems should make it compulsory for team leaders, managers and decision makers to spend time and effort developing their workforce and key fellow-travellers.

4:   *Workplace learning must provide meaning, self-worth and sustenance*
In a world where the value of being part of a stable and supportive family and community is often being eroded, many citizens are looking to the world of work to provide some extra meaning, self-worth and sustenance in their lives. To offer this, workplace learning must focus on a wider range of issues. Traditional programmes that aim solely at technical and functional skills are too narrow to meet the demands of today's rapidly changing environment.

Programmes must explore broader areas, such as increasing self-esteem and building self-worth, in order to engage the true learning potential of employees. Coping with change requires a broad repertoire of skills, including conflict resolution, learning how to learn, and general life-skills management such as career planning, overcoming burnout and maintaining physical well-being. Workplace learning must now address the 'whole person' to be successful.

Workplace learning initiatives must be available to all employees and other contributors to the business. Whether it means making available an excellent online service on the Internet or conducting face-to-face seminars, modern change requires workplaces to approach learning with a trusting and boundaryless attitude. Resources need to be invested in the workplace to ensure that learning is seen as a normal part of everyday activity.

5: *Workplace learning must be learner-driven*

The ultimate goal of workplace learning should be to help each person develop a clearer understanding of his or her own true learning potential. Therefore, learning in the workplace should value the integrity of mental diversity in each person. With this commitment, people will be more likely to see learning as a joyful and beneficial experience that builds self-belief, no matter what happens and no matter how busy we are; taking the time and effort to invest in our learning is the best way to resolve challenges and open up opportunities.

Guiding people to take greater responsibility for their own learning can take significant time and effort, particularly when trust is low or where there is a lack of leadership within a business. No workplace can afford to take a 'wait and see' approach when it comes to learning. We must all take charge in undertaking whatever learning is necessary to get the job done, be it formally sponsored education, e-mailing someone to find out an answer or holding a personal conversation. We must all take the initiative when it comes to our personal and workplace learning.

6: *Workplace learning must be competency-based*

The identification, development and assessment of relevant and measurable competencies is central to the success of workplace learning reform in organisations, industries and nations. To reap the benefits of competency-based learning, organisations need to ensure that:

- The application of competencies is seen more widely than just as 'training'.
- Designing and stating competencies is seen as only half the battle and that the war is not won until learning outcomes are assessed and updated.
- Reproducing industry and best practice competencies and using these as the sole benchmark for workplace learning is avoided. This strategy may be wonderful for consistency but may not enhance actual business performance.

To gain the full benefits of competency-based learning, all desired knowledge, skills and attitudes must be tied to the unique business challenges confronting the organisation.

7: *Workplace learning must be 'just-in-time'*
Organisations now require workplaces to be accountable and manage
their learning 'just-in-time' or right now. To succeed, such learning
systems must be driven by a commitment to uphold the values of
collective intelligence, partnership and dialogue. This commonly
involves improving communication channels and opening up access
to corporate knowledge networks. Approaches include establishing
simple ground rules for respectful listening right through to regular
review and upkeep of an online helpdesk. This is particularly important given that workplaces are increasingly 'virtual' and dispersed,
and more and more work is being performed by people in different
time zones and places.

8: *Workplace learning must expand into new frontiers of knowledge*
The final barometer for the success of workplace learning is measured
by an organisation's capacity to mould a 'business brain' that traverses new frontiers of understanding while acknowledging the
lessons of the past.
   The threshold of knowledge is expanding to a point where organisations must see the management of the organisation 'business
brain' as a important part of business strategy. This includes
well-thought-out and flexible work practices that encourage
networking and discussions, with an unlimited array of resources
and conducts. Whether it is through an industry gathering, a joint
venture, an electronic mailing list on the Internet, people within
business need to be encouraged to search and share their wisdom
whenever possible.

People who work in the modern organisation can no longer accept formal,
insular and inert structures as the way of doing business. To survive in
chaotic times, the workplace must have structures that are flexible and
self-generating. They need to be free of controls and they must create
knowledge-based systems that are nurtured by cross-fertilisation,
networking and celebration. These key factors will stimulate a better
response to the unlimited opportunities of informal learning that occur
well outside 'formal' workplace learning systems and rituals.

SUMMARY

Before any organisation can consider transforming workplace learning, it
must engage in serious soul-searching about whether it wants to 'unleash
the true potential' of its people. If the enlightened approach of supporting
workplace learning has been actively chosen, the organisation must then

be prepared to 'call the bluff' of people whose actions do not match this intention.

The best way of cementing effective workplace learning is to follow the above eight principles or mindsets, which will allow the change process to unfold in the modern workplace. These mindsets are fundamental to the strategies discussed in *Learning Unlimited*.

2

Leadership And The Learning Agenda

> *Empowerment is the collective effect of leadership.*
> Warren Bennis

KEY PRINCIPLES

- Help people to stay calm and clear.
- Focus on the needs, vision, actions and results of change.
- Demonstrate a visible commitment to learning.
- A positive learning environment provides hope for the future.
- Invest in self-nurturing behaviour.

BEING A SUCCESSFUL CHANGE AGENT

Gaining sustained support for workplace learning takes tremendous resolve, resilience and leadership. Ultimately, our personal capacity to influence the agenda for change will dictate whether we are successful in bringing about positive reform and renewal.

The modern workplace needs people who not only complete tasks but are able to build trust and maintain relationships. Successful management of performance and change requires empathy and tolerance as well as commitment to results. Or, in other words, just because someone has commitment does not necessarily mean he or she will deliver the outcomes desired. Better change agents are sensitive to the fact that it is easy to become paralysed or smothered by the enormity of what needs to done. By keeping things simple and clear, and by helping other people to stay calm and centred, you will be taking huge strides towards being a successful change agent.

There are many other attributes that make a successful change agent. A change agent:

- takes responsibility for his or her actions, avoids blaming others and refrains from justifying his or her own behaviour to hide his or her role in the change process;
- actively listens and understands people's values, hopes and fears;
- has courage and is not afraid to lead 'up front' and to express an opinion;
- earns respect by being able to build joint outcomes between different viewpoints;
- is persistent and willing to 'chip away at the edges' to bring about change;
- is aware of his or her own strengths and develops mutually beneficial partnerships with others to compensate for his or her weaknesses;
- is passionate about overcoming obstacles;
- learns and shares information from a wide range of diverse sources;
- has high self-esteem and resilience;
- reads organisational politics astutely;
- is generous when success is achieved, acknowledging the contributions of other drivers of the change process.

THE KEY INGREDIENTS OF LEADERSHIP

In addition to understanding the traits of a successful change agent it is important to have leadership that is well considered, dynamic and flexible.

Work by Beckhard and Harris (1977), Kotter (1986), Leibowitz, Farren and Kaye (1986), Wheatley and Kellner-Rodgers (1996), de Geus (1997) and Theobald (1997) has helped reshape the role and style of leadership thinking within 21st century workplaces. Using their wisdom plus my own study in areas such as building learning communities (Rylatt, 1998b) and navigating the frenzied world of work (Rylatt, 1997), the following framework offers a way to use leadership to implement workplace learning initiatives. Similar in nature to the transformation model discussed in the introduction to this book, this adapted model provides the change agent with a dynamic way of implementing and inspiring change. It gives a powerful insight into why leadership must constantly evaluate and update its approach to staying abreast of trends and business challenges. The model is explored under the headings of needs assessment, vision, action and results.

Needs assessment

Before any organisational change or transition can occur there must be an excellent understanding of the beliefs, values and rituals driving existing behaviours and attitudes within an organisation. Care must be taken to avoid stereotyping or labelling organisational culture. Change agents must be flexible and responsive to people's fears, anxieties and dreams. The best way of guaranteeing this flexibility and responsiveness is to use a range of needs analysis techniques, including interviewing people for information, surveying views, feelings and skills, watching and measuring current performance, and reviewing the quality and output of current systems.

Having completed a well-researched needs assessment, change agents are then better able to:

- reflect an understanding of key stakeholders, customers and workforce;
- articulate clear values and reasons for reform;
- develop precise benchmark measures for success;
- determine how to better serve the needs of customers.

Alternatively, data collected from a needs assessment can provide ammunition to terminate a process entirely, or begin a renegotiation process that may lead to a reordering of priorities.

Vision

Envisioning change requires confident leadership, excellent design skills and the active involvement of a wide range of people. Communicating a good vision sets the scene and through active consultation engenders enthusiasm for a future that everyone can connect with, based on their own perceived reality. Developing a vision includes:

- describing a powerful picture of the future, based on a deep conviction and clearly embodying a desirable central purpose;
- showing how the workplace needs to change;
- unfreezing fixed attitudes that may be inhibiting positive change;
- providing promise, hope and enterprise.

Action

Developing a skilful blend of implementation strategies will ensure that change becomes reality. Deciding which action plans to implement is largely determined by the degree of support given by key individuals both within and outside the 'core' organisation. Good action planning achieves key milestones that engage the hearts and minds of people along the way. Successful action planning requires the input and contribution of a community of people, including individuals, groups and key decision makers. Strategies that add credibility to action include:

- obtaining visible key decision-maker support in all stages of design, delivery and evaluation, involving community leaders and customers as well as employees and shareholders;
- appointing a high-influence driver for the process (possibly in the form of a project team or steering committee);
- clarifying a body of principles by which behaviour and actions will be assessed;
- identifying potential resource requirements and timelines;
- brainstorming new strategies for action while considering ways to overcome potential obstacles;
- setting clear milestones and celebration points during the process;
- enhancing versatility and adaptability to changing circumstances.

Results

Cementing the long-term success of change requires excellent design, powerful systems, rigorous evaluation and high-impact marketing. In many ways the 'result' is endemic to all aspects of the change process. Focusing on results and continuous improvement of all initiatives will minimise wastage and help maintain ongoing and satisfactory momentum.

To benefit from this model of change management, it is imperative that all four variables are seen as a living formula that requires constant feeding and supporting. As reflected in Figure 2.1, the change agent must ensure that needs assessment, vision, action and results are positively influencing the desired transition. Although the relative importance of each ingredient may vary from time to time, all four variables interweave with each other during the change cycle.

Given the impact of each variable, none of them can be forgotten. Neglecting any variable, or an over-reliance on any single variable, could send a change process into the abyss. The personality of the change process will be determined by the nature of the change and the demands placed on it by the culture and the expectations of the key opinion leaders and stakeholders.

All four ingredients of the change process are best managed within a 'shared leadership environment', where teamwork and active consul-

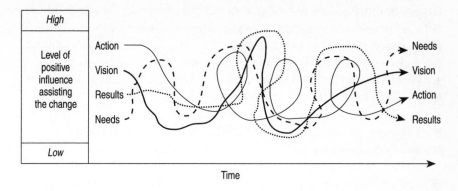

Figure 2.1 A dynamic view of handling change

tation is the norm rather than the exception. This is especially important when the drivers of change are motivated to be involved in only parts of the change. For example, a change agent may enjoy the creation of ideas but ignore quality control.

DEMONSTRATING OUR COMMITMENT TO LEARNING

The influence of leaders and champions is heavily affected by their personal zeal for discovery. In a world where learning is very much a process of being 'stretched' and taking new risks, the effect of good leadership is contagious and inspirational leaders demonstrate what they expect others to do. Obviously, when leaders expect others to learn they must also model the behaviours, attitudes and knowledge of being a learner themselves.

This is particularly challenging, given that we may be dealing with our own personal obstacles to learning. However, it is clearly our capacity to meet such pressure with resilience that will determine whether we are able to achieve our own peak learning potential.

Like everyone, I have confronted many such hurdles. Each in its own way has helped to improve my capacity to learn. Some of these hurdles include:

- ordinary results at high school;
- loss of a parent at a critical age;
- being in the wrong career on several occasions;
- working in a low-morale, low-learning organisation;
- lack of a mission or purpose in life;

- confronting organisational politics;
- coping with nine years of part-time study at university;
- balancing work and life demands;
- lack of self-esteem or self-understanding;
- breakdown in health or emotional well-being;
- career burnout;
- labelling, stereotyping and discrimination;
- unsupportive colleagues and friends;
- being self-employed.

In listing these common obstacles, it is my hope that I will establish some rapport with many of my readers. I am not suggesting for one moment that these hurdles are greater than, or less than those faced by others. However, by listing such experiences I hope to highlight that everyone, including me, needs to overcome a number of actual or perceived obstacles to achieve their goals. The solution to overcoming obstacles comes when we realise that it is not what happens to us that is important, but how we react to what happens to us. Our own thoughts create our reality and sometimes this perceived reality may not necessarily reflect true reality. With this in mind, it is imperative that leaders and champions of workplace change are prepared to unlearn outdated habits and thinking as well as taking up newer ones.

Seeing yourself as a 'learning business'

A wonderful way to demonstrate our commitment to learning, while fostering our learning potential, is to view ourselves as 'learning businesses'. Creating a 'learning business' is just like forming any business; it takes a significant investment of time and resources, lots of hard work, clear goal setting, planning and a belief in one's ability.

There are plenty of actions and behaviours that send a clear signal that you are committed to your own learning. Examples include:

- seeking new learning and personal growth in all aspects of life;
- constantly challenging and reviewing your assumptions;
- avoiding imposing assumptions and beliefs on others;
- actively expanding knowledge by encouraging inquiry, debate and reflection;
- distributing appropriate knowledge and discoveries to others;
- sharing personal books, workbooks, videotapes, audio tapes, Web sites and personal stories;
- demonstrating skills by modelling new attitudes and behaviour;
- disclosing personal successes and failures in learning;

- listening and offering assistance to others;
- setting challenging goals and stretching yourself wherever possible;
- openly stating where, how and why particular knowledge, skills and attitudes have been developed;
- using positive 'self-talk' to overcome self-doubt;
- sharing learning perspectives from a wide range of people (including children and people from different cultural and educational backgrounds);
- rigorously seeking out a wide range of mentors and networks.

How do you currently rate yourself as a learning business? What would your friends, colleagues and family say about your track record as a learner? Take a few minutes to explore these issues by completing Exercise 2.1.

Exercise 2.1: Reviewing your learning commitment

1. List the six behaviours that you believe most clearly demonstrate your commitment to learning:

- _____
- _____
- _____
- _____
- _____
- _____

2. What could you do more of to improve your learning potential and performance?

- _____
- _____
- _____

Writing affirmation statements

An excellent way to build confidence and commitment to learning is using written affirmations. The regular use of written affirmations provides a frame of reference that enhances your self-image and inner strength, especially when facing difficult or trying experiences.

An affirmation statement is a phrase that helps you to confront a learning challenge of some form in a positive way. The best affirmations are those that you write for yourself. It is surprising how many successful change agents and students of learning use affirmations as an integral part of their self-development strategy.

An affirmation statement normally begins with a phrase such as 'I am', and concludes with a desired state of being, as in 'positive about change'. For example, three affirmations that I have found useful are:

- I share what I know, learn from what I don't know.
- I can cope with whatever life deals me.
- I seek to make a positive difference to everything I do.

Affirmations have played a critical role in helping me achieve exciting goals but, more importantly, I have used them to build inner strength during high pressure or stressful times. Using affirmations has led to improvements in career, family, social and spiritual experiences. To capitalise on and strengthen my capacity to obtain the most benefit from the affirmation process, each week I place a key affirmation at the top of my 'to do' list as I undertake my daily duties.

TAKING THE TIME TO NURTURE OURSELVES

Transforming workplace learning requires a tremendous outlay of personal and team energy. Long-term commitment to our work can lead to burnout, fatigue and ineffectiveness unless we set aside time each day to nurture ourselves. Unless people are physically and emotionally healthy they will not be able to function effectively as change agents, leaders or team members.

I have met many people who have paid the price of not investing enough time in nurturing themselves. Whether it is ill health or not thinking straight, there are plenty of people who are doing the best they can without adequate reserves of emotional, physical or spiritual strength.

Any profession or work that requires people to constantly resolve other people's problems is highly susceptible to burnout. Dentists, team leaders or working parents – no matter what our role, we must look after ourselves. Being a problem solver takes energy and that means investing in your health regularly.

Being burnt out is no fun. Everything seems difficult or a chore. We all are given signals of when enough is enough. Sometimes we hear and pick up the message, while on other occasions we are tuned right out. We are so busy being busy that we are leaving ourselves open to a downturn in our quality of life.

A local coffee shop displays advertising postcards: one particular card caught my eye recently. It was for Mental Health Week and its motto was 'Achieve more, Attempt less'. When I reflected on this, I thought, 'How true!' We need to be less demanding of ourselves and give ourselves the choice of reflecting more, digging deeper and resting more before taking on greater volumes of work. For me, living life this way means a higher likelihood of being healthier and being far more open to possibility.

I give myself a 30-minute 'gift' of self-nurturing each day. Self-nurturing can be any activity that promotes well-being and celebrates who you are, while stimulating a resurgence of energy. Self-nurturing activities are diverse, and include exercise, diet, friendship and home-based experiences such as gardening or listening to music.

These daily investments help me become more balanced and more able to achieve important goals, not just at work but in my whole life. A minimum of 30 minutes per day for unconditional, self-indulgent and different self-nurturing activities is what a person needs to maintain and sustain their energy, focus and mental alertness. Of course more would be better.

What is classified as self-nurturing is a deeply personal matter and the selection of appropriate activities must suit each person's unique needs. The key is to create a range of experiences that stimulates a variety of good feelings. Burnout and fatigue can also be a team issue, so team leaders and members need to ensure that they are investing time and energy in team vitality and well-being. Exercise 2.2 gives you an opportunity to identify some suitable individual and team-nurturing activities. Remember: what makes an activity self-nurturing is that it makes you or your team feel energetic and revitalised. Make sure you set clear and measurable goals and that you review your progress on a weekly, monthly and yearly basis.

Exercise 2.2: Identifying self-nurturing activities

1. Examine the following activities and circle the actions that you would find nurturing.

*Suggested **individual** self-nurturing activities*

- listening to music
- contacting long-lost friends
- tai chi exercises
- redefining your affirmations
- reading
- playing a musical instrument
- soaking in a bath
- playing a motivational tape
- deep, relaxed breathing
- playing with children

- yoga
- playing sport
- going for a walk
- grooming a pet
- flying a kite
- smelling flowers
- buying yourself a gift
- seeing a play or film
- having a facial or massage
- going to a coffee shop
- a hobby
- watching television
- using an aromatic burner
- breaking the routine
- hugging someone
- playing a computer game
- meditating
- having a drink with a friend
- visiting your favourite restaurant
- having a nap
- window-shopping
- writing poetry or a letter
- saying no to unreasonable requests
- cooking
- lying in a garden
- listening to the radio
- painting or drawing
- writing in your journal

Given these prompts, list five (30-minute) activities that you could do on a rotational daily basis:

- _____
- _____
- _____
- _____
- _____

2. Examine the following activities and circle the actions his or her your team may find self-nurturing.

*Suggested **team** nurturing activities*
- establishing a process to help each member confront his or her own learning challenges
- making self-nurturing a team responsibility
- undertaking job rotation and multiskilling
- organising life-skills management training
- renegotiating roles and responsibilities
- saying no to unreasonable requests
- encouraging mentoring and mutual support
- making self-nurturing a team responsibility
- listing your achievements

- bringing in outside assistance
- a regular social gathering of fun and information exchange
- discussing team and individual goals as a team
- organising a best practice visit

Given these prompts, list three suggestions for discussion at your next team meeting:

- _____

  _____

- _____

  _____

- _____

  _____

CREATING AN EXCELLENT IMAGE

An excellent measure of whether an organisation is providing leadership towards the learning agenda can be determined by examining the image of that organisation.

Have you ever been socialising when you hear someone talk about their workplace in less than pleasant terms? Some time ago I met Jo at a party. After initial introductions, she candidly shared the inadequacies of her on-the-job learning and the formal training in her organisation. During her story telling, examples of poor leadership, lack of feedback and unethical behaviour were quoted. The current employer was compared unfavourably with all past employers. After several minutes, other party goers joined in and shared similar experiences from their workplaces.

While listening, I pondered the impact and damage that such a discussion could be having on the image of these organisations. Irrespective of how true these stories were, the disruptive impact of such discussions cannot be underestimated. It could be argued that such disclosures should not be made. However, such stories are commonplace in everyday life.

Not only can the image of workplaces be affected negatively, but such stories can also be indicative that people often blame others rather than taking at least some responsibility for overcoming an apparently hostile and unfriendly situation.

As leaders and change agents we should be especially sensitive to how the quality of workplace learning affects the internal psyche and external image of an organisation, and tune into both formal and informal conversations unfolding. Organisations that spend significant time and effort developing their capacity and that of their people are promoting a positive self-image. A positive internal and external self-image does more than just develop current performance. It also provides greater 'hope' for the future. In many cases this hope can be the best tonic a workforce can have as it confronts its own challenges.

To help us develop a positive image, we need to constantly seek out organisations and change agents with excellent track records for transforming workplace learning. We need to take time to learn from them while sharing and celebrating our own successes. Success in leading the learning agenda will be highly dependent on our ability to develop mutually supportive partnerships with such people.

SUMMARY

Gaining a commitment to workplace learning reform requires courage, the ability to overcome obstacles, persistence and an understanding of the dynamics of successful change.

The energy for successful change management comes from three prime sources:

- being 100 per cent clear about what it takes to be a successful change agent;
- using written affirmations to build self-confidence and inner strength;
- confronting burnout on both a personal and team level.

A successful change agent must also demonstrate a passion and commitment to learning. If leaders and change agents fail to do this, the internal psyche and external image of organisations will be adversely affected. Change agents and leaders should therefore allocate time to develop relationships with people who are living role models of the benefits of lifelong learning.

3

Meeting The Demands Of Change

> *Nothing endures but change.*
>
> Heraclitus

KEY PRINCIPLES

- Modern workplaces need flexible and adaptive learning.
- Develop a shared understanding of both the business and the individual.
- Career success requires constant renewal.
- Job fit is the cornerstone of all workplace learning.
- Foster the chemistry of dynamic personal growth through support and encouragement.

LEARNING AND CHAOS

The pace of chaotic change is alarming. For some people change is frightening, but others may experience it as wonderfully exciting. Irrespective of how we react, how well we learn as individuals and as workplaces is a major factor in how well we cope with change.

To survive and thrive in modern frenzied change, everybody needs a learning approach full of enterprise and creativity. Daily practice that expands our resourcefulness, networks and choices is demanded of us. Practices should include finding good mentors, engaging in self-initiated discovery, tapping into the riches of the Internet, participating in special projects and exploring new possibilities and scenarios. All these together provide a mix of methods to enhance our knowledge and talent in a fast and efficient manner. As already discussed, we can no longer use a 'wait and see' approach; if we need to learn something we must take charge straight away.

While living in modern chaotic times can at one level seem quite complex with much blurring and confusion, at another level change can be quite simple. We learn to focus on high-priority items and instead of trying to communicate everything, we spend more time communicating key values while creating processes that support greater risk taking and self-management.

Individuals who have been brought up in a world of control and command are slowly seeing that a new style of leadership is required, where time is spent coaching people to take responsibility for their learning and work systems that stimulate the exchange of knowledge are established.

The modern workplace has a very low tolerance of people who are creating division, trying to hoard information or only rely on a small number of people to get things done. Running any business like this can quickly lead to inertia, apathy and helplessness. The primary drivers of outstanding workplace learning and re-engineering are trust, openness and partnership. The drivers create organisational capacity to adapt to never-ending chaotic change. Where they exist, work generates greater challenge and excitement rather than fatigue, fear and vulnerability.

BALANCING ORGANISATIONAL AND INDIVIDUAL PERSPECTIVES

As well as understanding how the ground rules of workplace learning have shifted, it is equally imperative to understand the delicate balance between the needs of the individual and the organisation. Particularly important is grasping the transitory nature of the labour market. Increasingly, the talent used for business comes from people who are hired on a short-term or project basis. Advances in telecommuting and increased part-time and contract employment have meant that people are often hired at a moment's notice to fill shortfalls in knowledge and skills, rather than relying on a large pool of full-time employees. Employers and individuals have found it necessary to create more flexible and reviewable employment contracts, where all parties work together in partnership. In this new world, performance, employability and co-operation are seen as a joint responsibility.

Figure 3.1 represents the workplace learning process as a set of scales that constantly measures and balances the consequences of organisational and individual career trends. To do this successfully, workplace learning processes must adapt to the ever-changing world of work.

Maintaining this balance is no easy task, of course, and requires a high-quality, two-way communication process between the needs of the organisation, and the individuals and their teams.

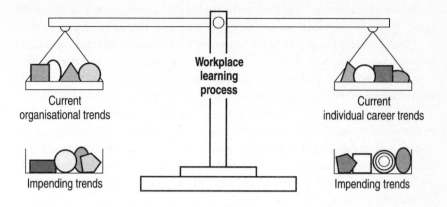

Figure 3.1 Balancing workplace learning trends

Figure 3.1 paints a picture of workplace learning as a balanced relation-ship between the individual and the organisation, but in real life this is rarely the case. The scales are often unbalanced, with either one or both of the parties disillusioned or unhappy or feeling poorly served. If unre-solved, this imbalance leads to friction, poor performance and high or rapid turnover of key personnel.

Also reflected in Figure 3.1 are a number of current and impending trends that affect the balance of the scales. As each new trend affects the business, a range of new policies, strategies and practices will be required and old ones will need to be reviewed to bring about a high-quality work-place learning process. Managing this constant measurement and review requires a shared understanding of the values, the uniqueness and the legitimacy of both worlds. It is no longer possible to regard individual and organisational trends separately.

The following story (inspired by Dick Knowdell, the Director of Career Research and Testing in San Jose, California) demonstrates how employ-ment has changed and continues to do so. It also shows how the shift from predictability to chaos has transformed the workplace learning environ-ment.

A story of change

The way individuals manage their careers has undergone a major trans-formation. In the past, employees would catch a large 'career bus trip' through life. The itinerary and duration of the trip was in the control of the employer. Most of the people who boarded the bus did so at an early age and stayed there for life. Some individuals loved their bus trip while others just came along for the ride. There were, of course, many people who were bored and unhappy but they had no choice but to sit out the trip.

The rules for travel on the bus were carefully stipulated: employees were told where to sit, where to stand and how to behave. If the passengers wished to change position they would have to ask the driver. When people broke this rule they could quickly find themselves at the back of the bus.

The terrain was very predictable and the roads were very wide. The drivers had extensive log books about past journeys and were expected to follow the same travel route meticulously. The rigid itinerary included scheduled meal stops and set educational tours. In regard to the educational tours, the bus driver had a prescribed script and everyone received the same information at the same time. Occasionally, the bus would have a different driver, but this would make little or no difference to the nature of the journey being undertaken. Interestingly, there were a few select people (mainly men) who seemed to get better treatment. They received better meals, nicer seats at the front and clearer information on where the bus was heading.

In today's world, the bus transportation system is no longer suitable. Although there are still many bus trips being undertaken on the main roads, the number of passengers has shrunk to about half. It is generally thought that the 'career bus' is now too uneconomical, too big and too inflexible. One of the prime reasons for the change is that the terrain and climate have become much more rugged, unpredictable and hostile.

As a consequence, many people now own, drive or ride their own vehicle, some opting for a four-wheel-drive, others using mountain bikes, some even walking, but all enjoying their own degree of freedom, versatility and mobility. Most importantly, each individual can travel up hills, down hills or cross-country, as desired.

There is an ever-increasing band of people who are not travelling at all. They sit quietly at home and, using the latest advances in telecommunications, they manage their life in a way that suits their life goals and work plans.

Given this background of balancing individual and organisational perspectives in chaotic environments, we will now shift our attention to identifying the major trends affecting workplace learning.

MAJOR TRENDS AFFECTING WORKPLACE LEARNING

Contemporary trends in workplace learning fall into two main categories:

■ worldwide workplace trends;
■ individual career trends.

Worldwide workplace trends

Some of the major driving forces affecting workplace learning include:

- increased pressure to demonstrate productivity, performance, customer service and quality;
- the globalisation of the marketplace, which has meant an increase in the amount of mutually beneficial networking and benchmarking;
- managing more services and products with fewer resources and smaller workforces;
- a serious shortage of talent to perform the work required, in both the lower-paid and high-paid ends of the spectrum;
- increased use of virtual organisations and temporary teams to get the job done;
- increased incidence of decentralised work locations (particularly home-based employment);
- increased use of managerial systems that increase quality and responsiveness;
- increased pressure to transform information into knowledge that adds value to the corporate IQ, and the competency and sustainability of the business;
- increased diversity of cultures and educational backgrounds in the workplace;
- increased requirement for compliance with government, environmental and industry standards;
- greater employee expectations in securing more interesting, well-paid and meaningful work, while employers look to save the investment in labour;
- increased power and flexibility of digital technology.

The implications of organisational trends

Looking at the number and nature of these trends, it is not hard to see why learning has become such an important issue. It is also understandable that some people are overwhelmed by them, particularly when you add industry-specific workplace issues. To resolve this complexity it is important to identify and 'red flag' the most critical issues for action.

The recurring tragedy is that even after such rational and logical processes have been undertaken and discussed, some decision makers still may not be motivated enough to support the agenda for reform. A common example of this behaviour is when decision makers prefer to fight fires and be crisis-stimulated rather than meaningfully address real long-term change. This form of avoidance is a common cause of long-term innovation problems in organisations. Practical tips and best practice information on how to manage this situation are provided in Part 2.

Individual career trends

The following career trends are now dramatically affecting workplace learning:

■ Careers now operate within a maze of options. Promotion is only one of the options available to individuals. Others include: developing and improving skills; remaining up-to-date in one's current position; renegotiating better use of skills, interests and values within one's current job; new and challenging special projects; a rotation or transfer to develop skills; and taking a new job that offers greater work/life balance.

■ Career paths are now shorter in duration, more flexible and multi-skilled.

■ Career choices are exploding beyond the traditional 9-to-5 full-time employment option. Choices include: subcontracted temporary employment; small businesses and franchises; a home-based career; job sharing; part-time employment; and network marketing.

■ Employment and rewards are based more and more on merit rather than seniority and security.

■ The number of dual-career couples is increasing (that is, both 'live-in' partners are working).

■ The number of careers within a single working life is expanding.

■ Individuals are increasingly expected to take full responsibility for their own learning by constantly updating skills, researching career options, setting goals and reviewing progress against organisational realities.

■ The employment marketplace now operates within a global domain.

■ There is continued expansion of multicultural workplaces.

■ There is developing reassessment of traditional gender roles in employment.

■ The incidence of compulsory retirement continues to decrease.

■ The potential for long-term unemployment continues to grow, particularly where employees have lost touch with the culture and expectation of holding a job.

The implications of individual career trends

These individual career trends add their own flavour to the workplace learning equation. The pressure of managing a career in today's world can bring many emotions and responses to the surface. Common words offered by individuals to describe their feelings include 'frustrated', 'stimulated', 'scared', 'tired' and 'exhausted'.

So, what impact is today's world of work having on individuals? And what are the key lessons that must be learnt?

Having conducted many hundreds of career coaching appointments and over 100 career planning programmes, the following issues seem to me to require urgent action if we are to successfully reach our full potential:

■ *Developing resilience.* Managing careers in today's rapidly changing environment requires an extensive range of life management skills. Important resilience skills include accepting career accountabilities, developing self-esteem, assertiveness, goal setting, confronting career burnout, learning how to learn, negotiating, networking and developing mentors, coping with information overload, stress management and financial planning.

■ *Getting a life.* How does one remain sane and healthy and stay employable? There is no point in burning people out to the point where they cannot perform. In the decade ahead, the focus of career development will become increasingly holistic. Attention will shift to issues such as finding a balance between work and non-work time. In other words, towards 'getting a life' among all of the pressures of modern living.

■ *Working for hope rather than fear.* One of the most mortifying aspects of today's world is that often the individual works purely for survival and not for pleasure. In other words, many people are working under duress, discrimination and fear rather than for hope and joy. Sadly, as a result, individuals feel powerless and out of control. People talk about their career as if it were a private and public hanging. They express powerlessness and helplessness as they talk about how the employer or the system is tying a noose around their neck. This perceived lack of control over one's future and destiny has a serious effect on levels of self-worth and well-being. A greater commitment to building community in the workplace is needed in order to break this destructive cycle – in simple terms, treating people with respect and creating opportunities for them to share their feelings and shape a better future for the benefit of everyone.

■ *Expanding our knowledge network.* One of the consequences of rapid change is that the amount of knowledge we need in order to do our work is rapidly increasing. Even if we take the trouble to read a couple of articles in our area of interest each week, we are still likely to be falling behind in our thinking. As a result, finding colleagues and other people to share and build on each other's understanding is a vital factor in career sustainability.

■ *The working poor.* The emergence of the global economy and the desire to keep labour costs down by renegotiating contracts, working longer hours, or shifting business off-shore means that employers must be increasingly sensitive to the impact of a commercially driven business philosophy on people's time, money and energy. All the exciting business ventures and workplace learning initiatives in the world will not make a scrap of difference if people feel their quality of life is reduced.

■ *Redefining success.* Promotion, increased responsibility and higher wages are not the only measures of success. Other career outcomes must be recognised as equally successful motivators: achieving a greater balance with leisure, obtaining more stimulating work, finding a career that provides greater financial or geographic predictability and, finally, obtaining greater autonomy and freedom.

Exercise 3.1 will enable you to explore the current career management issues in your life. This activity has been adapted from material from a coaching session at Worklife, a career coaching service based in Sydney.

UNDERSTANDING JOB FIT AND PERSONAL GROWTH

Translating the knowledge of workplace trends into real and meaningful learning requires an understanding of job fit and personal growth. Without this added understanding, the capacity to achieve quality on-the-job learning will be low. To do this requires excellent communication skills combined with a desire to make positive changes. Understanding job fit and the personal growth cycle is the nucleus of all transformation in the workplace, as it is here that the most potential for learning occurs.

Exercise 3.1: Clarifying your career management needs

1.   After reflecting on the following concerns, circle the ones of most importance to you:

■ clarifying my career direction
■ selecting a course of study
■ defining what success means to me
■ developing a strategy to overcome boredom
■ setting goals and priorities
■ writing a résumé
■ developing a strategy to make a career change
■ determining the skills that are transferable to other fields or jobs
■ finding ways of spending better quality time with my friends or family
■ preparing for a career development discussion with my manager
■ preparing for a job interview
■ identifying multiple career paths

- writing a career plan
- finding suitable mentors
- learning how to learn
- reviewing past achievements
- writing a self-development plan
- moving from a dead-end job
- undertaking a career exploration
- overcoming a hostile boss
- developing a better balance between work and other activities
- identifying the skills that I need to develop most
- locating more interesting unpaid work
- improving self-confidence and self-esteem
- joining a suitable professional development network
- developing a support network for my current change
- reviewing a previous career plan
- clarifying career ambiguities
- resolving dual career issues with my family or partner
- discovering important career values
- determining criteria for a career change
- working towards more inner peace
- researching career trends in my field
- planning for a job placement or rotation
- developing a mission in life that will assist my career
- changing or improving my personal relationships
- improving my interview and job-seeking skills
- securing greater spiritual meaning in my life
- stress management
- overcoming burnout

2. List any other issues or concerns that are important to you:

_____

Job fit

Without doubt, the match between an individual's values and abilities and the job's key results areas (KRAs) will determine whether work is done with passion and motivation. Figure 3.2 illustrates the essential features of the job fit process.

The input of the person and the job

Into every project and workplace people bring their own unique strengths and weaknesses, likes and dislikes. Mirroring this personal input are the demands made by each job. Each job has its own unique blend of KRAs and tasks that seek to improve performance, system development, innovation and learning. The degree of job fit between the person and the job will vary from situation to situation and from time to time.

Locating untapped potential or areas of avoidance

Figure 3.2 shows the job fit between the person and the job, an example in which the job fit is about 50 per cent. This means that half of the job outputs suit the natural style of the person, while the other half do not. The 50 per cent that does not fit is made up of two sections: 25 per cent is 'untapped potential' and 25 per cent is 'areas of avoidance'.

Untapped potential is that part of a person that lies dormant. To access this untapped potential, the organisation and individual need to consult and develop a strategy to use more of the individual's natural repertoire on the job. Possible strategy options include special projects, cross-training or the development of multiskilled teams. Obviously, the greater the flexibility, the greater the opportunity to develop untapped potential. If the organisation runs a bureaucratic and rigid process of on-the-job learning, the chances of discovering and using hidden talent will be far more restricted.

'Areas of avoidance' are those where a person has little or no preference or aptitude for a skill or KRA. This could be demonstrated by a lack of interest, regular procrastinating or avoiding doing a specific task. For example, as a consultant, I enjoy training and facilitating or coaching, but I have 'historically' avoided marketing. However, marketing is an important part of the consulting process.

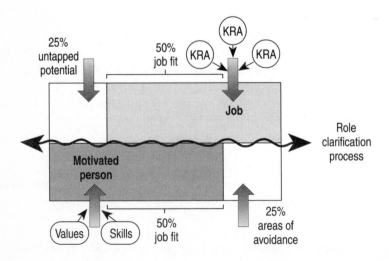

Figure 3.2 The job fit process

Role clarification process

Central to the job fit is the negotiation process. The more frequent the communication process the greater the capacity to design workplace learning, stimulate motivation and enhance performance management. Job fit thrives on a quality two-way consultation.

The chemistry of personal growth

Figure 3.3 shows how the personal growth process is assisted by a number of factors, including taking risks, having opportunity, being prepared to try diverse developmental experiences, negotiating job fit, giving permission to be stretched, going outside one's comfort zone, receiving sufficient coaching, accessibility to quality learning resources, and sharing how one feels about the workplace learning process. Figure 3.3 shows how the personal growth process comes alive and evolves into a dynamic and energising experience. With appropriate transitional support, the growth of an individual occurs in essentially two ways: first by extending his or her skills and confidence level, and second by extending the job boundaries. With extended job boundaries there is increased likelihood of improving adaptability to change by multiskilling and supporting workplace innovation in line with business requirements.

FACING UP TO OUR RESPONSIBILITIES

The demands of change are best met by forming a partnership between the organisation and the individual. A joint approach increases the likelihood of job fit and personal growth while creating a synergistic relationship that stimulates innovation and performance improvement, irrespective of the type of employer and the status of employment.

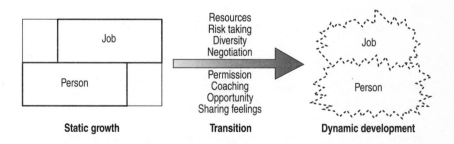

Figure 3.3 The chemistry of personal growth

A learning bill of rights

A useful strategy for developing a partnership approach is to have all employees face up to and accept their shared responsibility in the workplace learning process. A way of cementing this accountability is to develop a learning 'bill of rights' that establishes a standard of excellence and code of conduct for workplace learning. The following learning bill of rights is a discussion document that can be negotiated, finalised and circulated within your organisation. This learning bill of rights has been adapted from the work of Marlys Hanson and Associates in Livermore, California.

A bill of rights for workplace learning – a shared responsibility

To support workplace learning the *organisation* must:

- accept that workplace learning is an important part of business activity
- communicate goals, strategies, policies and values
- provide resources, tools and systems that support workplace learning and knowledge management
- provide practical advice on suitable mentors or contact points for further development
- provide adequate and timely information about career opportunities
- reward team leaders and managers who coach and develop.

To support workplace learning the *individual* must:

- perform on the current job
- take responsibility for his or her own development by showing interest and action in personal growth
- assess interests, values and personal preferences for learning
- request and gather ideas that improve service
- develop, implement and review action plans.

To support workplace learning the *on-the-job coach* must:

- communicate the short- and long-term vision of the organisation
- help individuals gather the information they need to manage their learning
- establish a supportive environment to help people identify resources and tools, and encourage reflection and action

---

- provide honest feedback on performance and advice on how skills can be enhanced
- hold ongoing development discussions
- allocate or recommend work assignments that stimulate learning
- support the implementation of agreed action plans.

SUMMARY

The demands of chaotic change help set the agenda for workplace learning. The reasons for implementing organisational and individual career workplace learning are very diverse and interdependent. Examples of current workplace trends include such organisational issues as increased productivity, performance management, customer service and quality, as well as career trends, such as adapting to shorter and more flexible career paths.

The best way of handling the complexity of change is to form a partnership between the organisation, the individual, and the on-the-job coach so that a win is gained for all parties.

4

Championing Knowledge Work

> *The wise see knowledge and action as one.*
>
> Bhagavad-Gita

KEY PRINCIPLES

- Information does not always translate into knowledge.
- Create conversations that stimulate insight and self-awareness.
- Balance the creation of new ground with the reflection of wisdom.
- Tap into the informal network.
- Use leading-edge management technology.

SECURING A STRONG FUTURE

Knowledge is fundamental to the survival and success of every business. There can be no doubt that in the world of virtual teams, constant restructuring and changing business, the intellectual capital of a workforce and its 'business brain' is its lifeline to the future.

The management of knowledge has many dimensions, including how to create, store and share discovery, as well as applying advances in digital technology. People need to think beyond just 'managing' knowledge and think more about its creation, sharing and application. We need to seek out meaningful discovery that adds value, rather than smother others with indiscriminate information. Decision makers need to be prepared to let go of old thinking and be prepared to open up decision-making channels. And it must be recognised that knowledge work will not just happen by itself; it needs trust and a desire to mediate key messages and lessons learnt along the value chain. Everyone needs to be given clear responsibility to ensure that when important knowledge, research or discoveries emerge, they are delivered, integrated and used on time where it matters most.

Finally, there needs to be a clear recognition that knowledge work does not happen by chance. It demands strong dialogue, consultation and accountability. People must understand clearly why they need each other. Key internal and external customers should be seen as important connections and networks in the business brain. Commitment to an expansive work culture that nurtures and develops people as knowledge assets and not as costs must be demonstrated by organisational leaders.

So what does knowledge work mean in practice? The following discussion articulates what needs to be done to build a culture where knowledge work becomes a living and transparent process.

MOVING PAST THE SMOKESCREEN

There is something magical about dancers weaving their spell on the stage, or a basketball team combining its years of experience into a champion unit. When used and displayed, knowledge is not only fun but it leads to the reinvention of human talent.

In business, focused knowledge work creates a workplace full of promise and innovation. Business improvement rarely happens by accident. It requires people to make the transition from merely undertaking tasks and activity, to experimentation, reflection and the sharing of understanding.

Work activity may appear to be knowledge management, but it is not. Just because a person is responsible for building a bridge, or a clerk takes the trouble to send an e-mail, or just because a chief executive calls a meeting, it does not necessarily mean that knowledge will be shared, enhanced and acted upon. For knowledge to unfold, there must be the chance for deeper meaning and improved competency that leads to some act or application. Karl Erik Sveiby, author of *The New Organizational Wealth* (1997), says 'the vast majority of knowledge management is information management'. One of the enduring challenges of the modern workplace is that knowledge work can never be assumed. We need to go past this smokescreen that constantly calls people 'knowledge workers' and start making the process of learning full of discovery and insight.

People often say that they understand knowledge management but more commonly the 'words' and 'actions' are worlds apart. To make this transition, here are 10 behaviours that can help a person become a knowledge worker:

- undertaking the daily ritual of personal reflection on what has happened and what has been learnt;
- taking time out to experiment, try out new ideas and check understanding;
- posing questions that re-form the boundaries of what is and is no longer required;
- trusting one's own wisdom and insight as well as fostering that of others;
- accessing knowledge and storing it in our long-term memory;
- abandoning outdated concepts, skills and data;
- building trust and partnerships to share ideas and enhance skill transfer;
- using digital technology to stimulate better communication, synergy and creativity;
- asking questions that help identify what is desired and where the source of knowledge may lie;
- using our findings or skills to shape considered action.

DISCOVERING WISDOM

One of the recurring lessons of the last century is how poor organisations are at surviving the perils and the demands of their times. In recent times, very few can say they lasted for a decade or more without some major upheaval. The capacity of an organisation to survive is intrinsically connected with the ability of its people to discover wisdom that helps them adapt. This is particularly important given that much of the discovery needed is either forgotten, unpractised or completely unknown at the time it is required.

For wisdom to develop there must be a balance between quickly creating new ground and sound reflective practice. Both these knowledge work approaches are discussed below.

Creating new ground

Exploring new frontiers, envisioning new possibilities, practising new, unheard-of skills, and invention are critical parts of improvement. They require a continual learning dynamic that stimulates inquiry, exploration and imagination. Without it, the knowledge work process can quickly grind to a halt.

For me, the Wright Brothers were shining lights of this frontier of creating new ground. During the days when they were building their flying machines, they would orchestrate animated 'face-to-face' discussions in which they would passionately argue their ideas, and they trialled their ideas in various simulated environments. A comprehensive testing and modification programme was run on the flying machines. To highlight the creative tension of their learning dynamics, each of the brothers would often take an opposite point of view to the one he had taken the day before. With such a culture of knowledge work, it is not surprising they succeeded in being the first people to create a flying machine that would carry a person.

Workplaces can learn from the Wright Brothers' approach by creating an environment where people are encouraged to think, and where creative tension stimulates greater openness and creativity. Practically, this means people must be given the permission to 'field test' their ideas, while understanding that forced answers or quick fixes seldom work. Most of all, they need to have a process that allows people to discover together in a constructive fashion.

Benefiting from reflective practice

Complementing the desire to create something new is the practice of reflection. Whether it is drawing on one's own experience, recalling history, or researching a new field, reflection is a vital contributor to knowledge work. All we need to do is ask the right questions and have an open mind.

A common example of reflective practice is when people choose to hold conversations in teams or small groups. When done properly, it can lead to valuable shared insights. Interestingly, the practice of such exchanges comes not from modern business but from the customs and traditions of local tribes and indigenous communities, who have over thousands of years perfected this kind of group learning into an art form.

Reflective practice itself reveals that ancient cultures can teach us much. Yet the lessons do not stop there. Traditional cultures also provide wisdom in areas such as environmental management and chaos theory (to name just a couple).

Of course, you do not need to go back thousands of years to find answers and perspectives for modern challenges. Your supply of wisdom may come from a more recent source. Exercise 4.1 will help you explore this field of reflective practice.

Exercise 4.1: Sources of reflective wisdom

Using the following questions as prompts, consider the merit and value of applying a number of wisdom sources to address your current personal and business challenges.

Your life

■ What story have you heard or lived that can help you deal with the current situation, and what lessons did you draw from this?

_____

_____

■ How do your personal goals, mindset or values shape your current viewpoint or stance?

_____

_____

_____

■ What evidence do you need to promote a greater inquiry of your current knowledge?

_____

_____

_____

Corporate/industry memory

■ What is your core business?

_____

_____

■ What is your business trying to become?

_____

_____

■ What is treasured as vital knowledge? What is its worth?

_____

_____

■ What have you discovered that works or does not work?

_____

_____

■ How would you view your current strengths, weaknesses, opportunities and threats?

_____

_____

■ What would your customers say about you?

_____

_____

■ What outdated knowledge is tied up within existing systems and databases?

_____

_____

■ What wisdom can be learnt from past managers and practices? Can you contact them?

_____

_____

Quotations and/or words of wisdom

■ What has been said or written that can give you instant inspiration or inquiry on a matter of concern?

_____

_____

Strategic alliances

■ What people or workplaces could be a source of inspiration for your current challenges?

_____

_____

■ How could you go about finding case studies or fellow-travellers who could assist you on your journey?

_____

_____

■ If the answers you need do not appear to be available from your current contacts, where could you go to find new insights?

_____

_____

Traditional wisdom
Indigenous cultures

■ What lessons can be learnt from the stories, beliefs and customs of ancient or existing cultures in helping deal with your challenges?

_____

_____

The arts

■ What insight can be formed from the symbolism of the arts?

_____

_____

■ What wisdom exists in music, literature or film that can help you in your daily challenges?

_____

_____

Myth, archetypes and symbols

■ What insight can be extracted from folklore, metaphor, religions or methodology (such as Ancient Greek or Roman methodology) that can help you deal with modern times?

_____

_____

_____

Universal principles
Sustainability

■ What does nature tell us about how to lead and maintain modern chaotic workplaces?

_____

_____

■ How do you balance economic, societal, environmental and community concerns and still achieve business success?

_____

_____

Trends or phenomena

■ Can we learn from the cycles of boom or bust?

_____

_____

■ Do you have a product life cycle?

_____

_____

■ What are the implications of trends such as Internet growth, global warming and expansion of worldwide conglomerates on your life?

_____

_____

_____

_____

■ What apparently wacky scenario do we need to consider?

_____

_____

_____

_____

STIMULATING KNOWLEDGE FLOW

There is no real point in discovering new ground, creating a new insight or developing a new skill if people are unable to make use of it. Strategies must be user-friendly and flexible to help people share the discoveries. In some cases people can share their insights by putting the outcomes on a planning sheet, or drawing visuals, or incorporating lessons learnt on the company intranet. Individuals may keep a journal; companies could produce checklists and stories, sharing them in a newsletter.

To make smart use of knowledge, wisdom must be shared between the formal hierarchy and the informal 'grapevine' network that exists in every business. Tapping into the informal network is a key communication priority in business restructuring, ensuring that old bureaucratic and functional structures do not block and stifle knowledge creation. In doing so, you increase the chances of involving a wide range of people in the knowledge process. One of the greatest tragedies in workplace learning occurs when people are given little or no chance to participate in a range of knowledge-stimulation processes. Five popular strategies to tap into the informal network include:

1. establishing learning networks where staff, customers and suppliers run discussions and circulate discoveries by a newsletter, an open forum, by e-mail or by mentoring on important issues;
2. setting up helpdesks and offering Web access to business contributors at work and at home, giving them 24-hour access to key trends and issues;
3. using project and action learning teams to pool talent and diverse interests to learn and make decisions together;
4. conducting regular audits of the communication methods and processes being used to advance knowledge, and by appointing people to follow the message through the value chain, from research to application;
5. providing guidance on the skills of being a knowledge worker, while encouraging greater levels of trust, honesty and open communication.

Many more strategies and advice will be provided in upcoming chapters, such as in Chapter 9 where 20 ways for creating a thirst for sharing knowledge are listed. Appendix 2 provides a checklist for the intelligent implementation of a digital technology infrastructure to help improve learning and knowledge work.

ALIGNMENT WITH LEADING-EDGE MANAGEMENT TECHNOLOGY

A very practical way to improve the quality and focus of knowledge work is to search out and align business practice with leading edge management technologies. An example is offered by an international movement that has spent 30 years developing and updating excellence frameworks and awards for the benefit of businesses and workplaces in every corner of the globe. In doing so, it provides a consistent language, knowledge and global understanding for better innovation, customer value and sustainability.

This worldwide movement has resulted in a consistent and comprehensive approach to improved excellence, whether by a formal annual awards process or by its enduring legacy of helping workplaces explore positive reform. The primary beneficiary of aligning with such processes is that it provides 'ways and means' to foster better knowledge management, innovation and performance, while creating a workplace identity that is constantly adapting and improving.

International organisations that pursue similar ideals are in:

- the USA, the Baldridge Award;
- Japan, the Deming Prize;
- Europe, the European Quality Award;
- Australia, the Australian Business Excellence Award;
- New Zealand, the National Quality Awards.

According to the Australian Quality Council, which administers the Australian Business Excellence Award, the principles that are fundamental to better innovation and long-term success include, but are not restricted to, the following:

- Clear direction allows organisational alignment, and a focus on the achievement of goals.
- Mutually agreed plans translate organisational direction into action.
- Understanding what customers value, now and in the future, influences organisational direction, strategy and action.
- To improve the outcome, improve the system and its associated processes.
- The potential of an organisation is realised through its people's enthusiasm, resourcefulness and participation.
- Continual improvement and innovation depend on continual learning.

- All people work *in* a system; outcomes are improved when people work *on* the system.
- Effective use of facts, data and knowledge leads to improved decisions.
- All systems and processes exhibit variability, which affects predictability and performance.
- Organisations provide value to the community through their actions to ensure a clean, safe, fair and prosperous society.
- Sustainability is determined by an organisation's ability to create and deliver value for all stakeholders.

SUMMARY

Knowledge work has become a major focus of transforming workplace learning. For knowledge work to occur, diverse and creative processes must be used to access, store and celebrate discovery. It is particularly important to move past the rhetoric of knowledge management and ensure that people enact being better knowledge workers. This requires communication processes that are inclusive and adaptable. It means taking your time to reflect on the best method that can be implemented. Aligning workplace practice to leading-edge management technology is certainly a solid place to start.

5

Helping The Wounded Learner

> My life has been a constant effort to illustrate how a very mediocre
> person with very mediocre talents, which I have, can create quite a lot
> if they drive themselves.
>
> Sir Edmund Hillary

KEY PRINCIPLES

■ Reframe thinking that inhibits learning.
■ Overcome our fears with evidence.
■ Workplace learning needs to mould self-directed learners.
■ Explore different ways and methods to engage 'true learning'.
■ Accept and embrace a wider view of human intelligence.

REMOVING THE HURT AND THE STRUGGLE

Mention the word 'learning' and some people suddenly stop breathing
normally. For these people, the word 'learning' triggers a long list of
'negative' and 'wounded' feelings and memories. Most of my feelings of
learning 'struggle' come when I write. I have now written three books, but
to get to that milestone I have had to dig very deep many times to overcome self-doubt and aversion. In time, I have been able to prove to myself
that I am not only a writer but an author, and my self-doubt has been
slowly replaced with increased confidence and skill.

Much has changed since I completed over a dozen drafts for my first
book in 1992, but there is a part of me that still believes I should not be
doing this thing called 'writing'. Yes, I am very committed, and yes, I am
full of ideas, but a good speller or someone who has a rich vocabulary, I
am certainly not. Yet here I am again writing away, and in many ways

contradicting how I see myself. At the end of the day, nevertheless, another paragraph is written. Maybe I am defying the odds or maybe I am forming a new self-identity. Whatever is happening, learning the skill of writing has changed me forever.

The story of my writing is not unique and I am not going to claim I am more or less talented than anyone else. As we undertake our personal journey of transformation in life, our response to learning creates a roller-coaster of conflicting and complementary emotions. As we stretch our boundaries, we not only have our emotions played and pulled in every direction, we also have a precious opportunity to redefine our sense of our own capabilities.

Whether the learning experience is writing, dancing, training or chairing a meeting, wounded learning behaviour inhibits people from reaching their true potential. It is not what we are learning that is important, but how we react to learning. The good news for us is that we can overcome many of these so-called immovable obstacles by taking the right action. For me, one of the pleasures of life is that it provides us with a blissful opportunity to confront these challenges head-on and reinvent ourselves. To help put this in context, here are eight starting beliefs that helped me deal with my learning:

- Discover your motivation and let it calmly drive you.
- Set realistic goals and then glue them in with a written action plan.
- Search for mentors, books and resources for new sources of wisdom.
- Never forget that your mind is full of inner voices: some help you and others hinder you. You choose which ones you wish to listen to.
- You do need to take a risk occasionally.
- Be clear on which conditions help you learn and when you need to develop capabilities that stretch you beyond your comfort zone.
- Celebrate progress and use positive self-talk to help move yourself forward.
- At the end of the day, it is your unique talents that will shine.

The remainder of this chapter explores some of the common causes and remedies of 'wounded learning' behaviour. Two key issues will be examined: rebuilding learner confidence and understanding mental diversity. These issues will be discussed through the eyes of a person who is interested not only in transforming workplace learning but helping people in every aspect of their lives.

REBUILDING LEARNER CONFIDENCE

A 'wounded learner' is not dissimilar to someone who is physically injured or hurt. He or she needs the right medicine, the correct advice and plenty of character to return to health quickly. To improve the health of a 'wounded learner', we must first accept that his or her behaviour is a situational response rather than a personality disorder and, second, we must develop an excellent understanding of his or her unique motivation and learning preferences.

The origins of wounded learners are varied and they are located in every area of human endeavour. Each person has a unique range of learning preferences, motivations and values that are ready to be discovered and used in life. When people are aware of what interests and excites them they are more likely to seek out those choices in their life. However, for those people where the opposite occurs, they can spend the majority of their time performing demotivating tasks, which leads to fatigue, stress or boredom.

To build learning confidence in the workplace several transformational processes need to occur. As discussed in Chapter 1, there must be a preparedness for people to unleash their true potential. As highlighted in Chapter 2, there must be wide-ranging support if a person is to grow in a dynamic and proactive way. Offering the right support requires a good understanding of motivation, values and key result areas (KRAs). Third, there must be an inherent flexibility in workplace learning policies and activities to enable people to grow in a way that suits and stretches their learning styles, and this can only occur if organisations value their talents and capabilities.

Case study: Questioning our beliefs about learning

Some years ago, I counselled a woman in her mid-fifties about her career. She had contacted me a week prior to our coaching session and asked me whether I would be prepared to give her some pointers on how to learn. She had just taken up a university postgraduate correspondence programme and this was her first return to 'education' since attending school as a teenager. It had been 35 years since she had experienced any formal education.

In the first few minutes of meeting her, my initial impression was that she was articulate and highly proficient. Her current career was in the field of relationship counselling and her chosen course of study seemed highly relevant. However, I realised after the coaching session began that this was not going to be an ordinary appointment. Up front, she openly shared again that this was the first time she had attempted such a challenge and as a result was quite nervous and apprehensive about how she should go about it.

She went on to say that many of her friends and work colleagues advised her not to take the study on, as they felt it would be too demanding of her. She listened to their advice but decided that for her own self-esteem and confidence she wanted to do the programme. As she spoke I could feel her tremendous courage and determination.

I asked her to describe how she undertook her first assignment, which she had just completed. She was keen to share this, as it had been quite a struggle and had caused much stress and anxiety. After 10 minutes, the need for the coaching session became crystal clear. My client had undertaken her assignment the same way she did at school 35 years previously. As she talked, I could not help but think of the many people I had met in the workplace and in educational institutions who had spent their time trying to conform to a system that in many ways was not geared to fully appreciate and adapt to the natural talent being paraded within it.

We then paused and summarised the coaching discussion so far. We spent the next 30 minutes clearing away various assumptions that were blocking her learning. Examples of her assumptions included:

- to pass at university, you must learn a set way;
- to pass at university, you must study only the one official textbook;
- never mark the textbook as someone else may need to use it again after you;
- to learn you must continuously write and rewrite your notes.

Having listened for a while longer, we both agreed that the current learning methods were grossly inefficient and did not suit her. At this stage, I searched for her learning strengths. To do this I asked her to describe how she had learnt to cope with some of her past and current challenges in life. One of them had been a serious illness. At this point, she became alive and talked with joy and passion about her love for music and her enjoyment in developing structured thoughts into debates.

I then suggested to her that she use her learning strengths in her current university assignments. Why not? Read and make notes to music, canvass a range of views by phone and fax, and conduct research face to face. At first, these suggestions startled her, but, as we talked more and more about learning preferences, she became more and more empowered and stimulated. When she left our coaching session it was apparent that she felt more confident and was ready and primed for action.

In some small way, this 90-minute discussion had changed my client's view of university learning from an 'imposition' to a 'joyful' discovery process. Yet all I did was to allow her to rekindle and discover her own strengths and natural talent.

If people are given the opportunity to explore and discuss their motivations, values and learning preferences there is always potential for increased confidence. In the workplace, the lesson of this story also 'rings true'. If people take the time to listen to each other, both the individual and the organisation can benefit. Employees become much more confident and improved workplace innovation, performance and potential result.

Confronting your fears

We all struggle at times with our capacity to adapt to new or different situations. This struggle is often tied very closely to fear of the unknown or fear of failing. Fear is a common enough word, but what exactly does it mean? The *Concise Oxford Dictionary* defines fear as 'painful emotion caused by impending danger or evil, state of alarm'. So why do some people become fearful of learning or change but others do not? To overcome fear we need to find the 'evidence' that helps people gain the confidence to deal with the perceived challenges.

As a consultant, career coach, and learner myself, I have found it useful to define FEAR as:

F   False
E   Evidence
A   Appearing
R   Real

The process of removing FEAR requires people to locate the evidence that best supports a change in a belief that may be inhibiting their potential to change. In the case of the woman who was attending university for the first time, she discovered that there was more than one way to learn at university, while also recognising that she had many strengths that she could call on to meet her learning needs.

Removing FEAR has transformational qualities. Whether it is an individual learning a new skill or an organisation moving into another frontier, the outcome is the same. Removing false evidence that appears real assists positive discovery and change.

Removing learning fear and building learner confidence requires the recall of positive learning successes that have been achieved in the past. With this information, individuals are better placed to 'ignite and kindle' the spirit of learning. For some people, these stories and achievements might be well hidden, but they are there to be discovered. People must also be open to question the way they label themselves. In doing this they are more likely to find out the truth about themselves.

Some additional tips for developing learner confidence

Additional tips for developing learner confidence include:

- 'Coaches' and 'advisers' must demonstrate 'up front' that they are committed to learning themselves.
- Be prepared to invest in functional and basic literacy to build the bridge to further learning.
- Remind the learner of his or her role and responsibility in the process.
- Include early successes in each learning process that is undertaken.
- Practise, practise, practise.
- Seek out and use relevant resource materials to support discovery, personal growth and application.
- Take every opportunity to celebrate what has been learnt.
- See each of life's experiences as a learning opportunity.
- Examine outside influences that could be inhibiting learning.
- Be wary of learning fatigue and burnout by setting clear and achievable action plans.
- Vary learning techniques and self-assessment processes.
- Maintain a record of learning achievements.
- Set learning goals that stretch abilities.
- Write out action plans that anticipate barriers and resources.
- Encourage learners to support and coach each other.
- Remember there is no set formula for learning. It is important to be flexible and adaptable at all times. When a strategy fails, always be prepared to re-evaluate your approach.

Becoming a self-directed learner

When people develop the skill of overcoming perceived personal growth barriers, they are well on the way to becoming a self-directed learner. Ultimately, if organisations are to achieve transformed workplace learning, employees and the people they interact with need to feel confident about managing their ability to confront any learning challenge.

This transition to self-direction and self-management does not happen overnight. Recognising this, the challenge of helping people from dependency through to self-directed learning requires a versatile range of support strategies. For example, if someone asked me to present a 30-minute training presentation on time management, I could do that task easily. However, if someone asked me to tile the office cloakroom, that would be a different matter. Left to my own devices, the cloakroom would end up a real mess, unless I made a major commitment to research and develop new skills. If this was not possible, I would need plenty of direction and support to finish the job on time and to the appropriate standard.

So the journey towards self-direction and self-management will potentially require a number of coaching, advising and facilitation interactions between the learner and others. These include:

■ expert assistance if the material is unfamiliar;
■ motivational support if there is a perceived level of risk or self-doubt in the discovery process;
■ resourcing the learner so that he or she can become self-directed and self-reliant;
■ delegating the whole learning task and establishing clear review points.

UNDERSTANDING MENTAL DIVERSITY

In many ways this final section on understanding mental diversity is a fitting climax to Part 1 of *Learning Unlimited* because it builds a strong bridge to Part 2, 'Proven implementation strategies'.

Without first understanding mental diversity it is very difficult to transform a 'commitment' to workplace learning into 'implementation' and 'action'. Knowing the concepts and mindsets is of little value unless people can translate ideas into action. To achieve this goal there must be correct coaching, training, influence and education derived from an excellent understanding of mental diversity.

As the new millennium begins, it will be the capacity of our organisations to value and treasure the richness and wonder of the human intellect that will ultimately determine whether true learning will occur.

Much has been said in worldwide communities about the importance of cultural and gender diversity. However, it is time to extend the diversity debate to include 'mental diversity'. With this in mind, the final section of this chapter examines five frameworks that provide a concise and powerful insight into this area. Each framework, in its own way, has withstood the test of time and provides an important perspective that enhances our tolerance and versatility.

The mental diversity frameworks to be discussed are:

■ the Kolb learning model;
■ the Honey and Mumford learning styles;
■ Neuro Linguistic Programming (NLP);
■ the Herrmann whole brain model;
■ Howard Gardner's model of multiple intelligences.

The benefit of exploring these five frameworks is that each opens an array of potential solutions. If you are perplexed about how to deal with a learning challenge, refer to these frameworks, and you will usually find a key that opens a door to further discovery. To use such frameworks ethically it is very important not to label or box people. People are too precious and unique to be stereotyped into categories. If used ethically and intelligently, such models and frameworks can foster and enhance our understanding, without being manipulative or invading the rights of others.

Given the infinite nature of mental diversity, there are no formulas or packages that can instantly fix learning or discovery challenges. However, when an understanding of mental diversity frameworks dovetails with the right support, we do increase our options for improving the hopes and choices facing a learner in the workplace.

The research data from all of these five frameworks suggest that the applications are not biased by any cultural or educational background issues. The models can be applied to any person, of any origin or age. Remember that the five frameworks measure preference only, not ability; it would be inappropriate to assume that the frameworks demonstrate learning expertise or competency.

The Kolb learning model

The Kolb learning model, illustrated in Figure 5.1, describes learning as a never-ending cycle of four stages: concrete experience, reflective observation, abstract conceptualisation and active experimentation. Kolb's highly popular model suggests that all learning should mirror this cycle. If you are teaching a skill, you could follow the model by:

■ practising current skills (concrete experience);
■ asking the learner to reflect on how the process went, or provide an example of what could be done differently next time (reflective observation);

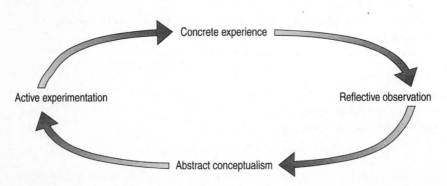

Figure 5.1 The Kolb learning model

- linking current desired learning behaviour to a theory, guideline or principle (abstract conceptualisation);
- practising, experimenting and applying the new information (active experimentation).

The Honey and Mumford learning styles

Instead of focusing on the 'total process' of learning that occurs in the Kolb model, Honey and Mumford, in their Learning Styles Questionnaire, describe four different learning styles.

- *Activists* learn best when they can use trial and error to discover something. They prefer to be exposed to lots of variation, and practise and enjoy the encounter of new challenges.
- *Reflecters* learn best when they are given adequate time to digest, consider and prepare. They need adequate resources and information to carefully consider their thoughts and opportunities. They would rather watch, listen and anticipate feelings, before demonstrating.
- *Theorists* learn best when there is a sound structure and a pattern or purpose. They respond well to complex ideas or concepts that stretch or question current thinking or have a strong research basis to the learning.
- *Pragmatists* learn best when they can be given real-life and practical issues to discuss and are supplied with practical tips and suggestions.

The Honey and Mumford model can assist the design, delivery and assessment of workplace learning by ensuring that methods and techniques are adaptable to each of the different learning styles. There is evidence to suggest that people do change their preferences over time, especially if they have undergone significant developmental experiences. In addition, people vary in their map of preferences, from some individuals who are dominant in a single learning style through to learners who are quite diverse and multi-dominant. Quantum leaps in personal growth can occur if people are encouraged to try out those experiences that are not their natural learning preference. For example, if someone normally avoids reflection, giving him or her a chance to develop some expertise and confidence in this area may open up a whole new world of insight and growth. This form of 'shadow boxing' can be invaluable to those wishing to expand their potential much further.

Neuro Linguistic Programming

Pioneered in the early 1970s by Dr Richard Bandler and John Grinder, Neuro Linguistic Programming (NLP) has become an oft-used and respected tool among a large number of counsellors, trainers and communications consultants. NLP studies how our mind and body are conditioned to respond to certain language or information signals. When applied to the workplace setting, NLP can provide a number of important guidelines on how people may process learning. One of the most commonly applied guidelines of NLP is the concept of modalities. This suggests that learners have at least three basic preferences that may affect how people input, store and output information. In exploring these modalities, it is important to note that the most likely scenario will be that a person will be able to identify with at least a number of the points made in the Visual, Auditory and Kinesthetic discussions.

- *Visual learners* are more successful inputting and outputting visually, for example painting or recalling a picture in their mind. Visual learners prefer representations such as pictures, diagrams and graphs. Learning is enhanced when the visuals are improved with the use of colour, patterns and adjustments to brightness and size. Visual learners also prefer to read rather than being read to. They traditionally need the whole picture to learn effectively. They are good spellers and fast, successful readers. They have vivid imaginations, are good at copying visuals and can recall detail better than people who prefer other modalities.
- *Auditory learners* are more comfortable communicating by sound and will pay more attention to things like tone of voice and combinations of speech. They prefer to learn by either explaining or listening to the material. When recalling, auditory people will recall the information by 'replaying the tape' of what they heard in the past. Their learning is amplified by using the spoken word, which is varied in pitch, volume, rhythm and speed. They like to repeat things back as a means of recalling information. Auditory learners prefer the spoken message to the written message. Traditionally, auditory learners are the most talkative and enjoy discussions, use phonetic approaches and rhythmic movement to spell, enjoy reading aloud, but are often slow readers because of sub-vocalising.
- *Kinesthetic learners* communicate more in feelings, touching and doing. They like to get their hands on things and try them out. They prefer movement and action and to be entertained and have an enjoyable experience. They prefer closeness, touch, smell and taste more than learners in other modalities. They normally communicate with large movements and gestures. For example, when spelling they

count out letters with the body and check their internal feelings; when writing they tend to have pressured, untidy handwriting; and when storytelling they usually act out the images with their bodies.

To be successful in applying the modality principles of NLP, workplace learning needs to be sensitive to communicating in all three modalities: visual, auditory and kinesthetic. In his book *Righting the Educational Conveyor Belt* (1991) Michael Grinder suggests that in a typical group of 30 people, an average of 22 learners will be able to move comfortably from the visual to the auditory to the kinesthetic modality. However, between four and six learners will have very dominant preferences for one modality, and as a result will turn 'on' and 'off' as the communication channel changes. The remaining two or three learners may have other factors that are influencing their communication, such as some recent emotionally draining experience that needs special attention.

Care must be taken not to assume that all learners input, store and output in the same modalities. For example, an individual may receive auditory information, store it visually and output it kinesthetically.

The Herrmann whole brain model

Herrmann, in his initial book *The Creative Brain* (1990) and the subsequent book *The Whole Brain Business Book* (1996), developed a powerful explanation of mental diversity by using a four-quadrant whole brain model. Herrmann has taken the work of such experts as Dr Roger Sperry and Dr Paul McLean and developed the metaphorical model detailed in Figure 5.2. Looking at this, it can be seen that Herrmann has separated mental preference into four quadrants: the left and right sides of the brain, the 'upper' (cerebral), and the 'lower' (limbic) divisions.

Through exploring the combinations and characteristics of these four quadrants, a learner can develop a powerful insight into his or her own unique mentality. Data collected by the Ned Herrmann World Wide Group since the 1970s indicate that the people of the world have a 'collective whole brain', constituting an unlimited range of learning preferences and mental dominance within the four-quadrant model.

The Herrmann whole brain model will be explored further in Chapter 17, 'Getting results from training', where the issue of designing, delivering and assessing whole brain learning will be discussed. Other areas of applications of the Herrmann model include creativity, teamwork and personal growth.

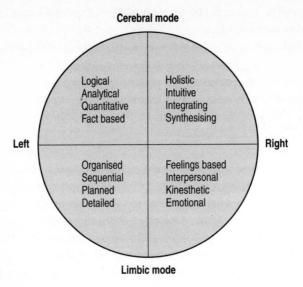

Cerebral mode

Logical Analytical Quantitative Fact based	Holistic Intuitive Integrating Synthesising
Organised Sequential Planned Detailed	Feelings based Interpersonal Kinesthetic Emotional

Left ... **Right**

Limbic mode

Source: The Whole Brain Business Book, © 1996 McGraw-Hill, reprinted with the permission of the author, Ned Herrmann, of the Ned Herrmann Group.

Figure 5.2 The whole brain model

Howard Gardner's model of multiple intelligences

Howard Gardner has made an important contribution to understanding human intelligence, detailed in his book *Frames of Mind* (1983) and in subsequent books, *Seven Ways of Knowing* (1991) and *Seven Ways of Learning* (1994) by David Lazear. This pioneering work expands the categorisation of human intelligence to areas well outside typically discussed areas of IQ. Gardner's framework is based on extensive research study and provides organisations with a richer view of human potential than may have been the case in the past. His work on multi-intelligence has made seven important contributions to workplace learning:

■ Traditional IQ measures are a very limited measurement of general intelligence.
■ Each learner has his or her own unique map of multi-intelligences, of which there are a possible seven at least.
■ Learners can indeed be smart and not so smart at the same time.
■ The range of learning options can be legitimately viewed as very extensive.
■ Broadening our view of intelligence expands the possibilities of building a better and mentally diverse workplace, which in turn

increases the capacity of organisations to adapt to change with greater flexibility and certainty.

■ There may be an urgent need to rethink existing policies and practices on recruitment, selection and workplace learning since they may be based on inappropriate perspectives on intelligence.

■ Intelligence can be taught and learnt.

Gardner identifies seven areas of multi-intelligence:

■ *Spatial/visual intelligence* deals with the sense of sight, and the ability to form images and pictures in the mind. An individual particularly gifted in this area may be able to visualise outcomes with clarity or measure the distance between objects with accuracy.

■ *Linguistic/verbal intelligence* acknowledges that some individuals have an ability to explore different ways of expressing themselves using language and are stimulated by the spoken word. A good example would be an individual who can articulate a dynamic presentation with the use of a story and metaphor.

■ *Intrapersonal intelligence* involves an understanding of self. This area of intelligence is demonstrated by the individual who has an excellent ability to reflect on his or her own unique thoughts and feelings and then develop action to take control of his or her own learning. Intrapersonal intelligence is viewed as the gateway to personal growth because it requires self-awareness.

■ *Musical/auditory intelligence* includes such capacities as the recognition and use of rhythmic and tonal patterns, and sensitivity to sounds such as the human voice and musical instruments. A person who has a major preference in this area is likely to enjoy using music to stimulate relaxation or learning.

■ *Bodily/kinesthetic intelligence* is the ability to use the body to express emotion, or play a game, to create or to do an action. A person who is talented in this area can make and build objects more easily than individuals who have low facility in this area of 'knowing'.

■ *Interpersonal intelligence* involves the ability to work co-operatively in a group, as well as the ability to communicate verbally and non-verbally with other people. A person who is strong in this area of intelligence would be able to empathise with the complexity of values, feelings, fears, anticipations and beliefs of others.

■ *Logical/mathematical intelligence* has been traditionally highly acknowledged in both educational institutions and workplaces. It is often associated with scientific and sequential thinking. As evidenced in many organisations, individuals who are proficient in this area can easily make objective observations from data, draw conclusions, make judgments and formulate hypotheses.

SUMMARY

Helping a wounded learner requires a skilful mix of motivational learning and coaching strategies. To improve the health of a wounded learner we must recognise that such behaviour is a situational response rather than a personality disorder.

An excellent way of expanding our options in dealing with learning challenges is through the development of our knowledge and application of different mental diversity models. This awareness acts as a bond and linkage between knowing the concepts and frameworks of workplace learning and implementing the strategies that matter.

PART 2

Proven Implementation Strategies

There are unlimited ways to transform workplace learning, ranging from the simple to the very complex. To help you discover the best options, the following 14 chapters cover a full spectrum of considerations. Depending on the nature of your business and work you will be able to choose the idea, technique or strategy best suited to your needs at this time, while allowing yourself the freedom to return to *Learning Unlimited* at a later date and consider fresh alternatives.

Part 2 shifts the discussion from developing a true commitment to workplace learning to the ideas or best practice strategies that add value to the transformation process. The material has been carefully selected for its practical and innovative nature. However, none of the suggestions should be seen as a stand-alone solution. Each idea, exercise or story needs to be considered in light of the unique variables and business issues arising within your organisation and industry.

Part 2 begins with a chapter on identifying business needs. This is followed by material on gaining and maintaining political support and ensuring employee participation. A number of different angles are then explored in the area of implementation, including stamping out bad practices, benchmarking best practices, competency-based learning, using digital technology, team learning, celebrating learning, building learning communities, mentoring and coaching, and managing on-the-job learning and formal training. To complete the discussion on proven implementation strategies, Chapter 19 details ways that organisations can build a knowledge pool that best meets the future business challenges of the workplace.

The material has been structured in a logical pattern, but given the interactive nature of workplace learning, it is not always possible to follow the sequential flow. To assist in this regard, links and cross-references are provided to aid your understanding. Simply go to any topic that interests you.

Part 3 then provides a range of exercises to assist in the development of measurable and challenging action plans.

6

Identifying And Evaluating Business Requirements

> *Survival is not about survival of the fittest, but the most adaptable.*
>
> Anon

KEY PRINCIPLES

- Develop an excellent understanding of financial, customer, community and environmental needs.
- Consider multiple futures.
- Identify a 'felt' need.
- Involve key people in accurate measurement of learning outcomes.
- Use a range of high leverage evaluation strategies to measure business results.

START BY TALKING SMART

One of the practical realities of modern business is that there are many organisations that do not place a high value on workplace learning. Unless the reason for the learning is to ensure some immediate redress, or meets some legislative obligation such as Occupational Health and Safety regulations, workplaces will often turn a blind eye to serious and systematic skill enhancement or knowledge building. As a result, people within these workplaces either become too busy or too uninterested to think about learning, innovation and skills enhancement. When stuck for talent these organisations may go searching the labour market to 'quick-fix' the capability hole that they are experiencing. This can often lead to frustration and disillusionment when the right people cannot be found, or will not stay.

Turning around such an apathetic approach to workplace learning requires a smart approach. Strong evidence must be found to educate key decision makers that workplace learning is an imperative that they cannot ignore.

In my first job as a training manager, I vividly remember catching the lift to the top floor of a large office building to meet my senior manager for the first time. My personal goal for the meeting was to gain some insight into what was expected of me in the area of workplace learning. Being a new kid on the block, I thought that I would start with an open question that would demonstrate my desire to make positive change. So, I asked the senior manager what skills he believed were needed if the organisation was going to be successful in meeting its five-year plan. After a very awkward silence, he came back with a response that totally startled me. He said in a quiet and monotone voice, 'Alastair, nothing much changes around here; we will be doing the same things in five years' time'. As the next five years unfolded, the workplace underwent massive changes, including a reduction of staff from 6,200 to 4,000, with the outsourcing of many functions including maintenance, training and recruitment, and the incorporation of performance-based contracts. The old insular and bureaucratic culture of the organisation has now been replaced by a new outward-focused and commercial culture. Ghosts from the past and so-called truths have been replaced by a new set of values that are more aligned to today's rapidly changing world.

This story is, of course, not unique. Every industry is affected every microsecond by internal and external drivers for change. Recent trends such as virtual organisations, e-commerce, green reporting, ethical investment and the need for joint ventures and mergers are indicative of how organisational structures and business processes have needed to reinvent themselves to survive. These pressures have resulted in a need for businesses to have a measured understanding of the financial, customer, community and environmental factors, as well as alignment of internal business processes, corporate culture and innovation and learning processes. Only then are organisations positioned to have the sustainability to pass the test of time.

Given the chaotic and uncertain nature of change, a one-track business strategy for a single predicted future is a very dangerous 'tightrope' to walk. Business planning and decision making must be open to the possibility that nothing is really certain, except more uncertainty. There needs to be a tolerance for a world of multiple futures. Only then will a business brain have the innate flexibility and 'know-how' to survive and thrive within chaotic change.

Questions that can help develop a clearer picture of what will happen:

- Where does the business need to be in two years' time?
- What are the global and regional trends affecting the business?
- What issues is the business frightened of finding out about?
- Which strengths and weaknesses does the business bring into the future?
- How are the customer and community needs and expectations changing?
- What business issues must be addressed in the next 12 months in order to remain viable?
- Which shortfalls in talent and knowledge could seriously hurt the business in this time?

BROADCASTING THE FELT NEED FOR CHANGE

The term 'felt need' has been carefully selected to highlight the fact that motivations for change may be based on emotional wishes and wants, rather than well-verified business needs. It would be very nice to think that people will listen and take action on what is required, but this is not always the case. To cater for this trait of human nature, people must remain sensitive to both the rational and the emotional side of the human spirit. Decision makers must be committed to the fact that key business needs and present realities must be the overriding consideration for all decision making.

As the story of my first experience as a training manager highlights, the pressures of change do work in strange ways. Although I did not find the first meeting with my senior manager particularly useful, I found in time that by 'red flagging' threats and opportunities for business improvement, I was able to influence the agenda for reform. This experience very much mirrors the principles of versatility that were highlighted within the models of 'transformation' and 'change management' discussed in the Introduction and in Chapter 2.

The high-profile business needs that are currently providing momentum for workplace learning include:

- adaptability to change;
- addressing community and environmental expectations;
- counteracting chronic skills shortages;
- consolidating core business opportunities against global pressures;
- effectively managing restructuring/downsizing;
- exploring new market segments;
- fostering a team-based work culture;
- improving customer service;

- improving quality;
- embracing information technology and e-commerce strategies;
- enhancing competitiveness and marketability;
- linking business activity to the mission and vision of the organisation;
- managing and sustaining a high-quality workforce;
- ongoing difficulty in attracting and retaining talent;
- overcoming a takeover threat;
- stimulating greater innovation, knowledge creation and management;
- targeting sustainability and long-term viability.

Irrespective of industry or organisation, all workplaces need learning as a vital part of business strategy. The 'felt need' may change, but the outcome of learning will not. No matter what the business and people needs in the workplace are, it will be necessary to develop many people to achieve new targets and goals.

Identifying needs rather than wants

Given the confusion that can result from sorting through such a large array of needs, it is imperative that information is gathered that describes accurately the key reasons for implementing workplace learning.

In upcoming chapters a number of high leverage ways to collect such evidence are canvassed, including performance management discussions, business planning processes, reviewing written and digitally available knowledge, undertaking best practice studies, forming co-operative partnerships, overseeing system change, conducting competency-based learning and holding team learning meetings.

In addition to these broad-range research strategies, there are also a number of complementary data-gathering methods that help identify business and people requirements. These methods include surveying employees and subcontractors, 360-degree feedback, conducting on-site interviews, focus groups, revisiting past needs research, and finally, examining performance indicators such as:

- productivity;
- absenteeism or tardiness;
- safety records;
- short-term sickness;
- grievances;
- waste;
- late deliveries;
- product and service quality;

- downtime;
- errors and repairs;
- customer satisfaction;
- equipment utilisation.

Having collected the information that helps identify priorities, the workplace learning process can then turn its attention to implementing and evaluating transformation strategies.

EVALUATING WORKPLACE LEARNING TRANSFORMATION

The aim of workplace learning must be to improve the business through the development of people. For too long, the evaluation of workplace learning in organisations has focused too much on how well the processes have been undertaken and not enough on behavioural change and business results achieved. In recent times the measures of business results have become more holistic in nature, with greater emphasis placed on the value a business provides to society in general. If neglected, firms can expect a public outcry or backlash if seen as greedy, unethical or out of touch. This is a recurring issue in industries such as banking, fast food, footwear, mining and government. Customers in modern times are far more informed and, as a result, expect the best.

The discipline of evaluation cannot be underestimated. Decision makers are now rightly expecting that business improvement is generated from all workplace learning policy and activity. To achieve this expectation, the evaluation process must follow seven guidelines. These are:

- Do not try to evaluate everything all at once. Allocate evaluation resources to policies, activities and processes that have the potential to be high business breadwinners.
- Carefully select the relevant measurement techniques and data collection methods. Select the evaluation techniques that can quickly resolve the answers you desire in a way that satisfies the decision makers' requirements.
- Do not fall into the trap of 'analysis paralysis', when hours and hours are spent producing reports that are never actioned or read.
- Involve the recipients and clients of the workplace learning process in the evaluation process. Where possible make them accountable for the design, implementation and assessment of the measurement process.
- See the evaluation process as a natural part of the total renewal and innovation cycle.

- Implement change by using evaluation as part of the consultation and empowerment cycle. Encourage all parties including employees, unions and customers to be part of the design, delivery and assessment of change.
- Wherever possible, quantify evaluation outcomes. Establish clear performance standards to be used as measures of improvement.

Taking a work-flow review

As described in Chapter 4, aligning yourself with leading-edge management technology is a solid framework for improving the quality of knowledge work and learning in the workplace. A practical demonstration of how workplace learning can be better evaluated by using a framework approach called a work-flow diagram follows.

A work-flow diagram maps out the stages of activity that occur while producing a service or product. By taking the work-flow diagram as a guide it is possible to evaluate wastage and continuous improvement in any activity that you may choose. For example, assume it was decided to implement a monthly team learning meeting within an organisation. Hypothetically, the team learning process may have resulted from an absence of workplace knowledge in a key technical area of expertise. Given this short background, Figure 6.1 could be a work-flow diagram that displays a six-stage continuous evaluation model for evaluating a planned monthly team learning process.

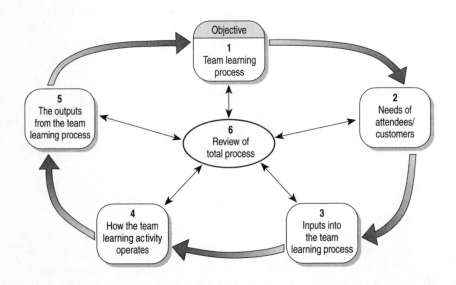

Figure 6.1 A team learning work-flow diagram

Taking each of the six stages of the work-flow diagram, a process of continuous improvement can be initiated by compiling and asking key questions in each phase of the process.

Stage 1: Objective for monthly team learning meeting

Examples of questions are:

- What business results are the team seeking?
- Is the objective of holding a monthly team learning meeting realistic?

Stage 2: Needs of attendees/customers

Examples of questions are:

- What are the learning needs of the attendees?
- What are the expectations of the attendees' customers?

Stage 3: Inputs into the team learning process

Examples of questions are:

- Are the right people attending the meeting?
- Do the team members have the confidence and skill to fully benefit from the meeting?
- How do the preparation and inputs compare with best practice?

Stage 4: How will the team learning activity operate?

Examples of questions are:

- How smoothly did the workplace learning meeting proceed?
- How do the agenda and process compare to best practice?
- Which skills are being used the most and least by the participants?

Stage 5: The outputs from the team learning process

Examples of questions are:

- How well do the outcomes achieved compare to best practice in team learning methods?
- What business milestones or projects have been completed since the workplace learning process began?

Stage 6: Review of total process

Examples of questions are:

- How successful was the process in meeting the overall objectives for the process?
- Which resources and activities were most and least practical in assisting business results?

- Was business performance enhanced or inhibited by the team learning process?
- What action is required for next time?

Take time to measure all levels of evaluation

In addition to evaluating performance and learning in a work-flow format you can also evaluate in terms of levels. As displayed in Figure 6.2, workplace learning can be evaluated at four distinct levels. This four-level framework of evaluation, developed by Kirkpatrick, provides a powerful method to review and measure workplace learning. This is especially the case when the Kirkpatrick method is used in combination with other leading-edge management technologies.

Level 1: Reaction

Reaction evaluation measures the feelings of the participants within a workplace learning process. This feedback gives data about the spontaneous and instant reaction of the learner to how well the process was perceived. This is the most used of all the evaluation methods. End-of-training course/programme questionnaires and employee climate surveys are common examples of the reaction evaluation process. To get value out of the reaction evaluation:

- carefully determine what standards you wish to measure;
- design a process where written comments and reactions are quantified;
- 'chase up' honest responses from everyone;
- measure reactions against standards;
- implement action on the recommendations.

Level 2: Learning

Evaluation of learning can be observed during an actual workplace learning process. Learning is measured by giving the learner tasks to complete during the process (for example, during a team learning meeting or a coaching session). To accurately measure learning:

- conduct a pre-test and post-test of knowledge, skills and attitudes, before and after the workplace learning process;
- use measurement processes that accurately measure learning objectives;
- conduct performance assessment for skills (that is, role plays and demonstrations) and tests for attitudes and knowledge;
- compare the results and improvement of the learners with another similar group of people who have not undertaken the process (this

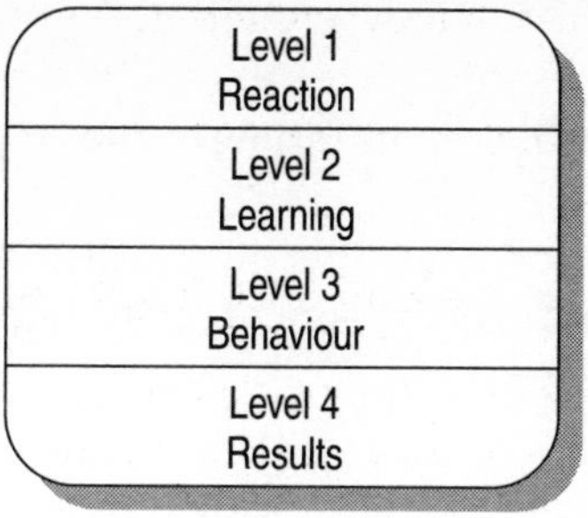

Figure 6.2 The four levels of evaluation

'control group' evaluation method helps validate actual learning by directly comparing the results with those not under the effect of the workplace learning process in question);
■ compare results with past workplace learning processes;
■ statistically analyse the data;
■ implement action on the recommendations.

Level 3: Behaviour

The third level of evaluation, 'behaviour', measures changes in on-the-job behaviour. To correctly measure behaviour:

■ conduct assessment of behaviour on the job before and after the workplace learning process;
■ allow a time-phased review of behavioural change by evaluating on-the-job behaviour 1 month, 3 months and 12 months after the process (this provides a more reliable measure of growth and enables a closer examination of factors that may be helping or hindering the application of desired knowledge, skills and attitudes on the job);
■ survey and/or hold discussions with the learners, their managers and major customers;
■ use accurate sampling processes, if 100 per cent evaluation is not possible;
■ hire a third party to do focused research or sampling;
■ implement action on the recommendations.

For further explanation of the background on the assessment of learning refer to Chapter 11.

Level 4: Results

Measuring tangible improvements in business results is the final and the most important level. Many of the principles discussed in evaluating behavioural change can also be applied in measuring results. These include using pre- and post-test reviews of business results, using control groups to measure business performance, and a phased review of business results over time.

To further explore evaluation, the final section of this chapter discusses the important and controversial area of quantifying business results from workplace learning.

QUANTIFYING RESULTS

As the allocation of resources within organisations becomes more and more competitive, so does the importance of gaining decision makers' attention. The pressure to demonstrate value and improvement are now a normal part of modern-day management. Within this process of barter and negotiation there is an increasing tendency to measure improvement. Workplace learning professionals are beginning to wake up to this trend and are slowly learning how to quantify the outcomes of workplace learning.

Developing meaningful measurement takes time and plenty of coaching. As a starting strategy, approach people who are most affected by business change and ask them to articulate how important outcomes could be better measured in ways that have greater impact and creditability, whether in financial terms or some other performance indicator such as social responsibility, corporate image or ethical practice. Line managers or major customers are often the best friends you have in quantifying returns that can be measured. A good way of developing the skill of quantification is to learn from various financial or performance wizards who are normally employed somewhere in an organisation or industry. Alternatively, you could ask people on the Internet via various newsgroups and lists that exist. To join a popular network for trainers send an e-mail to listserv@ lists.psu.edu with 'Subscribe trdev-l Your Name' in the 'Subject' heading.

Cost-benefit analysis

Using a cost-benefit analysis can be a useful supplement to the quantification challenge. Common elements of a cost-benefit analysis are explained in this section.

Costs

- labour consisting of all salaries, subcontract and consulting fees in all phases of design, production and development;
- set-up involving technology, software, hardware, equipment;

- material comprising all reusable items and learning aids;
- delivery and assessment including wages and salaries of all the people involved, travel costs, rentals, accommodation and digital network and telecommunications.

Benefits

- time saved;
- savings in material and resources used in performing a function;
- reduced staff turnover;
- improved productivity;
- improved environmental, customer or business costs.

A checklist for measuring or marketing in cash terms

Building on the comments on cost-benefit analyses, the following checklist suggests six practical ways in which business outcomes can potentially be measured or marketed in cash terms. This checklist should be used as a discussion starter only. As you explore real-life scenarios and consult with decision makers, the best measures in your industry will slowly emerge.

For many people, quantifying in cash-benefit terms may clash with their values and they may prefer to spend their energies on other projects, particularly when the real impact can be quantified in other ways such as value to society or improved business image. However, for me, great sadness arises when I see wonderful workplace learning processes going unrecognised and undervalued because they have failed both to measure and market the success.

Ethics play an important role in this quantification debate. Great care must be taken to ensure long-term integrity. Many professionals from all walks of life incorrectly claim successes from a process they are managing. Good ethics prohibit statistical theft! Decision makers may like meaningful numbers but they certainly despise statistical liars.

Area 1: New business milestones, critical incidents and testimonials

Examples include:

- increase in strategic and operational key result areas (KRAs) being achieved;
- achievement of newer and higher KRAs;
- increased customer satisfaction, resulting in reduced costs and resources to maintain and keep key customers, and/or reduced resources allocated to deal with complaints;
- continuous improvement successes including wastage savings, higher production milestones, greater consistency, faster introduction of new technology and innovation;

■ improved decision-making practices leading to measurable successes in better teamwork, improved communication of critical decision-making information and higher quality of staff participation in decision making.

Area 2: Savings in the investment in labour

The cost of labour provides a wonderful opportunity to quantify workplace learning. Given that hiring, selection and employment rates are easily calculated, many financial arguments can be calculated to demonstrate that workplace learning improves the return on investment in labour. Examples include the costs associated with the replacement of key personnel, downtime, staff turnover, absenteeism, orientation of new staff, retaining low-performing staff, internal and external hiring of full-time, casual and temporary staff, and the cost of subcontract versus full-time labour.

Area 3: Measuring the leverage of workplace learning

Comparing the investment in workplace learning with business savings and productivity increases, this method can be quite powerful when expressed in a per person figure. For example, the per person annual investment in workplace learning may be less than half the improvement in productivity. To use this technique ethically a minimum 12-month framework is recommended.

Area 4: Financial improvements benchmarked against internal or external competitive performance

In this regard, most industries produce publicly available information that gives indications of growth, potential, and service and productivity delivery.

Area 5: Improvement in the recall of learning

A workplace learning programme has increased learners' rate of retention. For example, using a new accelerative learning process, a training course has increased its 12-month period retention rate from 25 per cent to 50 per cent. This saving has led to cash savings in customer service, productivity and retraining time.

Area 6: Improvement in the efficiency of workplace learning

For example: instead of requiring 20 days to train an employee, it now takes 10 days, resulting in a cash saving.

SUMMARY

Ultimately, workplace learning processes demand proof to ascertain whether they are making a difference to the business. There are no easy answers to identifying and evaluating business results, only intensive data gathering and skilful communication of findings.

The challenge in evaluation is not so much how to measure something but finding the most ethical and most efficient way of performing the assessment.

7

Gaining And Maintaining Political Support

> *You are the organisation.*
>
> John Lizzio

KEY PRINCIPLES

- We are all players in workplace politics.
- Develop flexible management of 50–50 relationships.
- Get to know your stakeholders and fellow-travellers.
- Tap into the informal network as well as the formal hierarchy.
- Glue together your influence strategies with a marketing plan.

ACCEPTING THE INEVITABILITY OF POLITICS

Gaining and maintaining support for workplace learning requires a 100 per cent commitment to organisational politics. Unless you have political backing, your plans for workplace learning will not become reality.

So what are politics, and what role do they play in transforming workplace learning? Politics by themselves are not necessarily good or bad. It depends on how they are played. Politics can be defined as an influence and negotiation process that gets things done. Managers sending draft reports to senior executives for approval and a group of team leaders designing a new learning package are involving themselves in political activity, because they are influencing and negotiating with others to get things achieved. Politics are played in every organisation, from multimillion dollar conglomerates to small office partnerships.

Many people see politics as a dirty and nasty game of manipulation, where warring tribes fight battles to achieve goals. However, influence need not be exercised or perceived in this way. Politics can be played constructively, with integrity, and in a way that allows all of the parties to achieve positive outcomes.

Nevertheless, one thing is for sure – where there are people, there will be politics. They cannot be avoided. By simply taking a 'back seat', you are making a political statement. This may sound slightly paranoid, or part of some conspiracy theory, but true transformation only occurs when people recognise the inevitability of politics as a natural part of organisational life.

Learning Unlimited has already made a number of points that are important in gaining and maintaining political support. For example:

- understanding the process of transformation;
- clearly articulating your need and vision for change;
- using good project management and evaluation skills;
- taking the time to understand mental diversity;
- remembering to 'talk smart'.

The first step, however, in maintaining and gaining political support is knowing your principles and values.

KNOWING YOUR PRINCIPLES AND VALUES

Playing positive politics requires an astute understanding of your principles and values, and a genuine desire to be open with people. We recognise that politics can be played and battles won in a multitude of ways. A long-term and sustained impact on workplace learning is more likely when people approach transformation with caring and the desire to make a positive contribution to others' lives.

This requires integrity, trust and sensitivity. People need to serve the overall purpose or mission of workplace learning without trying to acquire some extraordinary personal advantage or glory out of the process. Generally, where there is destructive political behaviour, the organisation and individual suffer from a lack of synergy and co-operation in the design, implementation and evaluation stages.

The principles of positive political influence include:

- always enter a political discussion with total probity;
- wherever possible meet people face-to-face;
- seek win-win outcomes;
- actively listen and show empathy;
- opt for openness rather than secrecy;

- see the process as being a number of negotiation episodes over time, rather than just one;
- always expect the unexpected, and never take anything for granted;
- be quietly surprised when you receive thanks or gratitude, and never expect people to repay you for your deeds;
- recognise that your reading of the political situation may say more about you than it says about anything else;
- avoid overreliance on a decision maker for support; it is safer to develop a team approach by building a consortium of alliances with a number of people;
- accept judgments as black or white only rarely – always check and validate your assumptions;
- appreciate that political dilemmas rarely offer a perfect solution; for each situation there is more likely to be a series of right and wrong answers, which need to be 'weighed up' prior to action;
- avoid procrastination, show courage and move on.

TAPPING INTO THE INFORMAL NETWORK

A positive influence strategy means informing a wide range of people about what is happening. Traditional hierarchies and reporting channels have become grossly inefficient in getting the message out in a workplace. It is not because people in the formal hierarchy are poor communicators, but because gossip or grapevine is such a powerful medium for people to catch up quickly. You only need to stand in an open-plan office to find that out. Traditional corporate communication channels such as team meetings, corporate newsletters and decision-making processes are still important but the reality is that many people do not trust the official message, or they are uninterested, or simply do not have the time to tune in when you want them to. For many, talking to a colleague at the coffee machine, during a lunch break, having a drink after work, reading the daily newspaper or having a chat on the Internet is their best source of education and inspiration. The days of controlling what people say and do in workplace learning have gone. It is time to be far more creative in how and when we get our message out and understood.

The informal network has become an invaluable source of information, particularly when many people are so busy on multiple projects, travelling from point A to point B or are employed in capacities that make it difficult for them to participate in normal rituals of education and learning. When people are employed at remote locations, or are temporary employees, shift workers, self-employed or telecommuters, they often find it hard to be actively involved in traditional corporate communication processes. They are often out of touch and/or feel they do not belong within the corporate culture. In any attempt to shape corporate decisions it is imperative that effort is made to tap the power of the informal network.

To help you explore what you can do to tap into the informal network, here are some examples recently noted:

- e-mailing or mailing all staff directly;
- producing a reader-friendly newsletter in a 'tabloid' style;
- using plenty of visuals and key themes on computer screensavers and in public areas;
- producing an employee self-help guide;
- directly involving informal 'leaders' in communication processes;
- establishing special interest groups within the business;
- setting up a communication manager who audits and circulates vital messages around the business;
- holding videoconferences, or producing videos that employees can take home;
- holding friendly and social breakfast, lunchtime or after-work functions, or off-site retreats.

ADAPTING YOUR INFLUENCING STRATEGY

Being skilled in adapting to each person's needs is central to gaining and maintaining political support. It requires sensitivity to the interplay that occurs between people as they communicate.

Figure 7.1 shows that the arena of political influence that occurs between two people is attributable to both parties. When you are

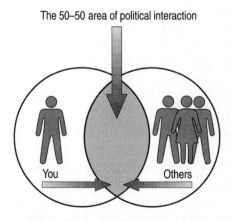

Figure 7.1 The area of political influence

negotiating with another person, 50 per cent of the dynamic occurring in your discussion is due to your perceptions and strategies. The remaining 50 per cent is due to the perceptions and strategies of the other party.

This highly interactive and interdependent 50–50 relationship is highly susceptible to tactics, attitudes and frames of reference.

Your ability to vary your tactics or thinking processes to gain greater leverage is critical. Gaining support for workplace learning is therefore a consequence of managing hundreds of different 50–50 relationships, while recognising that each relationship has its own idiosyncrasies and 'personality'. Imagine if an employee were to approach three decision makers with the same 'match plan' and in each case sell the same message, using the same script and approach. It is likely that the overall uniform approach would fail. Versatility and adaptability to the different needs and decision-making styles of each person are needed for success in negotiations.

There are many different influencing strategies that can be used. Just some of these include providing greater evidence and proof, demonstrating your own excitement and confidence, supplying a concise written list of options and recommendations, taking extra time to build trust, offering assurances, saying no, being informal and relaxed, writing a report rather than giving a verbal briefing, going away and doing more research, and taking the time to listen to the other person's needs before addressing your own.

WHEN SHOULD YOU STOP BEING ADAPTABLE AND VERSATILE?

Before proceeding, it is appropriate to ask one very important question: how much adaptability and versatility should a person be expected to exhibit in transforming workplace learning? In many people's lives, there are times when the amount of adaptability and versatility demanded is so extreme and so far beyond the comfort zone that it is necessary to re-evaluate the amount of energy and time being spent, before changing one's approach. Some people may feel that they have a limited capacity to adapt, and as a consequence choose to use only one influence strategy option. This, of course, can be appropriate when you find you are getting political backing, but totally unsuitable when you continuously fail to achieve endorsement.

It is important not to avoid politics prematurely, unless you find yourself doing things that are not legal, that are grossly unfair, or with which you feel totally uncomfortable. At the end of the day, we must look after 'number one', which is of course 'us'. Failure to do so can lead to fatigue and burnout.

If you are getting nowhere, even though you are maintaining a large number of 50–50 relationships, it may be time to rethink your approach and seek out appropriate personal development and coaching to help resolve these challenges.

LOBBYING POWERFUL STAKEHOLDERS

Getting key decision makers to demonstrate a visible commitment to workplace learning can never be overvalued, and it requires the right political strategies. Key decision makers and influencers can be found in both the formal organisational structure or the organisation's informal network.

A stakeholder can be defined as anyone who has an interest in either the success or failure of your project. Stakeholders should be constantly reviewed to ensure that the right people or areas are being targeted. This is particularly demanding given that stakeholders can be located both inside and outside an organisation.

Having identified the key stakeholders at each phase of a project, attention can then shift to forming the best political relationships. Part of this process is to recognise the power of fellow-travellers. Such people have special political allegiances, important reporting relationships, powerful decision-making authority, knowledge and insights, and power 'savvy' or charismatic power that can influence or lobby a stakeholder to get things done in the required way. This is particularly important in organisations or industries where you have no direct reporting relationship with a stakeholder. It is certainly possible to use a fellow-traveller as a prime target in bringing about transformed workplace learning on an industry or regional basis, rather than focusing only on a direct influencing strategy.

The following exercises have been designed to assist in the process of lobbying stakeholders and fellow-travellers.

Exercise 7.1: Stakeholder analysis

1. In the space provided in the diagram below, write a brief description of a workplace learning project/process.
2. Now identify on the diagram a specific phase in the life cycle of the project. A phase can be described in terms such as 'design', 'delivery' and 'assessment', or alternatively in time (weeks, months or years).

---

3. In the space provided around the outside of the diagram, list the people or groups or functions that have a stake in either the success or failure of your workplace learning project. Write down as many stakeholders as you can, remembering both internal and external options. If you need to draw more lines, do so.

Stakeholders

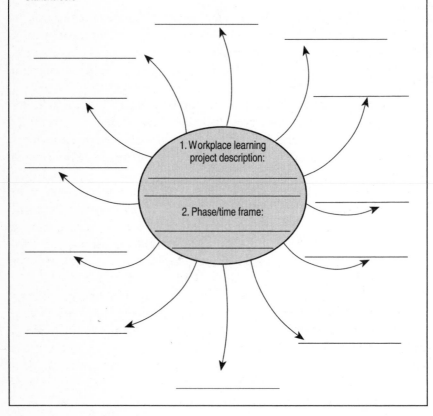

Exercise 7.2: Political influence assessment

1. Using the stakeholder analysis you completed in Exercise 7.1, identify the stakeholders who will have the greatest influence on the success or failure of your project:

_____

_____

_____

2. On the political assessment matrix below, plot the key stakeholders by considering both the vertical axis (that is, political clout) and the horizontal axis (that is, level of support).

Very high political clout
(a real mover and shaker)

Very unsupportive
of the workplace
learning process

Very supportive
of the workplace
learning process

Very low political clout
(unable to influence the
agenda on your project)

3. Next to each stakeholder on the matrix, note any fellow-travellers or third parties who you believe can potentially help you influence this person or area.

4. Given your assessment, which political strategies or tactics will you employ?

_____

_____

_____

_____

_____

GETTING DECISION MAKERS TO SHOW COMMITMENT

Like many change agents, I have been frustrated by influential decision makers who turn their backs on a workplace learning process after initial concurrence and support. Just asking for stakeholders' support is not good enough. You need to make them an active part of the process. Care must be taken to articulate how they, as individuals are expected to demonstrate their commitment to a workplace learning process by describing how you want them to contribute. Examples of commitment that could be demonstrated by a stakeholder include:

- participating in design, delivery and evaluation;
- personally endorsing the process by 'walking around' and showing interest;
- supplying adequate funding and resources;
- ensuring people fully participate;
- arranging work replacements for the participants undergoing off-the-job learning;
- communicating the expectation that action and results will be linked to business outcomes;
- scheduling and attending regular updates on progress;
- requiring that participants share and celebrate their learning.

Creating an organisational value statement

One of the most powerful ways in which an organisation can show commitment to workplace learning is for the senior executives to create and 'sign off' on *an organisational value statement that legitimises skill enhancement as an essential part of all business activity*. This way all people are either responsible for developing the vision or ensuring its execution.

The process of creating your own organisational value statement and involving all the people begins with the senior decision makers drafting a statement that they are prepared to back up with policies and action. This organisational value statement normally forms part of the mission and/or corporate philosophy, and as a result is widely publicised to make it an understood document to which people are accountable. For example, when a person is hired or a customer is approached, important values and expectations can be discussed and shared. In doing this you can develop a joint understanding of the key principles underlying business policy and initiatives and ways in which the workplace learning process is adding value. Such a statement could start with the following words:

- We are committed to ...
- We believe in our ...
- We will operate our business so that ...
- Our motto is ...

This high-level commitment assists organisational accountability and focus significantly. The use of value statements has become increasingly popular. Such statements are common in areas such as quality control, customer service, social responsibility and ethical management.

DEVELOPING A MARKETING PLAN

A wide range of perspectives on gaining and maintaining political support for workplace learning has already been shared. Marketing plans provide the glue to enable well-integrated action. A marketing plan is a management process that determines how the customer can be satisfied by meeting packaging, promotion, pricing and resource allocation needs.

When talking about workplace learning, the 'customer' could be an entire workforce, a selected target group or a stakeholder. Depending on the definition and location of the customer, the workplace learning process will require a special mix of marketing strategies to achieve a satisfactory outcome. A highly consultative communication process with the customer should be pursued at all times. There are four major components of a workplace learning marketing plan:

- excellent products and services;
- high leverage promotion strategies;
- appropriate pricing;
- resource management.

Excellent products and services

Products and services must meet the workplace learning needs of customers. The workplace learning activity agreed upon will therefore need to reflect a wide range of considerations including scheduling, location, time availability and packaging.

Part of the process of providing excellent products and services is understanding both tangible and intangible qualities. The tangible dimension is the knowledge, skill or attitude desired. The intangible component is everything else that appears to add perceived value to the process. Intangibles could include well-presented and best practice learning materials, using industry experts, quality equipment, lots of multi-sensory stimulation, catchy and exciting names, use of brands, recognition and rewards for demonstrated learning, flexible delivery methods, giving nurturing refreshments to participants, workbooks, and extra-ordinary on-the-job support services such as mentors and helpdesks. It is the management of intangibles that makes the critical difference in the popularity and effectiveness of products and services. Product and services delivery without spirit or emotional attachment rarely works, as Frances Rooney said about the footwear industry: 'Buying shoes has become an emotional experience. Our business is now selling excitement rather than shoes'. This wisdom is equally important in workplace learning.

High leverage promotion strategies

As already mentioned in the discussion on tapping the informal network, high leverage promotion strategies stimulate the necessary curiosity, foster excitement and generate the required amount of participation to ensure workplace learning transformation. Ideas not mentioned earlier include:

- sharing workplace learning successes at key decision-making events and public forums;
- writing articles for industry journals;
- issuing press releases;
- conducting briefing seminars for senior executives;
- having high-energy kick-off and milestone events;
- releasing videos, audios and workbooks;
- contributing to regular company communication processes.

Appropriate pricing

The pricing of a service or product can add significant impact to the success of a workplace learning process. A workplace learning process that is provided free, or is not costed, is often seen as having lower value. When a customer is required to contribute resources or funding it often increases commitment to the programme.

Pricing strategy is often used to reflect image. Rightly or wrongly, a high price suggests better quality. Unfortunately, this is not always the case. So it is important to 'shop around' and check the programme's track record.

Resource management

A good marketing plan includes a comprehensive costing and resource allocation estimate. This discipline helps make the marketing plan accountable and measurable by linking product and service, and the promotion and pricing strategy, to budget and resource constraints.

SUMMARY

Understanding organisational politics is important in gaining and maintaining commitment to workplace learning. Successfully managing organisational politics requires versatility and adaptability. Gaining political backing requires the use of a range of influencing and marketing strategies.

This chapter on gaining and maintaining political support, when combined with Chapter 6, 'Identifying and evaluating business requirements', identifies a number of strategies and considerations that can stimulate interest and momentum. Without well-formulated plans and actions in both areas, much of the effort on workplace learning can be wasted.

8

Empowering Ownership For Learning

> *True empowerment yields high trust, productive communication between individuals and teams and innovative results where each member of the team feels welcome to bring his or her genius to the table.*
>
> Stephen Covey

KEY PRINCIPLES

- Empowerment means the release of power and it needs a plan.
- Training personnel need to be performance consultants and learning facilitators.
- Champion 'movers' and 'shakers'.
- Use teamwork to synergise ownership.
- Performance management is the foundation stone of accountability.

PUTTING THE POWER INTO EMPOWERMENT

Some years ago I was asked to conduct a one-day seminar on empowered work teams in a large government enterprise. The brief from the senior executive was that he wanted more teamwork at the regional management level.

In the week prior to the seminar, I held one briefing session; both the senior manager and a senior human resources professional were non-committal about any prescriptive outcomes. Essentially, all they wanted was a highly participative and informative session. They advised me that the seminar would be attended by 29 people, including 25 branch managers, two trade union officials and themselves. During the remainder of the briefing session I quizzed both people about their reasons for having empowered work teams on the current agenda. This prompting led to a short discussion about the organisation's push towards regionalisation and increased middle-management autonomy.

When the day finally arrived, I started the seminar by asking the participants to split into small groups and to discuss what causes a team to be 'empowered'. After 30 minutes of interesting and often heated discussion it was universally agreed that the answer was more power.

I then asked the participants to describe what 'more power' meant when applied to the process of empowered work teams. After an hour of debate the group came up with four 'power' expectations:

- better-quality information on the direction of the organisation;
- increased development of team skills and greater provision of time to become proficient;
- greater decision-making authority;
- improved team-based reward structures.

A week later, the action plans were submitted to the senior executive for comment. The reaction was very cold. Some of the senior managers were quite disturbed and intimidated by the proposals. They felt that the branch managers who attended the seminar were trying to do the senior executives' jobs for them. The senior managers felt threatened because they felt they were losing status and power and some of their trademark or signature skills such as competence and creditability were being drawn into question. As a result, high levels of resistance were experienced. This is the paradox of empowerment. Empowerment can only genuinely occur by the release of power, the sponsorship of appropriate teamwork skills and a dramatic rethink of levels of decision making and authority existing in a workplace.

The theme of this story is not uncommon. Whether a workplace is restructuring or moving towards greater individual accountability, a key success factor in the transition is always going to be how much power people believe they have (and actually do have) as they try to manage themselves. Ultimately, devolution of power is linked to the level of trust and trustworthiness of the people involved, plus the level of anxiety that is associated with the change.

Making the transition to greater empowerment requires careful planning and consensus building. The development of an empowerment plan is particularly important. Concrete and observable milestones need to be formulated by describing in clear language what new skills and support are required to undertake the changes required.

Assume your goal is to bring about fundamental change in the level of individual or team empowerment over a two-year period. Before starting with implementation, a clear vision of the behaviours that will exist when people become truly empowered must be established. Areas that could be observed include: how decisions are made, the level of reporting, the level of joint ventures and co-operation with people outside the core business, self-management of budgets and development of a team charter or vision. As the process unfolds, you may end up with behaviours such as remuneration management, continuous improvement and long-term planning. Each milestone should provide tangible proof that things are happening on time and at the right standard.

Further strategies that increase ownership and commitment to workplace learning will now be explored.

DEVELOPING A NEW ROLE FOR THE TRAINING FUNCTION

During the last decade there has been a dramatic shift in the role and concept of the training function within business. Medium to large organisations have historically had a centralised training function that actively promoted and co-ordinated learning. It often resulted in line operators and teams washing their hands of on-the-job learning responsibilities; they saw it as somebody else's job.

People are increasingly realising that only when workplace learning becomes a natural part of everyone's responsibilities and accountability is there real potential for learning transformation. In other words, the training role needs to be viewed less as a function and more as a way of thinking.

Training professionals need to take on dual roles of performance consultant and workplace learning facilitator to stimulate this transition. Greater energy needs to be spent on:

■ linking workplace learning to strategic and operational business needs;
■ skilling all people to design, deliver and assess their own learning;
■ establishing networks for people to exchange views and enhance their capabilities;
■ mediating the creation and sharing of knowledge throughout the business;
■ ensuring learning methods are world class and have business impact;
■ ensuring the core values of the business are being followed;
■ championing excellence;

- organising appropriate mentoring and coaching;
- providing coaching on how to access and benefit from e-learning and the Internet;
- building learning resources that are freely available to staff;
- ensuring the values and benefits of workplace learning are understood.

MANAGING THE DYNAMICS

Genuine participation in and ownership of workplace learning will require people to travel though many new and often challenging frontiers. This is particularly true in organisations with a history of centralised and bureaucratic control.

To develop greater ownership of learning, several principles need to be understood. First, the push towards increased learning accountability may be initially resisted until the authenticity of the change is 'backed up' with the tangible release of power. Second, it is essential that any lack of trust and scepticism be seen as a normal and legitimate reaction when people are coming out of long periods of alienation and non-involvement. Third, the required level of trust is best built by people implementing and acting on policies and activities that demonstrate their trustworthiness. Finally, listening and communicating with line operators and workplaces will be a great start, but the journey is far more complex and multifaceted than just being consultative, well meaning and patient.

The following checklist offers 20 practical tips on how individual and team responsibility in workplace learning can be increased. Remember that a major proportion of the change towards greater empowerment is about changing how people relate to each other. This transition takes time and effort. At first, many people may feel this idea is silly, but in time they will behave differently as they see and experience the benefits.

Checklist for increasing participation in and responsibility for learning in the workplace

1. Use teamwork to the maximum.
2. Ensure that there is flexibility in the design, implementation and evaluation of workplace learning.
3. Set up a steering committee to drive the process. The steering committee must have the representativeness and the clout to get the process up and running. Carefully select the team so

---

that it is made up of 'movers and shakers' who are committed to making things happen.

4. Be very clear about the purpose and business reasons for the change. What is the joint legacy desired?

5. Create rituals and events where proof of transition can be seen, heard or felt.

6. Select people who have a track record of learning and coaching others to be change agents.

7. Give people plenty of opportunity to vent their feelings, anxieties, hopes and dreams regarding the change.

8. Actively support people who find the transition stretching. This is particularly relevant for people whose line manager role has changed from one of boss/subordinate to one of a coach or facilitator. Recognise that much of the resistance will come when people feel they will have to improve their coaching and learning skills. Some individuals will not like that, so be very tactful and supportive.

9. Ensure that all the people affected know the whole picture of the change process. Communicate simple and clear messages about why, when, how and what is happening. Avoid flooding people with multi-messages. Rigorously inject new energy into the change process by constantly selling benefits and consequences.

10. Consult with and involve stakeholders and fellow-travellers during the workplace learning process.

11. Learn from other organisations about how they managed the process.

12. Ensure individuals and teams are given sufficient information and time to make decisions regarding implementation.

13. Stamp out practices and policies that inhibit empowerment.

14. Anticipate the nature of resistance that occurs with increased empowerment. Use the guidelines contained in the transformation model (see the Introduction) and the change management model (see Figure 2.1).

15. Develop workplace learning systems that are user-friendly.

16. Regularly clarify changing roles and responsibilities.

17. Sell successes and results with versatility; reward and acknowledge people who champion the cause. Where appropriate, make sure key players and sponsors are praised for their contribution.

18. Identify milestones and constantly encourage celebration of success. Use celebration rituals to help sustain key players.

19. Link the process to business and people performance. Reinforce key messages and successes in workplace communication, and where possible use visuals and stories.
20. View the process of skills enhancement as having both short- and long-term benefits.

INFORMED CONSULTATION ON PLANNING AND DECISION MAKING

As discussed in Chapter 3, 'Meeting the demands of change', and in Chapter 6, 'Identifying and evaluating business requirements', it is imperative that people are kept informed of the impact and consequences of all workplace and individual trends. The more open and consultative the communication process on these matters, the more effective the workplace learning process.

Figure 8.1 details the link between workplace learning and planning. This link is highly interactive. The better the commitment to teamwork and continuous improvement the higher the potential for transformed workplace learning.

Two critical outcomes of effective consultation are high-quality planning and the achievement of high leverage key result areas (KRAs). These areas will now be explored.

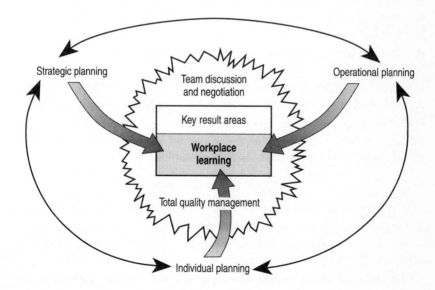

Figure 8.1 The linkage between workplace learning and planning

High quality planning

High-quality planning has three key components:

- strategic planning;
- operational planning;
- individual employee planning.

Strategic planning

Having a regular strategic planning process is an important foundation for workplace learning. The outcome of an excellent strategic planning process is the production of a vision and direction for the business that inspires and leads workplace learning transformation. The strategic planning process must reflect a first-rate understanding of the opportunities, threats, weaknesses and strengths that affect the organisation in the long term.

A good strategic plan includes a clear statement of vision/mission, strategic long-term objectives, and additional ethical and organisational value statements. As discussed in Chapter 7, the drafting of an organisational value statement is a flexible and influential way to entrench commitment to workplace learning.

The key workplace learning questions to be considered when creating a strategic plan include:

- What are the major strategic issues confronting the organisation in the next two to five years?
- What impact will these changes have on the organisation?
- How will workplace learning contribute to these changes?
- What competencies will be required to manage these challenges?
- What skills or competencies will not be required in our future?

The strategic planning process should be undertaken by senior executives every two years and should involve consultation with key opinion leaders from both inside and outside the organisation. The goal should not be just to produce a strategic plan, but to bring about empowered commitment and enthusiasm for the business direction.

Operational planning

Tied closely to the broader perspective of the strategic planning process is the operational plan. Instead of focusing on what the organisation is aiming for in the longer term, the operational plan is centred on how and when the goals can be implemented within 12-month intervals. The plan should include action plans and budget and resource implementation goals.

As in the case of the strategic planning process, the best way of discussing, implementing and evaluating the operational planning process is to view it as a team development process. Each team in the workplace should compare and review their operational needs with strategic requirements. Key questions could include:

- What impact does the information from the strategic planning process have on workplace learning activities?
- What competencies will be needed to meet these challenges?
- What changes need to be made to meet current workplace learning priorities?
- How can a balance be maintained between short-term immediacy and long-term strategic imperatives?

Individual planning

Employees and other contributors need to align their individual learning goals with the direction of the business. As discussed in the Introduction and in Chapter 3, 'Meeting the demands of change', for learning to become a natural and ongoing part of business activity there must be a close link between the needs and aspirations of the individual and the business needs of the organisation.

Teams again play an essential role in stimulating individual planning. As we will discuss in Chapter 16, 'Perfecting on-the-job learning', and Chapter 13, 'Embracing team learning', the skilful selection of individuals within steering committees, task forces and project teams helps provide employees with the necessary momentum to maintain fast and high-quality personal growth.

Formulating key result areas

As highlighted in Figure 8.1 and in Chapter 3, a central aspect of workplace learning is the identification and achievement of organisation, team and individual KRAs in line with strategic, operational and individual planning needs. In many ways, the formulation and achievement of powerful KRAs is the strongest way to unite the demands of rapid change with workplace learning remedies.

The process of identifying KRAs takes skill and finesse. Chapter 6 discussed the intensive research and active consultation on which KRAs must be founded. The power of determining KRAs lies in understanding both the measurement of quality and quantity. To get the best effect from developing KRAs, keep the tally to no more than six at a time. Give yourself permission to upgrade and downgrade as required. Exercise 8.1 provides some practice on setting KRAs.

Exercise 8.1: Determining KRAs

1. In the space provided below, list prospective individual or team projects and activities that can positively contribute to any or all of the following four areas:
   - investigating or implementing solutions to address key strategic and operational challenges

   _____

   _____

   _____

   - improving existing systems, technologies and procedures

   _____

   _____

   _____

   - designing and implementing new systems, technologies or procedures

   _____

   _____

   _____

   - developing and sharing critical knowledge, skills and attitudes.

   _____

   _____

   _____

2. From your analysis in the steps above, write down your most important KRA:

   _____

   _____

3. What measurable outcome do you wish to achieve at the completion of this KRA?

   _____

   _____

4. Describe why you believe that this KRA is so critical.

_____

_____

_____

5. List three active verbs (such as 'draft', 'liaise', 'train' or 'recommend') that best describe how you will go about doing your KRA:

_____

_____

_____

6. When will you know that you have completed your KRA?

- measurable outcome _____

- deadline _____

- time frame _____

7. In less than 30 words, draft a statement that describes your KRA. Use the wording you developed in the steps above.

_____

_____

_____

PARTICIPATION IN THE BUDGETING CYCLE

Involving people in submitting, reviewing and maintaining workplace learning budgets is an excellent way to empower participation and ownership. Coaching people in the skill of linking workplace learning funding requirements to enhanced business performance is central to the process.

Although the final approval of workplace planning budgets will usually remain with senior management, it is important that all funding requests are treated seriously. When information is incomplete or inconclusive, for example, relevant parties should be advised and counselled accordingly. This means that all parties should receive meaningful feedback on why their proposals were accepted or rejected. Budget proposals should include learning goals, competency outcomes and performance indicators.

The overall management of the budgeting process should be seen as a medium to stimulate knowledge of the business. This means ensuring the right advice and systems support in the advancement of talent and corporate IQ. In doing this, open and consultative communication is required to ensure that the best workplace learning is being conducted for the most important business reasons.

ENSURING ACCOUNTABILITY VIA PERFORMANCE MANAGEMENT

Good performance management systems are the best way of ensuring long-term accountability to workplace learning. The power of performance management is that it creates a discipline where the review, planning and appraisal of workplace discovery is tied to business activity.

The importance of the link between workplace learning and performance management may come as a bit of a surprise to some readers. However, linking workplace learning accountability to performance expectations should be seen as the lesser of two evils. Without this 'perceived sanction', many managers, team leaders and decision makers will continue to avoid their responsibility to workplace learning, which will in turn have a potentially disastrous effect on innovation, productivity, business performance and job satisfaction. The consequence of this 'perceived sanction' may cause some initial hostility, but in the longer term empowered workplace learning will lead to increased coaching and personal growth. At the same time, competence will be better acknowledged, clearer goals will be set and higher standards will be achieved.

Effective performance management systems are not about ticking and crossing people's traits or worth on a 12- or 3-monthly cycle of counselling. Performance management requires an ongoing commitment to performance enhancement and the development of potential on a daily basis.

All managers and team leaders must be trained in how to undertake this process properly. As long as performance management attracts the unfortunate label of being a punitive cycle, nothing will be stimulated other than the anxiety of the parties concerned.

Cementing performance management accountability

Best practice organisations use a range of ways to cement performance management accountability. In all cases substantial training and support is provided to assist the necessary development of skills and the reaping of workplace benefits. Three methods are listed here:

- *Linking monetary rewards or incentives to workplace learning.* For example, a high technology company pays its senior managers based on the following criteria: 60 per cent of salary is based on satisfactory completion of business goals; 25 per cent of salary is based on satisfactory completion of human resource management goals; 10 per cent of salary is based on how satisfactorily the senior manager collaborated and worked in partnership with others in the organisation; and 5 per cent is for satisfactory completion of self-development goals.
- *Providing an annual incentive or non-monetary recognition of employees.* Such incentives or recognition should be provided to employees who consistently demonstrate an extraordinary achievement in workplace learning and enhanced business performance.
- *Attracting, keeping and stimulating people.* Those people who have a track record of learning and contributing to the business should be targeted.

SUMMARY

Empowering ownership of workplace learning requires sharing of power with staff and other fellow-travellers such as suppliers, customers and community representatives. People must be given the time, information, resources and rewards to play a worthwhile and meaningful part in the change for this to occur.

Fundamental to successful transition to greater ownership for learning is excellent teamwork, knowledge sharing and performance management.

9

Stamping Out Practices That Alienate Learning

> *Successful knowledge transfer involves neither computers nor documents but rather interactions between people.*
>
> Thomas Davenport

KEY PRINCIPLES

- Organisations cannot tolerate debilitating practices.
- Unveil learning that has both intellectual quality and emotional value.
- Fix the system before trying to fix the people.
- People and business systems must be aligned and interconnected.
- Customise your knowledge creation processes.

CLEANING UP DESTRUCTIVE BEHAVIOUR

Many individuals are located in organisations where their contributions are highly valued and their learning, skills and the sharing of knowledge is rewarded on a regular basis. However, for many people the contrary is true. Here, the world of work is an imposition that reduces their self-esteem and is, in many cases, actually deskills them. As their working life unfolds, their capacity to contribute to workplace reform and change declines to a point where their contribution is neither recognised nor appreciated.

Many of us do not have to look far to recall times when we have experienced 'the good, the bad and the ugly' of workplace learning. Our personal stories, whether of an ineffective team leader failing to share his or her knowledge or an employee so task-focused that he or she never listened to alternative viewpoints, act as vivid reminders that effective learning can only be sustained in an environment where discovery, personal growth and performance enhancement are celebrated and acknowledged every day. No business can survive in the long run if it fails to embrace learning as a key ingredient of corporate and personal strategy.

It is surprising how much energy is wasted in actually stopping people from learning. Either people are justifying their own non-learning behaviour or they are deliberately blocking the professional growth of others. Eight notable examples of such behaviour include:

- people so immersed in protecting their territory and position in the organisation that they do so at the expense of the broader community, both within and outside the organisation; their actions reflect a scant understanding of the ramifications of their decisions on others;
- people continuing to deal with different issues with the same solution; nothing new is learnt because nothing new is tried;
- people failing to address issues at the right level of thinking, such as making transitions between operational and strategic thinking;
- individuals and teams blaming each other or justifying their own behaviour rather than accepting that it is they who should be taking greater care or should be changing;
- workplaces failing to recognise that impulsive 'fire-fighting' behaviour can lead to a major expansion of the original problem;
- workplaces not working and learning together as a team;
- people so engrossed with an idea that they are blind to different perspectives;
- mistakes generating fear and retribution rather than learning and discovery.

FINDING A SOLUTION

The eradication of behaviour that destroys workplace learning requires the commitment of everyone. A number of solutions have been addressed in *Learning Unlimited*, including:

- taking the initiative in leadership;
- actively communicating why learning is so important;
- understanding the difference between information and knowledge;
- skilling people to be tolerant and to celebrate mental diversity;
- providing incentives for people to share wisdom;
- developing versatility in dealing with organisational politics.

Notwithstanding this advice, the single most important way to clean up destructive behaviour is to fix the system and not to blame the people. You can have the best people in the world, but if they operate in an organisation where there are rules or systems that generate the wrong behaviour or there is a lack of trust, the problem will never go away.

As Leon Noone says in his report, '5 Proven Methods for Improving Performance on the Job' (1993), organisations must spend time trying to find out what is stopping their employees from performing and learning; constructing rewards that support learning; demanding that managers and teams enhance performance and potential; carefully selecting and recruiting employees who aspire to the positive values of the organisation; and finally, fixing offending systems before trying to 'fix' the people.

To gain a greater commitment to learning, intellectual capital and knowledge, change agents need to clearly understand corporate culture. Corporate culture is everything from how workplace memory is stored and how beliefs and values shape behaviour, to how workplace rituals reinforce and unify organisational identity. Understanding and working with corporate culture is fundamental to managing change well. Managing change demands a cultural fit between what you are trying to do and the actual behaviour being undertaken. A new and fresh commitment to learning may require a revamped vision, a higher business priority, a reallocation of roles or additional resources to stimulate the impetus for change.

A common mistake that people make in fostering a new attitude to workplace learning is that they spend too much time packaging programmes and initiatives rather than gaining and sustaining commitment. Building a shared view of why change is important is particularly valuable. Time must be spent sharing views, showing empathy and understanding, helping everyone see that they need each other and demonstrating that everyone will benefit from the change. From there attention can be shifted to supporting people during their adjustment, by providing awareness training, or leadership development, or just encouraging people to have a go and to use their initiative. To finish off the implementation cycle, attention then shifts to the custom design and packaging of the final product or service.

BUILDING TRUST

Where there is no trust, sharing knowledge and learning becomes an impossible task. People will naturally continue to do their own thing in a low-trust environment, and maybe pick up an odd tip or idea, but the true potential of knowledge development and learning is only manifest with teamwork, sharing and disclosure.

So how does one build trust, so that people respect, listen and exchange views with each other? We need to trust ourselves first, by exploring the attitudes that are driving our own biases, judgments and values. If we are not prepared to change our own thoughts, no real change will occur in our organisations. Most of the growth in building trust is from within. We need to be prepared to look for positive intentions in other people's behaviour (and our own) instead of assuming their intentions are negative. When we are mindful of these attitudes, building trust becomes much easier.

Other ideas for building trust include:

- as much face-to-face communication as you can manage;
- developing a joint goal that you are both interested in and wish to work for;
- being prepared to suspend judgment and forgive;
- telling others what you are and are not prepared to share, and why;
- noticing how your ego may be blocking you from trying a new idea or finding a fresh perspective – maybe you are finding it harder to change than you think!
- reviewing incentives that reward individualism rather than interdependence;
- dismantling the myth that 'hoarding' is the way;
- celebrating and acknowledging people who share their wisdom unconditionally;
- showing your trustworthiness by asking good questions and showing you understand;
- defending the absent by not talking about them negatively behind their backs;
- finding role models who are more trusting and discovering how they sustain their trust;
- spending greater time building relationships; 10 minutes listening to someone's story can make a world of difference in the long run;
- if you are not happy, saying so and explaining why;
- supplementing personal efforts with coaching and training.

As indicated in Chapter 2, 'Leadership and the learning agenda', the role of senior management in building trust cannot be underestimated. When the benefits of trust start to manifest and people begin to work and learn together, business and life can be so much more liberating. To build trust, senior managers need to live trust and partnering themselves. Conversations that help people to understand the real cost of trust's absence – business losses, fighting, failed opportunities, staff turnover – should be encouraged. These conversations may not be easy, as the politics of fear and secrecy can block people from acknowledging that their behaviour is inappropriate and counterproductive.

UPDATING THE INTEGRITY OF SYSTEMS

The quality and integrity of people and business systems have a major impact on the quality of workplace learning. Irrespective of the type and size of an organisation, the assumptions that drive decision making and business systems must preserve the integrity (intellectual quality or emotional value) of learning in the workplace.

To uphold the spirit of discovery and performance enhancement, all activities, policies and strategies should lead to improved insight, discovery, innovation and wisdom. Human resource or people systems must reflect both systematic and interactive qualities.

I can best explain the systematic and interactive mindset by telling my favourite fishing story. This story has been adapted from the original version told by Joshua Owen, a consultant based in Australia.

My favourite fishing story

One day a friend decided to spend his lunchtime fishing in a large pond at the back of his house. After a few minutes, his fishing line became entangled. Assuming that the hook had become caught on some weed, he slowly wound the line in. To his surprise, on the end of the line was a sickly looking one kilogram fish. It was hardly breathing. Taking a closer look, he found it was covered in oil and sludge. The fish smelt more like car oil than fish. Feeling sorry for the fish and its ill health, he placed it in a large tank in his shed at the back of the house, filling the tank up with clean water.

After a couple of days, the fish began to return to health. It swam faster and its eyes began to sparkle. Inspired by his success, our friend went down to the local fishing shop and bought some fish bait. He began to feed the fish, and the fish ate the feast with pleasure. Over the next week, the fish grew to the point where the tank became too small. Sadly, in time, my friend realised that the fish must be returned to the polluted pond.

Training courses, coaching sessions or the latest book can be like this fishing story. People consider and apply new ideas, concepts and skills, and when they are finished they have to return to their workplace to put them into practice. Returning to the workplace is like returning the fish to the polluted water. A place full of unhealthy beliefs, attitudes and systems kills any chance of someone being a better learner or knowledge worker. New hope or enlightenment can quickly fade.

After a couple of days of cleaning and feeding people with new information, ideas and skills, they are returned to their workplace – the polluted pond of learning. Unless there is a major environmental clean-up, it is quite likely that their efforts to learn will be wasted.

Workplaces need a positive environment. Any learning activity or event can be prone to failure unless a range of other supports is being used. Ensure that each day produces new learning and the creation of knowledge, and that the sharing of wisdom is not some afterthought or added bonus.

ALIGNING HUMAN RESOURCE SYSTEMS

Figure 9.1 shows how the array of human resource (or people) systems must pull together for workplace learning to occur. To help paint a picture of alignment, I often think of the chariot race in the award-winning film *Ben Hur*.Like the team of horses pulling in the famous chariot races, human resource systems must work together as a team. If one of the horses decides to change direction, steering a Roman chariot becomes haphazard and difficult. If the team of horses is clear about the required direction and speed of the chariot, it is harder for a renegade horse to have its way and disrupt the team effort.

As can be seen from Figure 9.1, systems driving the workplace learning agenda can be quite complicated. The names of the human resource systems can change, but what will not change is the need for exemplary workplace learning. This is the inner purpose that drives the alignment of all human resource and business activity in the one direction.

Human resource crossover points

Particularly important is the concept of identifying human resource cross-over points. As shown in Figure 9.1, crossover points are those outputs that

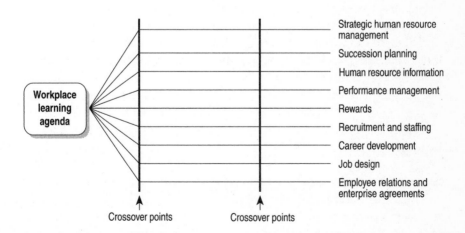

Figure 9.1 Systematic and interactive outputs of human resource systems

either help or hinder workplace learning. For example, a poor management policy will contaminate all associated human resource activity.

Identifying crossover points must be managed with both sensitivity and skill. As systems evolve, so will the number, range and impact of crossover points. The number of crossover points will be contingent on the number and complexity of systems involved.

A case example, based on a visit to a large petrochemical company in the USA, gives a practical explanation of this process. This company had undertaken a comprehensive review of its human resource systems. The impetus for the study came from unfavourable feedback from an employee survey in which people complained about limited workplace learning opportunities and poor morale. As a consequence of this feedback, a senior management task force was established to examine existing systems and redress problems.

The systems examined were career ladders, job classification and evaluation, promotion guidelines, performance management, multiculturalism and diversity, replacement and succession planning, remuneration, family policies, continuous improvement, recruiting, educational assistance policies, relocation and staff transfer policies, training and development, retirement policies, outplacement policies, and compensation and internal selection procedures.

After completing their review, a senior management cross-functional team found that the crossover points generated from career ladders, promotion, job classification and evaluation systems were inhibiting workplace learning. Changes were then made to these systems, including the introduction of an annual career development review process for all staff and a total review of retirement policies. It was found that a lump sum payout at 65 years of age was providing little or no incentive for workplace learning given that most of the workforce were very young and saw this incentive as essentially irrelevant.

Failing to examine crossovers is a very common phenomenon, particularly when the human resource systems are managed by a wide range of people and agendas both within and outside the organisation. Commonly, the situation is made worse when there is little time or interest in discussing how the systems are working against each other.

Examples of the crossover points that can support workplace learning include:

■ strategic human resource management linking people's development needs with those of the business;
■ clear leadership and guidance in developing succession planning;
■ human resources supplying up-to-date information to the business on people's interests, aspirations and concerns;

- backing up performance management with adequate training, on-the-job support and incentives;
- encouraging individuals to apply their learning within their workplace by use of both monetary and non-monetary incentives;
- recruitment and staffing improving the fit between the person and the job: where possible, post-interview coaching should be made available to successful and unsuccessful applicants;
- using career development systems to stimulate the power of on-the-job learning through interventions including individual self-assessment, potential identification programmes, internal staffing information exchange, counselling and coaching, job matching and development programmes;
- job design systems catering to ever-changing business needs with anticipation, teamwork and flexibility;
- employee relations and enterprise agreements recognising the close working relationship between conditions of employment, remuneration and workplace learning.

To help you apply the principles of human resource system alignment and identify potential crossover points, complete Exercise 9.1.

Exercise 9.1: Reviewing your human resource system

1. Given the existing human resource systems in your organisation, which of your current policies and practices support and cherish the value of workplace learning?

   _____

   _____

   _____

   _____

2. Which of your current policies and practices frustrate or inhibit the value of workplace learning in your organisation?

   _____

   _____

   _____

   _____

---

3. What can be done to make these crossover points explicit?

_____

_____

_____

_____

CREATING A THIRST FOR SHARING KNOWLEDGE

One of the most powerful ways to stamp out bad practices that inhibit learning is by creating a culture where knowledge is shared in a way that adds value for everyone. Whether it is consolidating corporate memory, exchanging the lessons of experience or building a new product, when created in the right spirit new knowledge can push individuals, teams and workplaces to a much higher level of insight, service and performance.

In many ways, knowledge culture is an outcome of the learning organisation when it works smoothly, helping people to become more competent, innovative and wise.

Part 1 of _Learning Unlimited_ showed that workplaces must clearly understand that knowledge is much more than mere information. True knowledge needs to add value and, most of all, it needs human processing and thinking to advance its status beyond information or data. Attaining wisdom requires people not only to break new ground but also to reflect on traditional wisdom, personal experience and the corporate story. Universal doctrines such as sustainability need to be constantly monitored and encouraged if excellent and well-formulated learning is to be maintained over time.

One of the ironic twists of the knowledge creation process is that people are often very keen to collect new insights, steal ideas, and listen to best practices, but are not so keen to share what they know or to do the extra thinking required to reach a higher level of insight. We need to implement rituals, strategies and processes that cut their way through this hesitancy, proving to the cynics and people who are hoarding information and knowledge that there is a more enlightened way to proceed, which results in stronger business performance and increased job satisfaction.

To help you do this in your workplace, 20 strategies for creating a thirst for knowledge sharing are listed below. Before reading through them, note that in the upcoming chapters we will discuss many more issues that have a significant impact on the quality of knowledge creation. Some of these areas include:

- benchmarking best practices combined with on-site visits and observation;
- competency-based modelling with carefully considered assessment and feedback;
- tapping into digital technology, distance learning, intranets, the Internet, multimedia and groupware;
- team learning approaches;
- celebrating learning as it occurs;
- establishing networks of common interests;
- project learning;
- storytelling skills;
- coaching and mentoring;
- formal training courses;
- maintaining family-friendly, non-discriminatory and flexible work practices.

Twenty knowledge-creation and stimulation activities

Here are 20 places to start. Exercise 9.2 follows, to help you implement appropriate actions in your working environment:

1. Appointing key knowledge management roles moves knowledge work from a fringe idea to a central business strategy. Appoint people to mediate the process of creating, codifying, sharing and measuring knowledge. In larger organisations, these roles are given titles such as Information Officer or Rights Manager. Other knowledge management roles include leaders of informal networks in areas of special interests such as emerging technologies or development strategy to meet business challenges. The final structure and role descriptions used will be determined by the nature and shape of your business, and the expertise required will vary from technical skills such as Web publishing, systems thinking and instructional design to outstanding leadership and communication.

2. Bringing a little fun into knowledge creation can help shift the spirit of the process from burden to joy. Some organisations create an award with some novelty attached to it. BP has a 'Thief of the Year', awarded for the best idea taken from somewhere else and implemented successfully. Texas awards a 'Not Invented Here But I Did It Anyway' prize to celebrate better practice and ideas from other companies.

3. Buying in expertise is a very common strategy to accelerate learning and knowledge. Options include hiring new employees, forming

partnerships or joint ventures with another organisation, or outsourcing a function to another provider. Similarly, seeking help from consultants, suppliers, and industry associations may be a sensible way of proceeding. Ensure maximum learning is achieved by developing a partnership based on trust and exchange, and where the wisdom of those hired is captured for either short- or long-term use.

4. Knowledge learnt on primary business issues such as improving quality or service delivery should be codified, preserving a healthy and safe working environment. Alternatively you may need to compile wisdom on some key processes in your value chain such as winning proposals, budgeting, competitive intelligence or policy clarification. This wisdom can then be distributed either in written or digital form to employees and contributors to the business.

5. Conduct awareness training on what it means to be a knowledge worker. Training should provide clear business reasons for the importance of sharing knowledge. The way the training is conducted must embody the principles of knowledge creation by having a learning design that encourages open sharing and celebration, not strict lecture delivery. People must leave with an attitude that knowledge work is much more than information dumping.

6. Consensus conferencing is a method for building understanding on complex issues. This method uses an array of people from a wide range of backgrounds to build consensus on what could be done or recommended on a matter under discussion. Consensus conferencing works with the assumption that all people, with the right briefing, can make intelligent recommendations on the most complex and controversial issues even, for example, Gene Technology in the Food Chain. Although more of a community consultation tool, this methodology has enormous potential to build a shared world of significance in workplaces. The process normally includes four ingredients and can take up to seven days:

   – A panel is carefully selected to ensure that it is diverse and representative. The panel may vary in number between 6 and 12 people.
   – The panel is then introduced to the topic or issue to be discussed. It gets familiarisation training to bring it up to scratch on basic principles and jargon, and on who some of the key opinion leaders may be.
   – The panel then takes over, choosing speakers or experts to participate in a series of informal conversations with them. The panel prepares the questions for the invited guests/opinion leaders/ experts in advance.
   – The panel generates consensus conclusions and recommendations. Minority reports are allowed.

7. Identify the true value of knowledge work by estimating the value of an organisation's tangible and intangible assets. This method pioneered by Skandia (a Swedish insurance and finance corporation) developed a framework for providing a more accurate idea of an organisation's true wealth by including measures of intellectual capital such as knowledge experience, customer relationships and the ability to share wisdom. This led to a stronger appreciation of what drives shareholder value and the intangible assessment of actual human talent and knowledge-based assets. Sveiby's book *The New Organizational Wealth* (1997) is a solid reference to begin your study in this area.

8. Formal training and external study are used extensively to build knowledge capability. To reap the benefits, people need to apply their learning on the job. This means providing opportunities to capture what they have or have not learnt and then their being given a chance to experiment or try out innovations or ideas. Regular skills audits or career planning discussions should be conducted to determine whether ongoing knowledge creation and application is occurring.

9. Filtering data sets is an important quality control feature of a good knowledge creation process. Regular review of existing knowledge banks is imperative to ensure that current data are up to date and of high value. This will mean tossing out knowledge repositories that have reached their use-by date or are no longer useful. Filtering processes normally are performed by a panel of experts which ensures that there is ongoing creditability to the knowledge management process. To assist the management of the filtering process, people need to be given training on how to have input into the corporate memory and knowledge banks in the first place.

10. Incentive plans encouraging people to create and apply knowledge should be considered to supplement workplace learning endeavours. Some workplaces link knowledge management into their performance management agreements. At Lotus, 25 per cent of performance evaluation is based on knowledge sharing, while at ABB engineers are evaluated not just on results but on how much knowledge and information was shared in the decision-making process. Some organisations hold an annual retreat or conference to thank knowledge sharers and have them show how business performance has benefited.

11. Job rotation and multiskilling is a very practical way of generating new knowledge networks. Moving someone into a new field or using someone in a different capacity by changing and expanding responsibilities can make new inroads in knowledge capabilities. Well-managed job rotation and multiskilling can forge new thinking, expanded networks or discoveries in different parts of the business.

Research at the Center for Creative Leadership in the USA shows that long-term growth requires diverse 'stretch' experiences supported by adequate coaching and counselling. To reap the full benefit of job rotation, peer assistance and multiskilling they need to be supported by coaching that matches developmental needs with the roles and responsibilities of the new area of learning.

12. Modelling, simulations and field research combined or used separately provide a great catalyst for knowledge enhancement. Technical and scientific professions commonly use modelling when variables can be controlled and comparisons made. Notable examples of simulations include flight simulators, virtual reality applications in safety training and economic modelling. Field research in business often uses customer feedback, process improvements and data mining to improve workplace performance and innovation.

13. Open space methodology, developed by Owen (1992), helps a small or large audience to share knowledge. All participants are given the opportunity to be heard, to discover new possibilities and work towards a joint understanding. After a broad purpose or question is raised for discussion, groups form and re-form to explore key issues pertaining to the question. The meeting starts and ends in a circle and includes group discussion, open forums and the sharing and constant renegotiation of key themes and areas to be explored. When skilfully facilitated, open space methodology can effect major shifts in thinking as well as creating group commitment and understanding. The duration can vary from one to three days and, space permitting, hundreds of people can attend. This method can also be used to help resolve conflict and develop scenario thinking and innovations. Group size can be as small as 20 and as large as 500.

14. Peer reviews are increasingly used for feedback on approach, behaviour and thinking. Popular methods include 360-degree feedback and observation of people using their skills in situations such as selling, medical procedure and aviation. To reap the best of the process, individuals need to develop a good rapport, where high levels of trust exist and where people are willing to listen to each other.

15. Retaining key knowledge workers is obviously the flip side of the creation and sharing of knowledge. Retention practices provide the emotional, intellectual and practical support to keep the right people as long as possible. An environment of open sharing and creation will help provide some form of sustainability irrespective of the turnover rate, but the loss of key talent is always going to be a problem, particularly if there is the loss of a relationship that can never be accessed again. To retain key knowledge workers, always keep a close interest in their welfare, desires and career plans, while maintaining a positive

relationship with past employees and other contributors to the business. That way you can reduce potential loss of experience and capacity.

16. Scenario thinking processes, referred to in Chapter 4, have become an important part of modern business planning. They are an opportunity to stretch knowledge and imagination. This is particularly important given that businesses cannot plan for a single-future reality. Scenario thinking develops a joint story or concept of the multiple realities that may occur. Approaches could include hypotheticals, where people are asked to make judgments based on an invented scenario, or the establishment of dummy committees to explore the same evidence that a real decision-making committee confronted.

17. Setting aside physical spaces to share in a workplace is another very practical way to stimulate knowledge work. From observation, employers do not think enough about the physical layout of their workplaces and how it helps or hinders organisational learning. Leading Australian authority in workplace learning, Bill Ford, notes that visiting many offices and factories is like a trip to the stables prior to a race meeting, with workers sticking their heads out occasionally to ascertain what is happening. Think about the culture of workplace learning you wish to create and make sure your physical layout complements it. Examples range from an open plan with flexible furniture options to redecorating staff restaurants into something more inviting and informal. If you wish people to share knowledge, you will need to provide physical environments that encourage informal communication as well as having formal places for people to meet.

18. Sharing events and rituals provides the time and place for people to network and share experiences. Such events could include trade shows, annual retreats, demonstrations or theme conferences. When properly managed, they provide outstanding knowledge opportunities. Success does not happen by accident: every minute needs to be orchestrated to ensure true wisdom and high-level thinking. Care must be taken to avoid information dumping and inhibiting people from sharing their stories and experiences.

19. Strategic alliances with research and development are a smart way of rapidly creating knowledge. Not only do large international conglomerates such as Motorola, Ford or Disneyland invest in their own universities, but many organisations that are much smaller have developed very affordable and workable joint ventures to help them stay abreast of the latest and the best. Examples may include local technical colleges, management schools or adult education colleges. The key to this is reaching a solid understanding of learning objectives

and then backing this up with solid reporting and accountability channels that promote active evaluation and quality control.

20. Use knowledge mapping to develop a collective view of how a process or task is learnt. Normally this is done by asking a wide range of people how they go about finding out the answers to a learning challenge. It is important to note that a knowledge map is not a formal display of how things appear on an organisational structure but is an accurate representation of the actual flow and sharing of knowledge. This process can sometimes be quite political as it discovers not so much who has the 'know-how' but, more importantly, who is prepared to share it. It can also show a state of play of existing co-operation as well as parallel or independent thinking. Knowledge mapping provides a visual tool for showing learning interdependencies as well as disclosing the networks and communities of knowledge that exist in a business. Such a tool can also be invaluable if a business is developing a new area of knowledge or where different networks of sharing need to be built or created.

Exercise 9.2: Creating an environment for sharing knowledge

1. Of the 20 knowledge creation methods listed above, which has the most immediate value to you and your workplace?

   _____

2. How would you gain commitment to this method? Which business issues would you need to link to? What work locations or teams would be a good place to start?

   _____

   _____

   _____

   _____

3. Which resources will you need to tap into to make this method work?

   _____

   _____

   _____

SUMMARY

This chapter has addressed many of the practices that alienate workplace learning. The process of stimulating workplace learning takes time and requires total commitment to changing systems and people's mindsets.

If poor and debilitating systems exist, behaviour will not be controllable unless major rethinking about how the culture shapes such behaviour and how better practices can be implemented is undertaken. Two key areas include: making sure human resource and business systems are aligned, and implementing knowledge creation activities and policies that help celebrate wisdom, creativity and insight. Strategies include: knowledge mapping, fostering events for sharing and having a good incentive strategy.

10

Benchmarking Best Practices

> *Desire is the key to motivation, but it's the determination and commitment to an unrelenting pursuit of your goal – a commitment to excellence – that will enable you to attain the success you seek.*
>
> Mario Andretti

KEY PRINCIPLES

- Discovery of lessons learnt is the lifeblood of workplace learning.
- Benchmarking is everyone's responsibility.
- Benchmarking requires well-trained people.
- Desire the 'relevant' and 'practical' over the 'quick' and 'trendy'.
- Be clear about what constitutes ethical behaviour.

PURSUING THE DREAM OF EXCELLENCE

For thousands of years, civilisations and explorers have invested significant time and energy in discovering best practices. In the 21st century this tradition will continue as the world of work seeks out excellence and innovation.

Discovering better practices and learning from less-than-perfect experiences is the lifeblood of learning. In workplaces, benchmarking best practices offers people a wonderful opportunity to improve products and services in line with the very best in regional, national and international business standards. Whether purchasing the latest in digital technology or visiting an award-winning best practice organisation, the lessons are still the same. To learn and grow, people need to extend their horizons and explore new ways of meeting their challenges.

GETTING THE BASICS RIGHT FIRST

The globalisation of the world economy has resulted in the passionate pursuit of up-to-date world-class practices and systems. As a result, benchmarking best practice has become very big business. Done well, the result can be very rewarding; done poorly, it can be a time consuming and very expensive burden.

At the world's largest training and development exposition, the American Society for Training and Development (ASTD) international conference, it can take an average of four hours to visit the hundreds of exhibitors located in one massive exhibition centre. As you walk around, you can quickly become bewildered, unless you are clearly focused on what you want.

Every industry is full of people who spend countless hours talking to colleagues, visiting trade shows, making industry visits and attending conferences in the hope of locating and implementing best practice solutions to current and future challenges. This process of research can be time consuming and is often wasted unless some forethought and subsequent review is undertaken. Occasionally, individuals stumble across a great idea, but often this unplanned research approach only identifies the 'different' as against the 'required'.

Given the expanding desire for better knowledge and improved learning, how can a person be confident that he or she is getting the best value out of their benchmarking process, while at the same time being assured that they are not falling victim to poor research or to a well-orchestrated and drilled marketing machine? The following eight principles should be considered before initiating any best practice or benchmarking investigation:

1. Benchmarking best practices must have the full support and involvement of key decision makers.
2. Exceptional discoveries and wonderful implementation only come from well-trained people.
3. Good benchmarking of best practice requires allocation of sufficient resources.
4. The quality of best practice study is directly linked to the quality of lateral thinking, teamwork and the standard of research.
5. People should be held accountable for all phases of the benchmarking process, from research right through to final implementation and ongoing evaluation.
6. The key outcome of best practice investigations should be to improve performance against agreed standards of excellence.
7. Good benchmarking comes from forming partnerships with people both inside and outside your organisation.

8. Always ask for proof and validation of best practice claims made by others.

MAKING SENSE OF THE PROCESS

So, identifying best practices is a challenging assignment, taking both time and effort. It is a mistake to push people too hard or too quickly for brilliant findings. The drive for rapid implementation commonly leads to the recommendation of the quick or trendy answer as against the most practical and high leverage one. A better way of viewing the benchmarking process is to see it as a process of continuous improvement.

Benchmarking can be viewed as a seven-stage process. This process has been adapted from *The Benchmarking Book* by Michael Spendolini (1992).

Stage 1: Starting the process

Before starting any benchmarking activity, clearly identify the current situation and desired business outcomes. The most common mistake made by people is to rush out and start talking to benchmark partners without first defining clear research objectives. Like any business activity, benchmarking should address the needs of both the internal and external customer. This outcome can only be achieved by involving the customer in the process, from start to finish.

Stage 2: Forming a team

Selecting and moulding a talented team to undertake a benchmarking study contributes extra vitality and clout to the process. The reasons for this are threefold. First, it adds political power and representative accountability. Second, a well-balanced and diverse team fosters greater creativity. Third, the synergy of the team process gives more opportunity for people to learn how to find and implement the best of the best.

The first step in developing a team is to choose a project leader who will manage the investigation from start to finish. The leader must have the capacity to influence key decision makers, be a good listener, and have the ability to act on key issues and recommendations as they arise.

From there, the rest of the benchmarking team can be selected and built depending on the needs of the organisation and customer. Benchmarking teams could comprise actual work groups, cross-functional teams, industry representatives and joint ventures with other organisations.

Each team member should be trained to ensure that he or she can:

- describe a commonly held understanding of the rationale, ethics and uses of benchmarking;
- clarify the roles and responsibilities of each team member in the process;
- demonstrate the skills of data collection and partnership building;
- use high-quality project management techniques;
- share and build on the knowledge and wisdom obtained.

In addition to formal training, the team needs to manage its own learning in an open and synergetic way. This can only be achieved when all of the team aspire to the beliefs of continuous improvement. Inhibiting beliefs such as 'we know it all already', 'we are unique', 'we have no competition', 'our customers cannot go anywhere else', 'we are number one', and 'we have tried all these things in the past' need to be stamped out.

Stage 3: Identifying the parameters for the study

The terms of reference of the benchmarking process need to be agreed by the team prior to starting any forum of investigation. The terms of reference should define:

- the key result area (KRA) of the study;
- the importance of this KRA;
- how the study will be undertaken.

Particular attention needs to be directed to developing a common understanding of the unique conditions, trends and challenges affecting the benchmarking investigation.

Depending on the nature of the study, the following questions may help clarify its parameters:

- What is the most critical business issue driving this investigation?
- What is unique about our workplace that will affect where and how the study will be undertaken?
- What current products, services, systems and applications are currently being used to address these challenges (both outside and inside our organisation)?
- What do our customers need and what areas of improvement will have greatest impact on their level of satisfaction?
- What would be the ideal scenario? What would it look like? What would people say about our organisation if the best practice study was totally successful? What will we need to do to achieve that outcome?

In addition to developing the terms of reference, the team should also develop a common understanding of budgeting, time frames and project milestones, communication and feedback processes, involvement of the customer, and accountabilities for implementation and evaluation.

Stage 4: Identifying powerful benchmarking partnerships

As will be discussed in Chapter 15, 'Building Learning Communities', finding powerful best practices means developing a network of people who are willing to share their wisdom. Internal benchmarking involves comparing current performance against similar activities within your organisation. External benchmarking extends the learning process to review and enhance performance against other organisations, for example turnover rates and amount per person spent on workplace learning.

Locating benchmarking partners involves resolving two questions. First, who accumulates the data you need? Second, who uses or demonstrates what you need? Having answered these questions, the challenge then becomes: How can an 'added value' benchmarking partnership be formed? The motivation to form a synergistic partnership comes from the desire to have mental and professional stimulation, the willingness to share, or just simple politeness. Although many meaningful discoveries are found outside an organisation, many people neglect vital inventions, inspiration and corporate memory sitting in their own backyard, that is, within the people in their own business.

The data collected can often raise a number of dilemmas before a final agreement can be made. Quite commonly, a benchmarking team must deal with too much or too little information. In both cases, the team may need to go back and revisit the terms of reference and approaches before continuing.

The quality of information and knowledge or insight gained from benchmarking best practices is also influenced by timing, personality and politics. An organisation may have been 'best practice' 12 months ago, but is now lagging behind. Best practices are often heavily affected by the charisma or special qualities of a change agent or champion driving the process. When these agents move on, often the best practice loses momentum. Finally, politics can raise their head many times during a benchmarking study. Examples of political issues include gathering information from a competitor and ensuring claims made by a benchmark are authentic.

Stage 5: Collecting and analysing information

The amount of time spent collecting and analysing information will be contingent upon the relative importance of the study to the business.

When the study area is seen as vital to the business you would expect that the investment made in gathering data would be substantial.

When sources of best practice information are located, people need to allocate sufficient time and resources to ensure that the data collection is undertaken effectively. A well-structured methodology combined with a well-functioning team has a better chance of reaching appropriate recommendations by extracting key insights than an individual acting alone. For example, if two individuals are communicating with two different organisations, care must be taken to ensure that both ask commonly agreed questions.

Exercise 10.1 provides an opportunity to identify external reference points that can assist in a benchmarking investigation.

Stage 6: Implementing recommended action

The implementation process should engage the principles of gaining political support, discussed in Chapter 7, and celebrating learning milestones, which will be discussed in Chapter 14.

Stage 7: Identifying the benefits of the benchmarking process

Evaluating the success of the benchmarking process is vital. To undertake such evaluation, the history of the costs and savings arising from a benchmarking study need to be quantified. These findings should then be compared with similar studies undertaken either internally or externally.

Be sure that the lessons learnt are passed on, to share your discoveries. It can be useful to write down some guidelines and operating procedures for the next study.

SETTING ETHICAL GROUND RULES

Conducting benchmarking requires integrity and a commitment to ethical behaviour. Benchmarking is built on the premise of sharing and trust, so ethical ground rules must be established and followed.

Exercise 10.1: Selecting information from external sources

1. Briefly describe a potential area of best practice study.

_____

_____

_____

2. List any budgeting, resourcing and time constraints.

_____

_____

_____

3. In the list below, circle any external sources of information and knowledge that may be useful in helping you undertake this study:

- industry journals
- trade unions
- overseas centres of research
- past employers
- overseas trade authorities
- your own organisational reports
- special awards (national, international)
- media reports (newspapers, magazines, television, radio)
- expert testimonials or citations
- retirees
- professional associations
- past employees
- independent consultant reports
- promotional material
- word of mouth
- industry periodicals
- consultants and other professionals
- overseas workplace learning contacts
- stock exchanges
- conferences, trade shows
- alumni
- networks
- chambers of commerce
- books, videos

- professional awards
- annual reports
- national local government agencies
- contacts among friends and acquaintances
- industry groups
- the Internet
- walking around and asking employees for their suggestions
- private and public training providers
- line managers
- suppliers, customers, distributors
- academic research
- information databases
- business information services
- data warehouses

4. For the sources of information circled in question 3, list some actual names or contacts:

_____

_____

_____

_____

_____

Suggested ethical ground rules include:

- Only ask questions and request information that you and your organisation would be prepared to answer yourselves.
- Always be totally open about why you are seeking specific knowledge.
- Declare 'up front' how you hope to use the findings.
- Never publicly talk about the discoveries you have gathered without your benchmark partners' approval.
- Never abuse your privilege by poaching staff or otherwise acting unethically.
- Use an independent third party to gather and report back appropriate information when anonymity or confidentiality needs to be protected.

SUMMARY

Benchmarking best practices is a high-impact way to improve workplace learning and the intellectual capital of your business. Benchmarking best practices must be carefully planned from start to finish. Spending time and effort to identify excellent terms of reference for all activities including research, implementation and evaluation in a way that is full of enterprise, creativity and integrity is particularly important.

11

Stimulating Competency-based Learning

> *It is not how people learn or what route which is important in a competence-based system but whether they can demonstrate competent performance.*
>
> Shirley Fletcher

KEY PRINCIPLES

- Workplace competencies must reflect business performance priorities.
- Competency-based learning provides an opportunity to share and develop wisdom.
- All outputs of human resource and business systems must support the development of key competencies.
- Competencies must adapt to each individual's learning needs and history.
- High-quality assessment and career development must be a key outcome.

WHY BOTHER?

Helping people to perform well is one of the primary outcomes of an excellent workplace learning system or method. One of the best ways to achieve high performance is to use a competency-based approach, defining and assessing those skills, knowledge and attitudes that are required for effective performance. By doing this you clearly map out what really matters in reaching higher levels of expertise and proficiency.

Improving the standard of performance can cover nearly every area of activity, from stockfeed batching and mixing in food processing to communicating with an aged person with dementia in care.

Benefits from investment in competency-based learning can be immense, especially when the standards and assessment are accurately described. Appendix 1 details the array of benefits for individuals and employees, workplaces, industries and the national economy. Done well, competency-based learning opens up frontiers of transferable skills, enhanced self-esteem and workplace innovation. People need to refresh their memories constantly and enhance their capability on a daily basis, so having a solid but flexible framework for what excellence means is a wonderful way to maintain business development and personal career planning in line with the demands of change. One of the realities of learning is that what was outstanding a few years ago may no longer be appropriate today. Special effort must be made to identify and assess those competencies that maintain employability, credibility and marketability. You only need to explore some of the themes of *Learning Unlimited* to realise that the skills required in today's world of work have changed. For example, competencies such as the following have become cornerstones of high-performance teams, organisations and individuals in the modern era:

- benefiting from the advances in digital and new technology;
- expanding one's adaptability to chaos;
- partnering skills and maintaining relationships;
- virtual teamwork;
- dramatically improving one's ability to deal with work pressures;
- understanding one's emotions, self-motivation and expressing empathy.

UNDERSTANDING THE FUNDAMENTALS

Competency-based learning may have many benefits, but it is no panacea. Without an approach based on accurate review and regular updates, the process can quickly become a bureaucratic and largely irrelevant exercise. An ongoing commitment to competencies that enhance the employability and marketability of the individual while improving business performance is needed to successfully manage the process. This can only be achieved by exemplary skill development, informed consultation and benchmarking best practice.

It is dangerous to claim that the benefits are guaranteed, particularly given the pace of change and resources required to implement competency-based learning effectively. Do not fall into the trap of trying to develop competencies for everything! Start by addressing the competencies of most value to you and your business.

The term 'competency-based learning' is used in preference to 'competency-based training', broadening the discussion from the issue of training to one of learning and assessing. Chapters 1 and 9 show that the articulation and assessment of competencies is more than just a training 'add-on'; it provides the structure and mechanism to align and cross over between a large array of human resource and business systems. This is reflected in Figure 11.1, where competency-based learning is revealed as the nucleus of all discovery, as it passes through many different systems and activities.

First of all, business planning and continuous improvement processes must identify the competencies that positively assist individuals to meet business challenges. This can only be done by being both flexible and sensitive to the unique environmental issues confronting your workplace.

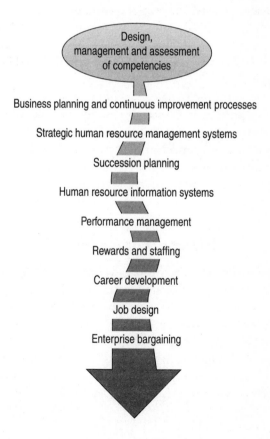

Figure 11.1 Viewing competencies as the nucleus of all workplace learning

As suggested in Chapter 1, 'New mindsets for workplace learning', simply accepting industry or national competency standards will not necessarily lead to improved performance. Many industry and national competencies are set to minimum standards only.

Strategic human resource management systems must ensure that the correct policies and programmes are created to develop key competencies and that the human resource information systems communicate competency and skill requirements on a regular basis.

Performance management and career development systems should encourage employees and the organisation to discuss and develop key competencies jointly as a major part of workplace learning. When people demonstrate their proficiency or when they help others to attain competency they should be rewarded.

The quality of recruitment and selection of employees is also tied very strongly to communicating and measuring competencies. Finally, employee relations and enterprise agreements should cement a close link between competency-based learning and productivity.

INGREDIENTS OF A COMPETENCY STANDARD

A competency standard template can include up to five ingredients. What is particularly important is that each competency clearly details what acceptable performance means, organises the task, provides a way of responding and reacting appropriately, and fulfils a role within the context of work. In other words, the competency standard must be relevant, clear and contemporary. The five ingredients of a competency standard will now be discussed.

1: Unit of competence

The 'unit of competence' refers to one aspect of competency contained within an occupation or job title. For example, Table 11.1 shows a unit of competence for front-line managers. This unit of competence is called 'contribute to the development of a workplace learning environment'. It is one of 11 units of competence developed to help Australian managers perform better in the global marketplace. Examples of other units of competence include 'providing leadership in the workplace', 'managing quality customer service' and 'facilitating and capitalising on change and innovation'.

Table 11.1 Unit of competence, 'Contribute to the development of a workplace learning environment'

Element	Performance criteria
Facilitate and promote learning	(a) Workplace activities are used as opportunities for learning
	(b) Coaching and mentoring contribute effectively to development of workplace knowledge, skills and attitudes
	(c) The benefits of learning are shared with others in the team/organisation.
	(d) Workplace achievement is recognised by timely and appropriate recognition, feedback and rewards.

Source: *Frontline Management Initiative – Frontline Management Competencies*, 1998, Australian National Training Authority. Reproduced with the permission of Prentice Hall Pty Ltd

2: Element

An element is a chunk of a unit of competence. This ingredient is necessary to enable a competency to be broken down to a level that is meaningful and measurable. In Table 11.1, 'facilitate and promote learning' is the element shown. Two elements of the unit of competence that are not shown are 'create learning opportunities' and 'monitor and improve learning effectiveness'.

3: Performance criteria

'Performance criteria' are outputs that give all employees a benchmark by which to gauge their proficiency. 'Performance criteria' are a dissection of the 'element'. In Table 11.1, four performance criteria are described.

The remaining two ingredients – range indicators and an evidence guide – provide the individual and the employer with the information to improve and assess learning in the workplace. Each one of these ingredients links directly to the performance criteria.

4: Range indicators

Range indicators provide a set of contexts or conditions for the performance of the competency standard. In the case shown in Table 11.1, a range indicator for the competence of 'contributes to the development of a workplace learning environment' could be described as a team leader whose responsibilities include functions such as being accountable for business planning and performance management. In setting out 'range indicators' you are ensuring that the competency standards can be completed in a realistic and true-to-life situation.

5: Evidence guide

An evidence or assessment guide is an agreed way in which an employee/individual can demonstrate a current level of proficiency against performance criteria. Depending on the learning outcome, there is a range of accepted ways to undertake assessment. These include:

- business plans and work journals;
- demonstrating a job-specific skill;
- direct observation;
- case study, role plays or simulation;
- diary entries and journals of learning discovery and application;
- finding fault or errors;
- group project or discussion;
- in-tray exercises;
- interviews with structured questions;
- performance management reports;
- publications or journal articles produced;
- previous experience explained;
- product or work sample;
- production of a kit or self-help guide;
- production of a video, or a Web page;
- proof of completion, certificate of prior learning (such as completed courses or training programmes) or samples of previous work that were supervised;
- written assessment of learning undertaken;
- written evidence of partnerships or ongoing work with clients;
- written feedback from clients;
- written or oral questioning;
- 360-degree feedback questionnaire results.

For the performance criteria in Table 11.1 of '(a) Workplace activities are used as opportunities for learning', suitable evidence might include developing links between work and learning, and using coaching and mentoring. Both of these could be assessed by a range of the methods listed above.

The remainder of this chapter highlights strategies that can improve the leverage of competency-based learning.

RISING ABOVE THE ORDINARY

Stimulating best practice competency-based learning requires excellent consultation, design, assessment and evaluation. To meet this challenge, the following four principles should be applied.

Focus on learning outcomes

Competency-based learning is concerned with helping to demonstrate identified skills, performance and attitudes. As a result, workplace learning must be managed in a way that helps people learn and achieve the competencies required. Competencies should not be used to initiate punitive action or control. When this occurs, the spirit that drives positive workplace learning will be lost. The spirit in which assessment is undertaken is paramount to this outcome. Care must be taken to ensure that, instead of passing judgment, learners should be given feedback on their growth and how competency can be improved.

There are several ways that this can be supported. One way is to list possible self-development strategies for each of the performance elements listed. These may mirror some of the assessment methods listed, as well as more generic approaches such as mentoring, shadowing (observing another performing the task to the right standard), staff rotation, books to read, action learning ('learning by doing' within projects) or a structured learning programme. Table 11.2 details an example produced for a client in local government. This is one small element of a self-development manual that was placed on the intranet for quick reference and easy updating.

Another way to help the evolution of learning within a competency standards framework is to articulate possible observable behaviour as an

Table 11.2 Self-development manual

Theme for learning – Future orientation

Behaviour: *Maintains an accurate diagnosis of operational and strategic constraints.*

- Using the business planning process as a guide, explore the plans in view of current realities, then identify issues that are strategic in nature and those that are more operational.

- Hold a meeting every three months with team leaders or senior managers to ensure that an accurate view of operational and strategic constraints is being maintained.

- Be involved in a wide variety of work assignments that give you a wide range of team, departmental and organisation-wide experience.

---

individual undertakes growth in expertise. A continuum of personal growth could start at the lowest proficiency (being totally unaware of the need to change) to the highest skill level (a shining example of best practice). Listing behaviours in such a fashion helps provide people with benchmarks by which to examine current competence and helps identify the next step in the development cycle.

Recognise prior learning

Competency-based learning must recognise that learning may have occurred before an activity or process is conducted. Imagine, for example, a young woman who has lived for many years above her parents' city bakery. It is reasonable to assume that she will have learnt quite a lot about baking while helping her parents in the bakery.

In traditional circumstances she would be required to complete formal training plus participate in workplace learning activities to become a qualified baker. Under competency-based learning, governed by the recognition of prior learning, she would only have to attend training when she could not demonstrate the competencies required.

Recognition of prior learning allows for flexible entry points and does away with the time-based formal training methods used in the past. Competency-based learning is not concerned with how long it takes to learn, only whether you learn. With this flexibility, competency-based learning methods are more adaptable to the learning needs of each individual.

Make competencies meaningful

Competencies should reflect essential business requirements and national and international best practice guidelines. The material produced should be freely available, clearly understandable and devoid of gender and cultural bias. Where appropriate, people should be allowed to customise a set of competency standards to reflect business realities and jargon more closely, but care must be taken to ensure that quality and meaning are not jeopardised. Any competency standard that promotes irrelevance or mediocrity should quickly be reviewed. The impact of competency-based learning will be most evident in such measures as productivity, innovation, observable skills levels and knowledge creation.

Use a range of data collection tools

Determining competency standards requires different data-gathering techniques. Some techniques include employee questionnaires, past research, on-site interviews, and forming external or internal benchmark partners. Given that most jobs involve 'hard skills' (such as 'prepare drawings'), which are easily observable, and 'soft skills' (such as 'conceptual thinking'), it is important that a 'unit of competence' details both. If this is not done, a tendency can easily arise where jobs are described in terms of strictly observable 'hard skills', while neglecting important 'soft skills' such as commitment, imagination and tolerance.

Developing competencies involves a combination of data-gathering techniques that are designed to break down work roles or key result areas (KRAs) into 'units of competence'. The choice of which method to use is weighted by a number of considerations:

- Which method is the most reliable and cost-effective option?
- Which option will inspire the greatest participation and stimulate the most interest in the development of workplace learning?
- Which method is most likely to lead to an agreement on the findings?

There are four regularly used techniques.

Develop a curriculum

The first technique is to develop a curriculum (DACUM) technique, which uses a facilitator and a group of expert job-holders to jointly review occupational areas and identify the general areas of competence. The group attempts to identify between 8 and 12 'units of competence'. Although the number is flexible, the intention is to refine the requirements into a workable number and eliminate duplication. When the group has identified the 'unit of competence', it then works through each of the statements to identify elements, performance criteria, range indicators and evidence guides.

Functional analysis

Functional analysis relies on a group process of expert workers and a facilitator examining a KRA in a work location or process. The group's discussion is centred around the question: What competencies are required for a KRA to be achieved? It is then determined which 'unit of competence' is required for each of the roles being performed. Each 'unit of competence' is then dissected into the ingredients discussed.

The critical incident technique

This technique involves employees posing questions about a critical incident that has occurred recently. An example could be a major problem (say, a serious workplace injury) or a major new opportunity (say, an increase in scope of operation). By examining the critical incident from start to finish, or by exploring the competencies required or not required, 'units of competence' can be developed.

The Delphi technique

The Delphi process involves pooling opinions from stakeholders who can make a 'best guess' on the future requirements or trends that may be required in a work function. These people meet either as a team or individually and are given a series of questions that identify the competencies.

The self-development manual in Table 11.2 came from an active consultation process with a team undergoing a change within local government. The team identified six 'units of competence' (which they called themes) as part of a comprehensive workplace learning process. One such theme was 'future orientation'.

The questions asked using the Delphi technique can vary, depending on the context. Questions commonly used to determine the profile of those who should be approached for further inquiry include:

- Who has a sense of where the business is going?
- Who understands the changing role of the business?
- Who understands the changing role of the occupation?
- Who plays a strategically important role in this work area?
- Are there any external stakeholders who should be involved?
- Who are the visionaries? For example, who understands the future requirements of jobs?

Having identified key contacts, further discussions can be set up. There, more probing questions are asked to determine the knowledge, skills and attitudes that would form the basis of a competency standard:

- Where is the workplace going?
- What needs to be changed in the way the work is done?
- What unique challenges is the business confronting?
- What are the greatest challenges that will confront our people within the next two years?
- What talents, skills and behaviour do people require to confront these challenges? Are these requirements trainable, manageable or hireable?

SUMMARY

The key to successful implementation of competency-based learning is to ensure that all the ingredients relate directly to best practice business requirements and that people are actively involved in the process.

To reap the full benefits of a competency-based approach it is important to accept that the process must foster ongoing learning. When implemented effectively, competency-based learning can make major inroads into every fabric of the human resource, business and continuous improvement strategy, while also providing an important impetus to career development and planning.

12

Accessing Digital Technology

> *The prediction I can make with the highest confidence is that the most amazing discoveries will be the ones we are not today wise enough to foresee.*
>
> Carl Sagan

KEY PRINCIPLES

- You are living in a global village that is becoming one big electronic classroom.
- You must have a digital infrastructure within a business to derive the benefits.
- Workplace knowledge archives must be constantly reviewed and updated.
- Digital presentations must be engaging, memorable and relevant.
- Even with all the advances, digital technology is no miracle cure.

A NEW WORLD ORDER IN WORKPLACE LEARNING

The birth and growth of the digital economy has dramatically changed the landscape of workplace learning. People have at their fingertips instant access to a digital revolution, which is redefining how, when and where people learn. Gone are the days when businesses could rely solely on the traditional classroom and on-the-job learning methods and the corporate information network. We have entered a whole new order in workplace learning.

Where the digital era will evolve in the decade ahead and what will happen to workplace learning is only limited by our imagination. We only need a moment's reflection on the advances in areas like the World Wide Web, very fast modems and digital television to realise how much the speed, delivery and access to learning have changed. Computer performance is doubling every nine months. Cost savings of 95 per cent in optic fibre and 25 per cent in digital radio links in the last decade have meant that hi-tech industry is offering a means of truly transforming the potential and capabilities of individuals, businesses and communities to levels never foreseen.

In many ways, the public face of the digital revolution has been the Internet via exciting advances in the World Wide Web. What was once text-based exchange has become alive with tools such as self-paced multimedia, videoconferencing and entertainment. The learning window of the world is now open to everyone who has access to a computer. In time, as affordability and access improve, the world will become one big electronic classroom. Time and place will not matter. Key factors will be the attitude of the learner, the quality of delivery and the content being offered.

To thrive in this new digital world, people must work across boundaries to forge new partnerships and gain greater wisdom and synergy. Individuals and businesses that hoard knowledge will quickly learn that this is a redundant paradigm. One of the greatest contributions of the digital revolution is that it smashes traditional hierarchies and 'top-down' thinking, forcing people to find fellow-travellers to achieve mutually satisfactory outcomes. In order to adapt and survive, the business brain must constantly feed people with vital messages and insights that advance thinking, 'drip feeding' them with knowledge that really matters.

The thirst for e-learning and e-commerce has reached a massive level. By 2010, 90 per cent of data transferred will be in forms other than simple telephone messages. It has been estimated that every 100 days, the volume of information on the Internet doubles. The ratio of knowledge workers to industrial workers is now 3:1 (Marquardt and Kearsley, 1999). But the digital era has hardly begun and as new advances in optic technology, security, privacy and smart features such as voice recognition and wireless delivery evolve in the years ahead, the way people learn and keep up to date will be quite different to contemporary practice.

Of course, the mere existence of digital technology will not automatically mean you will have outstanding learning. Access to the Internet does not guarantee that learning takes place and is put into practice. Businesses need a strong commitment to building the right digital infrastructure and capturing vital knowledge before corporate IQ and capabilities can improve. The benefits of digital technology will not appear overnight. Care, imagination, ingenuity and smart implementation are needed before success can begin to be measured. Naturally, a unity of purpose and a network of people who are energised by the opportunity that digital technology provide is a great start.

So, to summarise, all the latest technology and bandwidth in the world will not matter if you have bad information and a lack of purpose or creativity. As Lew Platt from Hewlett Packard (HP) once said, 'If HP knew what HP knows we would be three times as profitable'. And that quote comes from one of the world leaders in digital technology application.

We will continue with discussions of the major forms of digital technology. This will be followed by a special section on the use of adaptive technology for people with disabilities. Then we will summarise some timeless principles to help workplaces create a digital technology that supports learning platforms and business improvement. To finish, some predictions about digital technology in the next three to five years are made. To achieve this very wide coverage, comments will steer clear of the technical aspects of technology, opting for a broader, user-friendly approach. Given space constraints, older technologies such as audio conferencing, facsimile and radio broadcasting will not be discussed.

OVERVIEW OF DIGITAL TECHNOLOGY

Before commenting on the main forms of digital technology it is important to recognise two phenomena currently occurring. First, there is a massive increase in the complexity of networks. These networks are the communication pipelines and satellite wireless (cellular) frequencies that open up connections to different computer users. Second, there are the digital tools, applications and hardware themselves. The Internet is a good example of a network, while browser software combined with Digital Video Disc (DVD) hardware provides access to the World Wide Web (part of the Internet) in a highly interactive and stimulating way. If a business wants to reap the benefits of the digital revolution, it needs to connect the right network capability with the right technology with the right people. Only then will the very best in interactive, multisensory and convenient learning be realised.

Digital infrastructure

Let us explore the major components that make up a digital infrastructure platform.

Local Area Networks (LANs) and Wide Area Networks (WANs)

These are two common forms of networks used by workplaces. Depending on the final infrastructure, the range of services that may be available include: newsgroups, the Internet, shared access to databases, project management, an intranet, online training, satellite videoconferencing, proprietary programs, applications tools, e-mail and system protection software. One of the consequences of the quantum growth of digital technology is that the networks that serve it are fast becoming increasingly complicated to manage, particularly when they are loaded with massive demands for new data, voice, video and security. Network providers are exploring new methods to provide smarter ways to deliver single and more integrated networking infrastructure for businesses at a cost-effective rate. Some providers call this multilevel servicing.

Internet

The Internet has changed the way virtually every company, large or small, is doing business. Whether it is running an e-commerce service or using the World Wide Web for research, the Internet has profoundly affected the interdependence of modern business practice. In the area of workplace learning, the International Data Corporation has estimated that in the five-year period up to and including 2002, there will be a 95 per cent increase in the volume of Internet-based training. So, its impact on how and when people learn will be profound. World Wide Web (www) home pages will increasingly open the front door to the business. Web pages will need to be interactive and adaptable to customer needs by providing e-mail, video-conferencing or phone help as required. Such services will need to provide value for the time spent at the site, because if people do not like what they are experiencing they will quickly go somewhere else. Great care must be taken to make your Internet service engaging, memorable and relevant to the user. For the learner, the growth of the Internet is particularly important as it provides terrific freedom of choice.

Groupware and intranets

Groupware and intranets have been a major catalyst in knowledge management and learning initiatives within businesses themselves. Approved people have access to a common set of tools, presentations and spreadsheets, which means better access, quick application and knowledge transfer to a wide range of employees, contractors, customers, unions and suppliers – anywhere in the world. Specific uses include internal e-mail, online booking systems for training, search engines for lessons learnt, research and special interests. In some enterprises, workplaces can establish a private external network to serve this purpose (that is, an extranet) by offering secure direct access to selected people.

The Internet and intranets use similar software; the key difference lies in who has access to the network. Lotus Notes and Microsoft Outlook have excelled at data management, discussion groups, e-mail, integrated calendaring and scheduling, while Microsoft Explorer and Netscape Navigator are used for editing and browsing Web pages on both intranets and the Internet. Other brands that are available in the booming area of Web page development include Microsoft Frontpage, Cold Fusion, Net Objects, Tango and Macromedia.

In the future these capabilities will merge and there will be an 'out-of-the-box' solution to intranet and groupware creation, with improvements in workflow analysis enabling better overall management and quality control of the business.

As with other forms of learning, intranets and groupware can quickly be overloaded with information. If not managed correctly, these services can become dumping grounds for useless or, worse still, blatantly wrong information. This will lead to poor learning and performance outcomes. Excellent advice on how best to use and contribute to the databases, archives, tools and management systems must be offered to employees. Dealing with this challenge will be further addressed later in this chapter.

Electronic Performance Support Systems (EPSSs)

EPSSs use computers and associated technologies such as online terminals to aid learning on job-related tasks. Sometimes referred to by organisations as a 'helpdesk', performance support systems allow people to refer to 'how to' comments and policy matters in real time. EPSSs can advise you when you make a mistake in a transaction, popping up with a question or tip to advance your learning while rectifying any error. Increasingly, online capability is being placed on intranets using groupware or Web interfaces. The digital services now deployed range from simple online help functions such as tutorials on the specific task to sophisticated multimedia demonstration using DVD.

Electronic publishing

Electronic publishing enables increasingly user-friendly ways to produce professional-looking documents and Web pages by editing, reviewing and completing what you require in co-operation with some third party. Publishing services exist in many forms including text, graphics, audio, still photos scanned or lifted from a digital camera, video and CD. The final product can be produced and updated as required on CD-ROM, video disk, paper or via the Internet/intranet. Well-known software brands in publishing include PageMaker, QuarkXpress and CorelDraw.

Multimedia training

This uses the wizardry of digital publishing to produce self-paced learning opportunities accessible by CD-ROM, DVD or online. Multimedia training can be undertaken by the learner at a time of his or her choice at work, home or in an Internet cafe. Alternatively, the learner may join a larger audience that undertakes the same training at a set time via network connection.

With the high interactivity and flexibility of multimedia, growth in this area is now far outstripping that of traditional training, particularly in areas such as technical skills. This trend is set to continue as computer literacy, better availability and portability of equipment, better authoring tools, and extended network capability create a multimedia preference. In time, this preference will expand to more advanced fields such as behavioural change.

For a trainer conducting classroom training, a presentation can now benefit from the digital revolution. Powerpoint presentations with a large screen video projector (or LCD) combining text, photos, video clips and links to the World Wide Web, and CD-ROMs filled with libraries of great wisdom and music, can help transform the quality and impact of the learning experience. Lotus Freelance, part of Lotus SmartSuite, and Macromedia Director are other examples of multimedia software.

Another interesting new development in this field is SMIL, Synchronised Multimedia Integration Language. SMIL is a tag-based markup language, like HTML. It allows you to script multimedia presentations for streaming delivery over the Web. You can combine all the usual elements: sound, video, text, still images, animations, so it is much more flexible, and less demanding of bandwidth than streaming video, which is still too clunky for serious use. SMIL is absolutely ideal for developing training materials, and the ability to deliver over the Web is a major benefit. The client needs a browser, an XML parser and an SMIL plug-in. All are downloadable for free. There are no commercially available tools for SMIL development at this stage, but there will be soon, no doubt.

The digital era has enormous potential to enhance self-directed learning by providing feedback loops with online chats, live interactive video and telephone assistance. The versatility of multimedia has been driven in part by the emergence of a learning object approach to instructional design, which enables the instructional designer to give the learner greater choice as to which part of the learning module he or she wishes to attend and when. This cuts out the frustration of a learner having to go through a set curriculum on which he or she has already been assessed, or where there is already a high level of understanding and skill.

While the future of multimedia looks secure, and without dismissing the immense value of traditional face-to-face learning, the attraction of multimedia in digital form will continue to grow, particularly via the direct delivery of the World Wide Web.

Digital television

Digital television and its evolution from the old television medium continues to provide invaluable aids for unlimited learning and communication. However, digital technology in television now provides much more than was available in the past, delivering better picture quality, multiple channels, greater interactivity, smart agents, targeted advertising or promotion and access to the World Wide Web. Commonly used digital television features include satellite or multipoint distribution systems that allow the learner to interface with the program by use of data embedded in the television signal (possible applications include answering multiple-choice questions on an 'open learning' program by using a special key pad).

Learners will not only be able to watch and listen to the broadcast in real time, they will be able to download music, presentations, software and videos for future use. To do this learners will be able to use their computers and will not have to rely on their television set. Desktop video within your computer will enable frequent videoconferencing with other small groups and the transmission of broadcasts on the Internet.

Digital television also has much easier editing capacity and capability, allowing you to edit what is being received and to re-use it in another form at a fraction of the former cost.

Simulations and virtual reality (VR)

Simulations provide exciting possibilities to interact with a wide range of scenarios. Depending on the level of digital sophistication, they can range from airline flight simulators to dealing with case studies on the cause and effect of business decisions.

Like simulations, virtual reality is still evolving to meet the higher expectations of the digital age. VR is broadening its appeal from games to areas such as safety training. The advantage of virtual reality is that it gives the learner the impression that he or she is actually experiencing the scenario. Depending on the complexity of the virtual reality system, a learner is able to explore a world of vision, sound and touch within a 360-degree, multisensory world of discovery. The equipment normally associated with this technology includes eyephones, headphones and datagloves that measure the most minute movements with no risk. The eyephones enable the computer to know where the head is and where the eyes are looking. Headphones generate sounds of three-dimensional quality relevant to the experience. Datagloves measure hand and finger movements – for example the scalpel movements of a surgeon removing a brain tumour. A current software brand for virtual reality is Pie in the Sky.

Voice recognition

As already indicated, voice recognition is an emerging technology, though speech understanding and natural language still need to improve. In time, the days of the mouse and keyboard will be something of the past. It is estimated by Bill Gates that by the year 2010, 95 per cent of the World Wide Web will be voice-driven. Yet at this time much improvement is required before listening digital technology is the norm. However, the potential is enormous, particularly in the areas of technical training, literacy and publishing. Imagine being able to undertake a hobby such as car restoration or gardening by giving a cordless computer a verbal instruction to go and search for an answer on the World Wide Web or in a self-help guide. As well as voice, research is currently looking at interpreting gestures and smell recognition. Examples of current voice recognition branding include IBM Via Voice and Dragon Voice.

Expert systems

Expert systems use expertise based on experience to suggest approaches to a situation or case. This is done by finding relevant information on a specific area of expertise. Expert systems have the potential to aid decision making by reducing risk. They are widely used for diagnosis or in organisations where limited information or people are available to help. Expert systems are more easily formulated from a strong body of research or where there is some predictable logical path to follow.

Artificial intelligence

Artificial intelligence (AI) allows intelligent tasks to be performed by computers. Robotics, computers that understand images, learning systems that absorb information, voice systems that understand and generate speech, and expert systems are examples of AI. Artificial intelligence has yet to meet the hopes of the 1970s, particularly when fuzzy logic or non-linear difficulties are experienced.

Web site on digital technology

Michael Marquardt, co-author of *Technology-based Learning*, maintains a Web site at http: //www.gwu.edu/~lto/ which keeps up-to-date knowledge on digital technologies such as those discussed here, in the context of organisational learning.

CONSIDERATIONS FOR PEOPLE WITH DISABILITIES

In addition to the general benefits of new technology, there are numerous ways in which modern advances can be used by and for people with disabilities, thereby having a profound impact on their independence, efficiency and participation in both the workplace and in leisure. Adaptive technology is the term commonly used to describe the range of specialised equipment and software that has been designed or modified to meet the individualised needs of people with disabilities.

Most adaptive technology is designed to provide alternative ways to access the keyboard and the screen of standard computers. Now that so many jobs involve the daily use of a computer, effective computer access for people with disabilities is obviously critical. However, for true independence and equal access for the widest possible range of people, next-generation technologies will need to use principles of universal design. Just as modern buildings now contain ramps and elevators, so too will modern software and equipment need to be designed so that people of all ages, sizes, abilities, disabilities and backgrounds can access them with ease and effectiveness. That day isn't here yet, but efforts are being made to develop user interface approaches that can meet this challenge.

Today, for people who are blind or vision impaired, devices and programs are available to provide access to the computer screen as well as to provide feedback on keystrokes as they are typed. This is commonly achieved through synthesised speech, enlarged print or graphics on the computer screen or, less commonly, by the use of special equipment that displays Braille to the user.

For people who cannot read regular print, adaptive technology plays a vital role in ensuring independent access to information, either by converting computer files into an accessible format such as Braille, large print or voice output, or through the use of scanners and reading machines that convert regular print into a computerised form. Textbooks, computer manuals and other documents are often available on the high technologies already discussed. Use of emerging standards such as DHTML and XML (updated versions of the Internet standard HTML) and online publications have significant benefits for people with print-related disabilities, helping them to access educational material in a timely and reliable manner.

Developments such as these have widened the range of information-based jobs and study options for people who are blind or vision impaired – jobs and courses that were relatively inaccessible to them 15 years ago.

For people with physical disabilities that make it difficult for them to write, type or even speak, a variety of adaptive technology solutions are available to enable alternative methods of computer input in place of the standard QWERTY keyboard. Depending on the nature of the person's disability, switches, eye-movement monitoring systems and, more recently, speech recognition technology (which converts human speech into computer keyboard input) can be employed to enhance communication.

For people who are unable to talk, a variety of devices are now available that make verbal communication possible, even if these are still sometimes cumbersome and frustrating for the user. For people who are deaf or hard of hearing, text-telephones, videocaptioning and emerging technologies capable of interpreting sign language all allow increased communication options.

But adaptive technologies are no panacea. Adaptive technology, by its very nature, is usually a poor substitute for the sense or activity for which it tries to compensate. Nevertheless, if carefully selected it can often mean the difference between a person being able to do a job or not – being able to contribute in a workplace learning process or abstaining.

If these systems, the Web and e-commerce facilities are going to be usable by the largest possible range of people in our society, then we need to ensure that information is available in multiple modes – visual, auditory and textual – not only to address the specific information needs of different groups of people with disabilities, but to cater for the significant diversity of learning styles and preferences of all learners, disabled or not. For information in this field see the University of Wisconsin Trace Center Web site at http://www.trace.wisc.edu.

TIMELESS ADVICE ON IMPLEMENTATION

In reading and hearing about the advances in digital technology, or even seeing it work, it is easy to become carried away with the excitement and possibilities, but will the investment lead to improved business performance, knowledge creation and enhanced learning?

Without trust and partnering, digital technology will not transform learning. People need to be educated on the human interaction required to help advance understanding and wisdom. If people do not like what they see, they will quickly tune out and if digital technology is not aligned to business strategy, the efforts may well be wasted. Having much more information at your fingertips creates a new way of doing work. Those who once held power because they were the chosen few with access to information will need to change their thinking radically if they are to contribute positively in the new world of seamless, abundant and instantaneous delivery.

There can be no doubt that digital technology changes reporting lines and establishes a totally new network of knowledge workers. Not only does it shorten communication lines, it provides instant access to anybody at any time. While you can expect some resistance, many people will find the new way of interacting and sharing a revelation stimulating because, for the first time, they will have access and involvement in business processes and knowledge creation capabilities.

Organisations that lead in successful implementation of high technology are not necessarily the 'biggest' but may well be the 'smartest'. These organisations do not get hooked on the features of the technology, but are more concerned with the outcomes of enhancing decision making, stimulating creativity, pioneering best practices and increasing job satisfaction.

Highlighting this point of smart thinking is a 1999 study of knowledge management processes, commissioned by the UK Department for Education and Employment. During a three-year survey of some 14,000 companies worldwide, only 140 were deemed knowledge management businesses. The vast number were, at best, just information technology projects rather than a management process that shares knowledge. The study found the biggest problem was that everybody wants to get knowledge out but many were not prepared to put knowledge in. Only after trust has been developed will true knowledge work emerge and people start to fill knowledge banks and archives with powerful discoveries. The UK study concluded that if a business wants to create a knowledge work approach it needs to address four basic questions:

- How can you turn the knowledge you have into something that adds value?
- How can you generate knowledge, rather than flooding business with indiscriminate information?
- How can you create a knowledge-supportive organisation in which everybody is convinced of the contribution that knowledge can make to the success of the enterprise?
- How can you manage your people so that they will increasingly become knowledge workers or professionals, inspiring and motivating them to generate knowledge and share it with peers on a structured basis?

To further assist the intelligent use of digital technology, Appendix 2 has some advice on implementing digital technology with a view to improved knowledge creation, management and learning. Authors who most influenced the checklist include: Davenport and Prusak (1998), Marquardt and Kearsley (1999), Gates (1999) and Tapscott, Lowy and Ticoll (1998).

TRENDS AND PREDICTIONS

Making predictions on digital technology is a huge task. We only need look at the last five years to get some sense of the rate of change we are dealing with in the digital technology revolution. In the mid-1990s, Internet growth was only starting to skyrocket, the World Wide Web was not a household name, e-mail was rarely used, digital mobile phones were also rare and the facsimile was running hot with paper jams. In many ways, a week is a lifetime when it comes to high technology.

So what do the next three to five years have in store? One thing is for sure, the last 40 years of the deployment and usage of the computer has been a precursor for the main event. Here are three guiding observations that may help develop a mindset for the future.

Internet2

In 1998 the academic community joined forces with a range of corporations to look at the Internet2 (also called the Next Generation Internet (NGI) initiative), which aims to deliver information at 100 to 1,000 times faster than the current Internet by using leading-edge routing technology to produce a far more advanced research and development network.

Internet2 is working to enable advanced applications such as telemedicine, digital libraries and virtual laboratories, which are not possible with the existing technology. For the Internet2 project to be successful it will need to integrate a large number of advanced campus, regional, and national networks into one mega-network. This will require enormous research and development into joining together quite complex and different applications and engineering capabilities.

Just as today's Internet arose from the academic and federal research networks of the 1980s, Internet2 is helping to develop and test new technologies that will enable a new generation of Internet applications. Internet2's goal is to bring together institutions and resources to develop new technologies and capabilities that can be deployed in the global arena. The consequences of Internet2 on workplace learning should be profound, to say the least.

Searching seamlessly

According to Gates (1999), Microsoft and other system vendors are currently working on technology that will catalogue material across a variety of storage mechanisms: Web, file and database, and e-mail. This means a single search will be more likely to find what you are looking for quickly. It will be done by using Dynamic Hypertext Markup Language (DHTML) and Extended Markup Language (XML). What emerging versions of HTML will do is create a better linkage between layout and content, which means a better understanding of natural language and instruction. For example, as Bill Gates says, a search engine should be able to determine that 'the speed of chips has nothing to do with food'.

The exciting aspect of this research is that the learner will soon be able to find knowledge more easily because some interpretation will be done by the digital technology. By asking intelligent questions you will hopefully get loads of intelligent answers back. The other good news is that there will be a growth industry of search brokers, your personal librarian for searching the Internet, thereby saving you the time on the administrative part of the research equation.

Even more access

Imagine drawing on the combined knowledge of thousands of business partners before making a strategic move. This is the reality of the future in workplace learning. Whether you are sitting in your home watching digital television or you are hiking in Nepal, you will only be a mini-second away from instant access to vital knowledge or a person who is in the know.

As we are beginning to see, mobile digital providers have become less concerned with the physical features of the phone and more with the extra services provided. For example, a mobile multimedia service provided via mobile phones or other handheld devices can provide you with regular updates in your field of interest of the latest trends, sports results or competitive intelligence. This will become more of a reality as strategic alliances are forged between mobile network and Internet providers.

Wireless technology – cellular phones as small as earrings with voice recognition capabilities – will be able to respond to e-mail on telephone messages. Portable phones will be able to project Web images, including voice and video. It is predicted that the telephone of the future will contain voice, text, graphics, sound and moving 3D pictures and will be connected by a satellite wireless network.

Finally, people will be able to access vital knowledge at a much lower cost using a network computer, where the platform, training and applications are provided by an Internet provider or learning portal. People will be able to access applications and data from remote networks and learn from any machine in any office in the world. Considering that 96 per cent of the world population are yet to come on board the digital revolution, the range of possibilities is very exciting. The Philippines, for example, is currently implementing low-cost network computers to enable connection between 7,000 islands. This will create a network that can enhance communication, share insight and provide training at a level never before comprehended.

SUMMARY

Accessing digital technology is a business imperative in the modern workplace. Each one of us must see ourself as a knowledge worker who can tap into the riches of the global village. Some of the notable examples include the World Wide Web and technologies such as digital television and DVD. The reality of the digital age is that learning is no longer restricted to the upper echelons of the organisation and society. Managing this interconnected way of learning requires careful planning, integration and alignment at the individual, team and organisational level.

13

Embracing Team Learning

> *None of us is as smart as all of us.*
>
> Japanese proverb

KEY PRINCIPLES

- Workplaces must view teamwork as a way of life.
- Digital technology stimulates the deployment of virtual teams.
- Value diversity and balance.
- Learn from experience and develop reflective practice.
- Promote dialogue skills.

THE 'PRIZE JEWEL' OF WORKPLACE LEARNING

Team learning provides individuals and organisations with a wonderful way to expand their performance and potential. In many ways, the team learning process is the 'prize jewel' of workplace learning. History archives are full of people who have formed teams and produced wonderful results.

For thousands of years people have recognised the special qualities of effective teamwork. A key factor in the success of outstanding teams has been their capacity to learn from their experience and develop new plans to meet the challenges ahead. In this regard, the capacity of a workplace to undertake successful transformation is tied very much to its ability to cope with change – and that means learning.

In the modern digital era, teamwork has become more virtual and dispersed in nature, with people using e-mail, videoconferencing and telecommuting to communicate and share discoveries across time and place. In doing so, we need to ensure the quality and intention of the teamwork is not lost within the advances of cyberspace.

Figure 13.1 shows the workplace learning strategies that directly benefit from high-quality team learning. Take away the 'prize jewel' of team learning and the capacity to bring about positive workplace reform is seriously diminished.

Take a minute to reflect on the range of team-based structures that you have observed or heard of in recent times. Some that can be identified include:

- cross-functional workplace teams;
- action learning groups;
- task forces and project teams;
- consultative committees;
- focus groups;
- enterprise bargaining teams;
- customer support teams;
- joint venture partnerships;
- quality circle teams;
- creativity teams;
- semi-autonomous work structures;
- self-directed teams;
- informal and formal networks;
- strategic alliances;
- benchmarking teams.

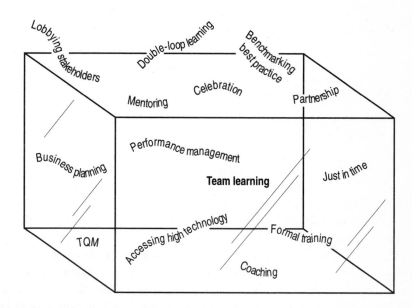

Figure 13.1 Workplace learning strategies

On the surface this list looks impressive, but in reality many of these team initiatives often do not produce the desired results. The cause of substandard team performance often lies in four factors:

- The change towards a team-based culture often requires a major shift in thinking and behaving.
- Each team must be committed to a common purpose and the desire to look at the process of teamwork as well as focusing on the task at hand.
- The learning journey for each individual and team is different. For some, it will be difficult and stretching because they are motivated to be independent contributors, while others find teamwork rewarding and empowering.
- Organisations need to acknowledge that teamwork is not about a 'special project' or a 'special event', it is about a 'way of life'.

To help in answering this challenge, this chapter provides practical advice on building high performance in team learning. The first step in this challenge is to establish a strong foundation.

ESTABLISHING A STRONG FOUNDATION

High-quality team learning is an outcome of excellent teamwork. Best practice team learning does not just happen; it is a consequence of both the organisation and team members being committed to making the process succeed.

The role of the organisation

The commitment of the organisation involves five key inputs:

- Senior managers and key stakeholders must show visible sponsorship. This principally means that all team solutions are encouraged, and followed up.
- The reasons teamwork is necessary need to be communicated. Appropriate publicity and marketing of team roles, purpose and activities need to be carried out.
- Work practices that alienate team learning must be addressed up front. Champions of teamwork need to be rewarded and the systems that are causing the non-team behaviour must be terminated.
- Key decision makers who are demanding more teamwork should be demonstrating those values themselves. This means trust, collective intelligence, quality, open sharing and a desire to achieve a common result.

■ Teamwork and the learning that unfolds is about contribution and not a life sentence. Ensure that time frames, milestones and resourcing are negotiated and reasonable.

The role of team members

Team members must take the responsibility to manage the effective functioning of systems influences, goals, roles, ground rules and procedures, interpersonal relationships and continuous improvement. Conquering these six areas leads to improved team performance and personal growth by increasing the confidence of your people. The enhancement of competence through self-awareness and the discovery of each team member's preferences and abilities is particularly important. Exercise 13.1 contains a team exercise on the six key areas but, first, let's examine the six areas.

Systems influences

A high-performing team understands the broader political, operational, technological and environmental constraints that affect team performance. This awareness results not only in an acute understanding of the team's perceived importance within the business strategy but also a level of insight into its place in the politics of the workplace.

Goals

A high-performing team understands and accepts responsibility for its 'goals'. As discussed in earlier chapters, all team members should be aware of how they fit in strategically and operationally. In time, this awareness will lead to greater involvement in everyday management and accountability, and performance enhancement.

Roles

The roles of each team member are understood and valued by the others. The process of negotiating and updating roles is seen as a necessary part of managing within a changing environment.

Ground rules and procedures

Ground rules and procedures that are needed to get the work done by the team are agreed. Areas of common agreement include making decisions, setting agendas for meetings, following up digital and face-to-face conversations, resolving conflict and managing 'just-in-time' learning.

Interpersonal relationships

All team members support and demonstrate group behaviour by encouraging high-performing interpersonal relationships. Each member of the team must recognise that he or she is jointly responsible for maintaining and improving group dynamics.

Continuous improvement

The team should be 100 per cent committed to better methods, processes and delivery in line with business requirements.

Exercise 13.1: How is your team performing?

Write down the name of the team you wish to examine:

Using a scale from 0 to 100, rate your current team's performance on each of the following 20 issues (0 points meaning bad performance, 50 points indicating satisfactory performance and 100 points indicating perfect performance):

Issue	Performance (points 0 to 100)

Systems influences

1. Are your team members aware of the major sources of power, influence and political support available to you? _____
2. Are the current opportunities and threats to your team clearly identified and understood? _____
3. Is there sufficient technological and operational support to encourage teamwork? _____
4. Are the team members fully aware of how their team links with business, strategic and operational planning needs? _____

Goals and continuous improvement

5. Are the team's goals clear and will people be rewarded and developed along the way? _____
6. Does your team communicate its goals clearly? _____
7. Does the team constantly evaluate outcomes and business impact? _____
8. Are the activities within the team evaluated and improved by regular specific, constructive feedback? _____
9. Are the team members fully aware of the learning needs of the team? _____

Roles

10. Are all team members' roles and responsibilities clearly defined? _____

11. Are all team members ready to negotiate and redefine their roles and responsibilities as required? _____

12. Are all the respective roles performed by each team member valued and recognised by the others? _____

Ground rules and procedures

13. Does the team have established and agreed guidelines for making team decisions? _____

14. Are there clearly understood channels for sharing information and building on each other's ideas? _____

15. Are necessary policy and procedure changes being implemented? _____

16. Are team meetings producing the required results and is the knowledge being shared for the benefit of the business? _____

Interpersonal relationships

17. Are team members committed to frank, constructive and open discussion? _____

18. Are all team members respected, supported and valued by each other? _____

19. Are the current styles, values and interests in the team balanced? _____

20. Are all team members accepting their responsibility for the ongoing improvement of the team? _____

Add any other issues that you think are relevant:

_____

_____

_____

Discussion questions
Analyse your team assessment and select the top three questions/ issues that require priority treatment.

_____

_____

_____

In your opinion, which strategies should be employed to confront the issues identified?

_____

_____

_____

_____

_____

How does your individual analysis compare with that of other team members?

_____

_____

_____

_____

THE FINESSE OF BEST PRACTICE TEAM LEARNING

Having the necessary finesse to produce best practice workplace learning requires something extraordinary and special. The inner strength, creativity and confidence to produce best practice learning comes from a range of additional factors on top of the issues already addressed. There are an additional seven factors.

Supporting diversity and balance

The best learning teams are highly diverse and balanced. The greater the balance and diversity the more the likelihood that there will be higher levels of creativity and innovation. At times the discussions may take longer but the chances of achieving better results are greater. Alternatively, it could be said that 'like-minded' teams produce only 'like-minded' outcomes. Albert Einstein once said: 'We will not solve problems using the same thinking which created them.'

In teams, the diversity issue extends past mental diversity, discussed in Chapter 5, into all other forms including cultural, gender and occupational background. Supporting balance through diversity enables greater performance and potential.

Considering both content and process

One of the greatest strengths of a team that demonstrates best practice learning is that it understands both content and process. On most occasions, teams concentrate on the task (that is, content) at hand, jumping into action 'up front' in a meeting and staying there right to the end. Often this results in the team getting nowhere because no team member is evaluating how the meeting is being run or how decisions are being made (that is, process). This can lead to frustration and hostility, particularly if people feel that their need for structure is not being met. Worse still, people often know that the team process is going astray but they are not encouraged to speak up and discuss how they feel. As a consequence, the quality of learning and decision making suffers. Figure 13.2 shows how the balance of content and process issues is played out in every team.

Balancing content and process perspectives is relevant to all forms of human interaction. This is very noticeable when people concentrate too much on the nature of the change and not enough on helping others come to terms with the change. A good example is the introduction of

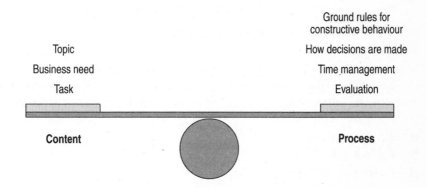

Figure 13.2 Balancing content and process issues

multiskilled teams. While organisations sell the benefits and features of the change (that is, content), they often neglect to supply adequate resources, time, coaching and training to allow it to happen (that is, process).

The development of team leadership

The skills of team leadership continue to grow in importance as the pace of change accelerates and organisational structures become flatter and more fluid. The traditional role of a manager or a supervisor as a 'boss' is being replaced by the role of coach and facilitator. Given this shift towards shared leadership, the team process needs to mould and build learning confidence as quickly as possible. Particularly important is that the competency of coaching is a team responsibility, and not just the team leader's. (For more information on coaching refer to Chapter 18.)

Forums for mutual exchange and support

Reviewing the lessons of discovery is fundamental to transforming workplace learning. Team learning needs some form of ritual or storytelling to share what knowledge and learning has occurred. Good-quality learning forums are characterised by group dynamics that advocate mental stimulation by framing and reframing assumptions and beliefs, bonding and building on ideas, exploring new paradigms, active experimentation, application and celebrating. (Sponsoring celebration is discussed in Chapter 14.) While the exchange can be done by e-mail or on the Web, nothing beats a well-chosen and facilitated face-to-face meeting in the right physical location.

Just-in-time learning

Best practice learning teams pride themselves on managing their own learning at the time it is required. The ongoing quality of 'right now' or 'just-in-time' learning is contingent upon all team members committing to the values of active sharing and skills enhancement. Particular skills that promote the self-managing capability of 'just-in-time' learning include:

- group solution-finding skills;
- leading effective meetings;
- interpersonal communication skills;
- conflict resolution;
- clarifying roles and responsibilities;
- technical training;

- performance management;
- Total Quality Management;
- staff selection;
- presentation skills;
- planning and budgeting skills;
- negotiation and influencing skills.

Developing the capacity to self-manage learning takes time and most of all it needs to start with a clear view of what the team is trying to become and clear identification of the skills that are needed to make the desired transition. Commonly, consultants or mentors are used to help the team manage the evolution of its learning, particularly if the skills required are lacking. The methods to develop these enabling skills include action learning, formal training, self-directed learning and team development programmes.

Where specialised team development is required it is strongly recommended that the programme be carried out with the actual team in question. Depending on their objectives, having participants from unrelated teams and diverse work locations attending a team-building programme is rarely as effective as running a formal training programme for people who are actually working together.

Forms of 'just-in-time' learning are shown in Figure 13.3.

A feeling of resilience and inner power

Having consulted with many businesses and communities over the years, I have found there is something precious about how an outstanding 'learning team' stands out from the rest. One quality that I have observed on many occasions is a sense of resilience and inner power. I have often pondered what drives this special aptitude. In my experience, this feeling of resilience comes from three important beliefs:

- All of the team members firmly believe that, irrespective of the pressures and demands that are placed on them, the team process is the best way to resolve current and future challenges. As Jack Welch, the Chief Executive of GE, says, 'Get energised rather than paralysed'.
- There is unconditional trust and respect for the synergy that teamwork generates. Allied with this is commitment and confidence in each other's capacity to contribute to the team's goals.
- Team members recognise that an effective team leads to a higher and more advanced level of decision making than can be achieved by someone working alone.

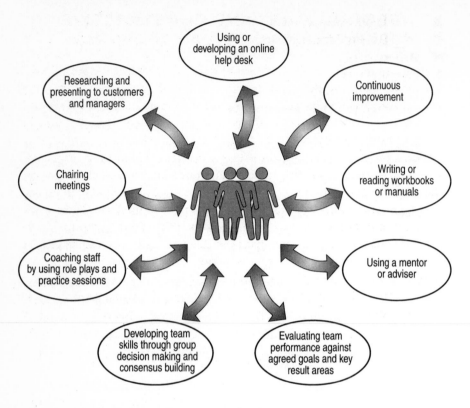

Figure 13.3 Just-in-time learning methods

Evaluating learning outcomes

Finally, it is imperative that teams spend time evaluating their performance on a regular basis. Teams that wish to aspire to best practice learning need to evaluate as many of the following issues as possible:

- innovations in systems and processes;
- improving the quality of service and product;
- demonstrating business improvement;
- increasing the quality of knowledge shared both internally and externally;
- enhancing team flexibility to respond to new challenges;
- reducing operating costs;
- a faster response rate to technological, political and environmental change;
- a more multiskilled and self-managing team;
- the capacity to attract, retain and motivate the best people;
- the creation of knowledge to build the corporate IQ.

GROUND RULES AND CONSTRUCTIVE BEHAVIOURS FOR TEAM LEARNING

Here we spend time on setting ground rules and constructive behaviours. This issue was first identified in Figure 13.2 – on the process side of the content-process continuum. It is the team management of the ground rules and constructive behaviours that will determine whether a team will demonstrate collective intelligence and reflective learning.

Peter Senge (1990, 1994) and Chris Argyris (1982) in their respective works on learning organisations provide some sound advice on how to get the most out of a team process. They do this by highlighting the difference between dialogue and discussion and providing guidelines. Their work strongly reflects the wisdom of indigenous communities who for thousands of years have demonstrated how dialogue skills such as respectful silence, suspension of assumptions, acting as colleagues and a spirit of inquiry can be invaluable in resolving conflict, building understanding and promoting learning. When discussion is value-laden it is more likely to lead to individuals tuning into only their own points of view.

Framing quality learning questions

Senge in his work *The Fifth Discipline* (1990) provides an excellent summary of how to use constructive questioning. He lists four ways in which questions can be asked to increase leverage in the power of learning. These are now summarised, with appropriate examples and questions or advice attached.

When advocating your view

- Make your reasoning explicit (that is, say how you arrived at your view and what data it is based on).
- Encourage others to explore your view (for example, 'Do you see gaps in my reasoning?').
- Encourage others to provide different views (for example, 'Do you have different data or different conclusions or both?').
- Actively inquire into others' views that differ from your own (for example, 'What are your views?').

When inquiring into others' views

- If you are making assumptions about others' views state them clearly and acknowledge that they are your assumptions.
- State the 'data' upon which your assumptions are based.
- Do not bother asking questions if you are not genuinely interested in the response.

When you arrive at an impasse

- Ask what data or logic may change their views.
- Ask if there is any way you might design an experiment (or inquiry) together that might provide a new perspective.

When you or others are hesitant to express views or to experiment with alternative ideas

- Encourage them (or yourself) to think with you 'aloud' about what they might be thinking (for example, 'What is it about this situation and about me or others that is making open exchange difficult?').
- Ask if there is a mutual desire to share or any other issue that may need addressing first.

SUMMARY

The capacity to develop quality learning within teams is a major factor in workplace learning. Team learning can assist strategies such as identifying business needs, gaining political support, gaining employee ownership and ensuring that just-in-time learning succeeds. Successful workplace learning requires effective teamwork and the commitment to building the right skills to encourage effective dialogue, innovation and application. The added challenge in the modern age is to ensure that the desire to communicate by digital technology does not jeopardise the quality and intention of what is being learnt, discovered and completed.

14

Celebrating Learning

---

*There are two things people want more than sex and money
...recognition and praise.*

Mary Kay Ash

KEY PRINCIPLES

■ Workplaces are full of celebration opportunities.
■ Celebrating milestones and achievement is the energy force of learning.
■ Celebrations promote further action and change.
■ Human beings learn best from stories.
■ Use metaphors to communicate meaning and understanding.

THE MAGIC OF SHARING DISCOVERIES

The theme for this chapter is very simple. Celebrating and sharing discovery is central to the process of learning. Irrespective of people's profession or occupation, they need to share to grow. True learning requires synergy, openness and celebration.

In many ways, it is the celebration of learning that provides the sustenance, energy and hope for workplace transformation. Unless celebration takes place as a normal element of personal and business growth, many of our plans will not bear fruit. Plans by themselves may not generate learning but the celebration of milestones on the way to our goals is an essential tonic for lifelong employee growth. The 'ritual' of celebration is a high-energy and simple way to stimulate learning in the workplace. Sadly, however, it is often overlooked.

During the last decades, I have visited hundreds of workplaces, community and professional groups that have either forgotten how to celebrate, or frowned upon it. For many people, each working day opens as if it were just another visit to the supermarket, with a long list of chores and errands. Like an illness, this lack of zeal and vitality can quickly spread throughout the whole business practice and if not dealt with can quickly contaminate the spirit of learning forever.

It is a mystery why there is such a lack of celebration in workplaces, particularly since it is so easy to do. Whether it is a group of employees discussing their daily achievements or an opportunity to exchange new-found knowledge, the workplace provides people with countless opportunities to celebrate.

CHOOSING THE RIGHT WAY TO CELEBRATE

The celebration of learning occurs in essentially two ways – in a planned and orchestrated way or in a spontaneous manner.

Orchestrated celebration

As discussed, individuals and teams can toil endlessly day after day without catching breath or sharing their knowledge and experience. Choosing the right milestone to celebrate can add important leverage to business and personal goalsetting. As indicated in earlier chapters, the creation, storage and sharing of knowledge, wisdom and learning does not happen by accident, whether it is face to face or via the World Wide Web. Outstanding celebration requires careful thought and genuine congruent communication.

Examples of potential orchestrated celebrations include:

- performance management discussions;
- team meetings;
- knowledge-sharing forums and placing results on an intranet;
- career development discussions;
- strategic planning processes;
- special research projects;
- implementation of pilot programmes;
- prototype and test runs;
- reports of best practice;
- study tours;
- producing company videos;
- think tanks;

- solution-finding activities;
- producing newsletters and publicity;
- training courses and their recall sessions;
- consultative processes;
- search conferences;
- team learning;
- awards ceremonies;
- symposiums between employees and customers;
- sharing stories of past experience and history.

To be successful, celebrations of learning must be conducted in a way that encourages openness, discovery and planning. There is nothing extraordinary or difficult about organising 'orchestrated' celebration. What is required are measurable objectives, excellent timing, good structure and maximum involvement.

A key skill in formulating an orchestrated celebration is the setting of clear milestones. A milestone involves the identification of key events or stages in the life of a project and/or job. A milestone signals a wonderful time to celebrate. The more vivid the milestone, the greater the motivational, self-nurturing and learning benefit.

To assist you to schedule and design an orchestrated celebration, the following two 'real-life' consulting stories are shared. These stories are then followed by Exercise 14.1 on designing and planning for an orchestrated celebration.

The first story occurred within a division of a major international conglomerate and the second within a small government agency.

Story 1:The strategic planning launch

Some time ago, I was asked to facilitate a strategic planning process over a five-month period with the senior executives of the Sydney division of a major international organisation. Towards the end of the process, attention shifted to how the initial findings could be best communicated to the 130 staff.

After some rigorous debate with the strategic planning team it was decided to hold an employee launch for the new plan. It was hoped that this would inspire the necessary level of interest and excitement for the upcoming change process. After considering a range of alternatives, it was decided to hold a three-hour launch for all staff on a Tuesday between 11 am and 2 pm at an off-site venue.

A day was spent with the senior executives planning and organising a celebration that would meet their expectations. It was agreed that the primary goal of the launch was to communicate the core themes of the strategic plan and to give all staff an opportunity to share their feelings, knowledge and experience on the proposals contained within the document. To achieve this goal the following took place.

Before the launch

After much discussion, the title of 'From Dream to Reality' was agreed to by the strategic planning team. It was felt that this theme best captured the spirit of the new plan. In preparation for the launch all 130 staff, plus 10 external stakeholders, received personalised written invitations from the Chief Executive. Buses were organised to transport staff from two collection points to the conference venue.

Design of launch

The launch was a multimedia extravaganza, orchestrated down to the very last detail, with carefully selected music, videos, presentations, group feedback discussions and a smorgasbord lunch. Each member of the strategic planning team was coached on how to present and lead small group discussions in an effective manner prior to the event.

Delivery of launch

The event started with each member of the strategic planning team delivering a five-minute presentation. They then held a series of small group discussions with approximately 10 staff each. The tables and seating positions of each of the 140 participants were organised in advance. Each employee sat at a circular table with a member of the strategic planning team and nine other employees from every function and division of the organisation. The goal of this arrangement was to promote cross-functional business understanding and exchange.

Just before lunch, a 20-minute presentation was made by a major external customer. The customer spoke freely about what he liked and disliked about the current service delivery – a theme of the new strategic plan.

After lunch, more small group and general discussion was held. All employees were then advised about the next phase of the planning process. This included information on the upcoming operational planning process, which was going to involve everyone in the organisation. At the end of the launch each attendee received a memento – a book with the 'From Dream to Reality' theme lettered in gold on the outside.

Evaluation of launch

Independent on-the-job feedback indicated that the launch was very successful, with most staff being able to recall the key messages from the day. There were four essential reasons for this positive response. First, staff enjoyed the event; second, they found the request for their involvement refreshing and useful; third, the level of senior executive commitment was seen as inspiring; and, finally, both staff and senior management found the talk by the customer very informative and insightful.

To me as the facilitator, this launch was a good example of how a carefully planned celebration can add significant value to a change process through quality learning and sharing. After such a celebration there was no turning back – the organisation had set in motion a strategic and operational plan that could not easily be reversed.

Story 2: The Eastwood experience

I was once asked to facilitate a cultural change programme with a small government agency undergoing a challenging major transition towards better client service. The recently appointed senior manager of the office was having trouble bringing about the required change because many of the long-established staff were unwilling to let go of the past. For many of them, the past held emotional anchors that were inhibiting their capacity to change. Particularly powerful was the 'ghost-like influence' of a recently retired senior manager who had debilitated and autocratically led the office for 15 long years. As a consequence, most of the longer-serving staff lacked both the confidence and the belief that they were capable of bringing about or adapting to the necessary change.

Upon my arrival in the organisation it was apparent that the retired senior manager was still haunting the office and was not allowing the office to change, even though he had left some six months earlier. So in a very real sense this office needed some 'ghostbusting' done! To do this, I organised a celebration for all 40 staff to attend with a choice of two one-day sessions. These were conducted at an off-site Sydney location in the suburb of Eastwood.

Design of celebration

The celebration was called a 'history trip'. The goal of a 'history trip' is to have each person share an event in the life of the organisation that they believe has profoundly affected the way he or she feels about the current workplace. To do this, each person is requested to write down and date an event of significance. Each is then asked to share his or her story publicly with the rest of the group. To add visibility to the process each story is marked on a time-line made from flip-chart paper attached across a very long wall. After reviewing the implications of the stories from the 'history trip', action plans are set and working parties established.

How it went

For two days, two different groups of 20 staff shared and listened to stories. Some deeply funny, others very sad, but all very personal, precious and informative. As each person told his or her story, people listened actively and asked questions of clarification and tested their understanding. People were given permission to say whatever they liked about their own story but not to pass judgment on others'.

Not surprisingly, various stories were shared about the retired senior manager but also, interestingly, several originated in the 1940s, long before anyone in the office was employed. So not only was the office dealing with the metaphorical power of the ghost of the retired senior manager, but also with other ghosts that floated around the corridors of power, some from the time of World War Two.

Both days created their own atmosphere of trust and bonding and the process of storytelling served its purpose of examining what was good and bad about the history of the office. For some, it was a profoundly emotional experience as the folklore was mapped out. For others, especially the new staff, it gave important meaning to how and why the office behaved the way it did. Most of all, the history trip gave the staff the information to make decisions for the future, by choosing to eliminate the ghosts that had been haunting them for years.

Endnote

Much has happened in this office since this workshop was conducted. The two seminars are now part of a new 'folklore' and the history trip is now called the 'Eastwood experience'. 'The Eastwood experience' is seen as one of the major turning points in the history of the office. Since then, the office has relocated, upgraded its facilities and has begun to reap the benefits of improved client service.

To help you plan for a potential celebration opportunity, complete Exercise 14.1.

Exercise 14.1: Designing an orchestrated celebration

1. Describe a project, job function or change process that you believe requires some form of celebration:

_____

_____

_____

2. Why is this the case?

_____

_____

_____

3. List, in sequential order, possible celebration opportunities that are available in the life of this project, job function or change process:

Activity   _Completion date_

_____

_____

_____

_____

4. Given your analysis, write down the best and most critical event or milestone to celebrate:

_____

_____

_____

5. What outcomes will you be seeking from this celebration?

_____

_____

_____

_____

6. Brainstorm the content and process issues that you believe will add quality to this celebration point:

Content   *Process*

_____

_____

_____

_____

_____

7. How will you engender participant curiosity before, during and after this celebration point?

Before

_____

_____

_____

During

_____

_____

_____

After

_____

_____

_____

8. What resources will you need to conduct a successful celebration of learning?

_____

_____

_____

_____

9. How can you sustain your own personal energy and drive throughout the project, job function and/or change process?

_____

_____

_____

_____

Spontaneous celebration

Every project that an individual faces in his or her working life requires careful attention to how energy is being sustained and managed. This is particularly the case in modern workplaces, where people are spending so much energy to work smarter and excel in a rapidly changing world.

Focusing solely on the task at the expense of how people are feeling can lead to a dramatic decrease in performance and learning. A common ritual I use is to have people share a major discovery or insight that they have learnt during the project at hand. In doing so, you are not only getting a quick gauge of progress but you are also celebrating in a spontaneous way what is being learnt.

Such rituals are imperative to stimulate renewal, hope and confidence with learning. There is nothing overly scientific about spontaneous celebration. All that is required is the permission to give out and receive praise, support and acknowledgment. This is all very simple and uncomplicated but a very powerful force in the process of workplace learning transformation.

So, whenever possible, take a moment to share and listen to people's successes and keep the spirit, feeling and joy of discovery alive and well.

The final section of this chapter explores how stories and metaphors add value to all forms of celebration.

USING THE POWER OF STORY AND METAPHOR

Since the dawn of time people have shared stories and metaphors to add meaning to folklore and increase their capacity to remember. Whether it is an Australian Aboriginal telling the story of 'the dreamtime' or a line manager describing the organisation as a 'well-drilled machine', we are still communicating an image or message. There is no doubt that, used effectively, stories and metaphors can add significant value to all forms of discovery. We need only to reflect on how history and experiences are told to come to the quick conclusion that human beings learn best from stories; particularly if they are communicated with conviction, elegance and passion, while also being empathetic to the listener's needs.

Stories and metaphors have a special place in the quality of workplace learning. For example, the two main consulting experiences described earlier in this chapter ('the strategic planning launch' and 'the Eastwood experience') used storytelling to revitalise and capture the imagination of the participants. In the case of 'the Eastwood experience', the metaphor of 'ghostbusting' was used to add clarity to what had been happening to the office over the previous 50 years.

Of course, the use of story and metaphor can be as simple as using video to broadcast a message or a team leader sharing where his or her knowledge or insight is founded.

Telling a good story

Storytelling is a craft and it takes practice to spin a great yarn. A good story is short, engages the learner and helps develop shared meaning. The benefits can range from entertainment, influencing, teaching, informing and renewal. The storyteller needs to use eye contact and body gestures to establish curiosity and maintain interest. Let your voice be an instrument, varying your tone and pacing to 'mirror' the emotion of your story.

You need not be a professional actor to tell a story. Quite the contrary, you are best placed to tell the anecdotes and experiences that matter to you, because when it is true or grounded in truth people will believe you and as a result your story will have integrity and impact. A good story can be used for a number of reasons:

- to focus thinking on a key point or an explanation of a key theme;
- to generate a desirable motivation or emotional state for learning;
- to provide a suggestion or advice about a challenge;
- to create empathy;
- to stimulate a new action from a learner.

To help you recall, develop and build your own stories, take a moment to complete Exercise 14.2.

Exercise 14.2: Creating a story

1. Reflect on a work or non-work experience from which you believe you have learnt something. Write down the background or sequence of events that made up this experience:

_____

_____

_____

_____

_____

2. In less than 10 words, describe the lesson that you have drawn from this experience:

_____

_____

3. Under what theme or heading would you place this story? (Examples of themes include leadership, motivation, teamwork, new strengths and overcoming obstacles.)

_____

4. Get a notebook or start a computer file index of your stories, adding and modifying them as required.
5. Set yourself a goal of adding one story to your index of stories per day.
6. Whenever appropriate, share and celebrate with others.

Using metaphors

Metaphors are a way of giving a description or label to a learning principle to demonstrate an infallible understanding. Metaphors can be short sayings such as 'team learning is the prize jewel of workplace learning', or a story such as 'My favourite fishing story' told in Chapter 9. In both cases, metaphors were used to explain a principle of workplace learning.

The benefits of metaphors are numerous. They include:

■ linking concepts and building bridges between old and new knowledge;

- evoking an emotion or a feeling that can help create positive learning;
- inspiring lateral thinking;
- creating a message that encourages a different perspective;
- helping the recall of information by activating the senses of sight, sound, touch, taste and smell.

Creating your own story or metaphor is both an enjoyable and positive experience. For a metaphor to be successful it must be simple, concise and appropriate. The four stages in developing a metaphor are:

1. Choose a concept that you need to explain.
2. Consider the background of the learners.
3. Brainstorm metaphors that link the learning concept with some unrelated object, which has some physical or emotional characteristics. The metaphor should closely align with the message you wish to convey. For example, in Chapter 9, comparing the management of human resource systems with a Roman chariot came after recalling the movie *Ben Hur*, where there is a famous chariot race.
4. Try out your metaphor on someone else and gauge their reaction and understanding. Ask them to describe which of the five senses were stimulated by the metaphor.

To help develop your understanding and use of metaphors, complete Exercise 14.3.

Exercise 14.3: Recalling metaphors

1. Write down the most memorable metaphor that you have heard or used.

_____

_____

2. What made this metaphor most memorable for you?

_____

_____

_____

---

3. How could you change this metaphor to improve the impact and quality of learning?

_____

_____

_____

_____

4. How and where could you use this metaphor?

_____

_____

_____

_____

SUMMARY

This chapter has highlighted the importance of celebration in the process of transforming workplace learning and the sharing of knowledge.

Quality celebration provides the impetus to maintain the momentum, drive and energy for learning. The opportunities for celebration are limitless, given that they can either be scheduled in advance or created on the spot. The best celebrations of learning are carefully structured and timed, and include excellent storytelling and the use of powerful metaphors.

15

Building Learning Communities

> *Reality is born largely from the beliefs and boundaries we co-create with those around us.*
>
> Robert Theobold

KEY PRINCIPLES

- Workplace learning must be a process of community building.
- Learning communities give people hope, inspiration and meaning.
- Create conversation that is vibrant, interactive and two-way.
- People who steal ideas at the expense of sharing are community killers not builders.
- Digital technology is a powerful medium to increase access and involvement.

REAPING THE BENEFITS OF THE NEW MILLENNIUM

Today's business environment is providing exciting possibilities for people to learn in new and innovative ways. Advances in e-commerce, digital technology and teamwork across the globe have meant that the number of people involved in learning has grown to levels that in the past would not have been possible. One minute you can be talking to a colleague in an office and a moment later you can be holding a conversation with another 10,000 miles away. Workplace success is now closely associated with how well people connect with each other and find new ways or rediscover old ones to confront the challenges being faced.

To reap the benefits of this new millennium, workplace practices must engage the hearts and minds of people irrespective of their background, status or occupation. This means extending your network of resources and personal contacts within a well-thought-out business strategy. We can no longer rely on the wisdom of people we know or can trust to get things done. Workplaces need imagination and insight to manage their own unique challenges and practices. As a consequence, taking a learning community approach to workplace discovery has become a major precursor to modern day innovation, sustainability and renewal.

The types and forms of learning communities that can be drawn upon can be as diverse as the people who live within them. A learning community could take the form of informal breakfast meetings, where once a month people join together to discuss a common area of interest, or it could be an organised process where customers, suppliers, unions and community representatives discuss an idea face to face or via a chatline on the Internet. Examples of learning communities that I have observed in recent times include: a school that joined students, parents and community leaders to redesign the recreational space inside the school grounds; a city council liaising with ratepayers in regard to a 10-year plan to become a learning city; a range of businesses that use groupware technology to formulate networks of knowledge sharers in areas of greatest common interest; and finally, the staggering growth of virtual universities. This last group are providers within an official university or non-aligned institution offering under- or postgraduate qualifications and short courses via the Internet. Examples include: The Global Virtual University Home Page at http: //www.gvu.ac.nz/ or California Virtual Campus at http: //www.cvc.edu, and for a broader listing of offers see http: // www.edsurf.net/ed.shack.

As you study learning communities, you sense beneath the surface something remarkably similar going on. It is a desire to save time and effort and pull together resources and knowledge to make a difference in whatever the cause being pursued. Here lies the driving reason for a community-based approach to learning. In order to cope with frenzied modern change, workplaces must pool resources, co-operate and share their wisdom in order to survive.

To further understand why the modern organisation needs to build a community approach to learning, see the discussion below of the organisation as a 'living human cell'.

The organisation as a 'living human cell'

To assist the conceptual understanding of the modern organisation it is useful to view it as a self-adapting living human cell (see Figure 15.1). Like a human cell, which needs constant oxygen, nutrients and the ability to self-organise, so the modern workplace needs the same ability to adapt, to remain alive and stay healthy.

The 24-hour clock

The 24-hour clock provides the perspective that organisational life is never static. That is, what was relevant yesterday may not be appropriate today. When decisions are made they need to weigh up the political and business implications for both the internal and external environment. To do this successfully, workplaces need to maintain very close links with networks of fellow-travellers and expertise, keeping a sharp eye on what is required to meet the demands of vital business challenges.

The internal environment

Like a 'living human cell', the internal organisational environment exists within a broader external environment of customers, suppliers and community. The challenges affecting the internal environment are heavily affected by external pressures. This causes a constant process of chaotic and never-ending change as the organisation tries to make sense of what is going on around it. Learning communities, digital technology and virtual teams have become a modern-day way of structuring the organisational nervous system, or DNA, in a way that can help the process of self-organisation and reinvention.

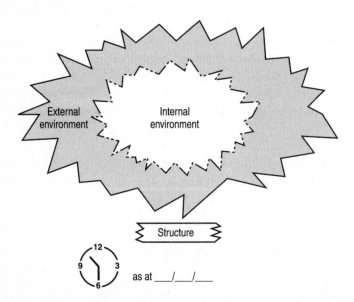

Figure 15.1 The 'living human cell' structure

SPARKING HUMAN SPIRIT

We can all remember a time in our lives when we were part of a wonderful community, whether it was at a sports club, in a local community or a workplace. There is something about the spirit of community that is contagious and memorable. When we feel part of a community we are inspired and find meaning in what we are doing. If we view a learning community as a cold-hearted process of just turning up to talk, or simply keying more words into the keyboard, we can quickly lose much of the spirit that makes the human connection of community so special.

For a community to develop, somehow the needs of the individual, teams and the organisation must be seen as benefiting a much broader aim or purpose than just individual pursuits. The legacy or vision of the community must be deeply attractive to all its members and when projects and activities are created they must foster vibrant and interactive exchanges. In doing this, communities are increasingly expected to gain the commitment of people they hardly know or over whom they have no direct control. As a result, relationship building and the ability to build trust are again vital.

So how does one build and sustain a community? Lessons include:

- ensuring the communities have a clear vision;
- listening to the various voices;
- making sure people are positively involved and not burning out.

To assist in building a learning community here are 10 ground rules that could be considered as a code of practice:

1. You must passionately desire community; if you are not 'walking the talk' it just will not happen.
2. If you are struggling to get the concept on the agenda, begin by having conversations about the merits of building community.
3. Practise respectful listening in everything you do.
4. Tell stories and express your thoughts and feelings about community. Help others to explore deeper meaning about themselves and what is happening around them.
5. Schedule regular times to discuss how people feel about change and what needs to be done.
6. Reach out and discover people who have different viewpoints and skills. Explore new frontiers, networks, friends and colleagues.
7. Praise and thank people who encourage others to share their ideas and perspectives. Make it known that people who steal ideas at the expense of sharing are community killers not builders.
8. Organise networking events or online virtual discussions to inform and consult. Actively involve contributors in the design, delivery and evaluation.
9. Establish meaningful tasks or shared areas of interest. Communities often fail because people do not know how to contribute or how to find people who can.
10. Community is about the commitment to listen and understand others. The greatest legacy of a community is not outcomes and bureaucracy but building a shared world of significance between people.

SUSTAINING SUCCESSFUL RELATIONSHIPS

Implicit in the efforts to build community is the preservation and upkeep of worthwhile relationships and/or partnerships. To do this requires trustworthiness, negotiation, ethical behaviour and reciprocity.

Within an organisation, a spirit of community or belonging can be facilitated by:

- setting up electronic networks discussions on the intranet or World Wide Web;
- organising a special event, such as a knowledge-sharing fair;
- forming project teams where people from diverse backgrounds consider real-life challenges;
- mobilising a wide range of customers and all forms of employees to work jointly on an area of mutual concern.

David Limerick, Bert Cunnington and Frank Crowther in their book *Managing the New Organisation (Collaboration and Sustainability in the Post-Corporate World)* (1998) suggest a number of common causes for unsatisfactory partnerships/relationships, which have a direct link to this discussion on the downfall of community within a workplace. These include:

■ a lack of guidelines on the reporting process between the partners, leading to ambiguity and confusion on boundaries of influence and control, resulting in people guessing how best to maintain the relationship;

■ some partnerships lead to extraordinary demands on either party, causing a breakdown in the synergy of the relationship;

■ given that partners are conducting their own businesses, it is quite common for some to put less effort into the relationship, resulting in the undermanagement of their contribution to the alliance;

■ a lack of equity on how some partners should service the needs of various alliances, for example, some parties may favour one partner in preference to another, thereby causing friction with other interested parties;

■ partners may fail to spell out the obligations, responsibilities and needs on an ongoing basis;

■ forming added-value partnerships can lead to the creation of a potential competitor in the long term;

■ some partnership relationships are too short-term focused and as a result are prone to undermanagement, poor evaluation and less than open exchanges. Having a long-term focus increases the likelihood of developing a good understanding of the organisational cultures and communication channels required to resolve business and learning needs.

FINESSING VIRTUAL COMMUNITIES

As discussed in Chapter 12, digital technology has fundamentally changed the fabric of learning. *Learning Unlimited* explores ways that the smarter uses of digital infrastructure can lead to dramatic improvements in discovery and innovation, resulting in a community of knowers or searchers being connected.

To gain some further insight into what is required to build and sustain virtual learning communities, let us explore the findings of a study in this field. In 1999, Arthur Andersen's Next Generation Research Group, in collaboration with Anheuser-Busch, Shell Oil and The Mutual Group, studied online communities of practice. The object of the study was to obtain insights into how communities within business organisations can generate more value by extending themselves virtually.

They found the following points of note:

- If a business wishes to build a virtual community it needs to concentrate its efforts on building the spirit of community.
- Stifling or trying to control communities will send them underground into something less visible and more informal.
- Virtual communities take significant investments of time and effort to maintain and improve service delivery.
- Members of the community must drive the agenda for it to be sustained. Everyone must be seen as equal.
- The speed of change fuels the acceptance of the virtual community. When speed of change is slower, people tend to hoard knowledge rather than share.
- There seems to be a cultural fit between people who use digital technology and those who embrace virtual communities.
- Community members often do not hang around and share their discoveries, opting to find the good e-mail contacts and move on.
- When the benefits of good conversations are located, it is a reward that has unlimited value.
- Virtual communities tend to be meritocracies, where people who are seen to have universal wisdom or merit have a high influence on how the network takes shape.
- There appears to be natural succession where members in time take a leadership role.
- The growth of virtual communities is based in part on a clear understanding of the needs of potential members.

As a closing activity for this chapter, Exercise 15.1 assists you to explore suitable partners for learning in whatever community you are currently or wish to be in the future.

Exercise 15.1: Establishing high-potential learning partnerships

1. What are the current KRAs within your workplace?

_____

_____

_____

_____

_____

_____

2. Given this analysis, which KRAs would most benefit from the formation of a partnership or the fostering of greater learning community?

_____

_____

_____

3. Why is this the case?

_____

_____

_____

_____

4. What workplace learning benefits would you hope to reap?

_____

_____

_____

5. What resources or information do you have at your disposal that would assist in the formation of relationships that are supportive of your cause?

_____

_____

_____

6. On the diagram below, make a note of possible partnership opportunities (and note that in some cases, a network contact could be grouped in one or more categories).

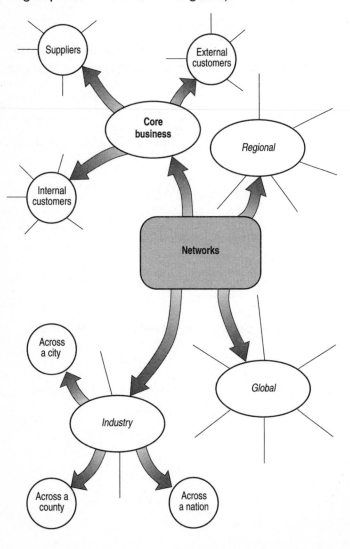

7. Given your analysis, what is the next logical step in the building of successful learning partnerships and exchanges?

   _____

   _____

   _____

   _____

8. In the next three months, what changes or improvements would you like to see and experience?

   _____

   _____

   _____

   _____

SUMMARY

Thriving on constant transition requires more than just adaptability: it requires that the pool of expertise and never-ending co-operation expand on an ongoing daily basis. Organisations and workplaces that do this best will be those that are better prepared for challenges ahead, by being far more resourceful and resilient. In order for workplaces to stay ahead and be contemporary in the years to come, they need to build communities of fellow-travellers who connect and share wisdom unconditionally on key challenges and concerns.

16

Perfecting On-the-job Learning

> *We are stuck with resources that we have forgotten how to use.*
> Jean Houston

KEY PRINCIPLES

- Excellent on-the-job learning requires reflection and sharing.
- Action learning is an excellent approach to blend learning and business priorities.
- Match learner motivation with KRAs.
- Emotional intelligence is a major factor in career success.
- Never undervalue the range of learning resources already available in your workplace.

A SOLID FOUNDATION

Stimulating on-the-job learning is the foundation of exemplary business performance. Excellence rarely happens by accident; it needs well-trained people combined with a work environment that cultivates reflection, innovation and knowledge creation. Already in *Learning Unlimited*, many strategies and practices have been discovered that make this possible. These include embracing a clear business focus; embracing digital technologies such as intranets and multimedia; and actively promoting celebration and team learning, to name a few.

To further assist you in perfecting on-the-job learning in the workplace, this chapter will explore some of the unique approaches that can cultivate personal growth and greater insight. In subsequent chapters on formal training, coaching, mentoring and building a flexible workforce more approaches will be explored to advance the cause further.

Before proceeding, it is important to consider the proposition that the real classroom is the job itself. Although formal training or delivery of e-learning by the Internet is a fantastic help, it is the reflection and experimentation that occurs daily on the job that will be the ultimate barometer of whether an individual learns and the business benefits. Seibert (1999), when talking about on-the-job learning, presents 'the skill of stepping back from an experience to ponder carefully and persistently'. Closely associated with Seibert's insight are the catalysts of outstanding feedback and celebration, which together help create a rich learning dynamic.

Ultimately, the skill of on-the-job learning is based not on what people are learning but on how well the environment of discovery and knowledge is created and maintained. Without skilful finessing of the processes of reflection and sharing, what is learnt is rarely noted and acted upon. People need to understand what their current strengths are, what lessons are being taught and what can be done to improve their performance and potential. By doing this we have a firm 'buy in' to the process of workplace learning.

ACTION LEARNING

An increasingly popular approach to on-the-job learning is 'action learning' or what is sometimes called a 'learning unit/set' approach. This involves using a group process to solve a work problem while at the same time focusing on what and how the people are learning. The positive appeal of 'action learning' is that it strongly links 'learning' with the 'business', and for the busy modern worker that is vitally important.

Action learning combines the team-learning principles discussed in Chapter 13 with a careful definition of an area to think and learn about, thereby providing a strong framework for discovery. By its very nature, action learning can take many forms, ranging from studies in known fields to ones that explore completely new frontiers. Examples of such topics include improving morale, reducing turnover, exploring best practice research and developing new systems.

According to Marquardt (1999) there are a number of steps in building an action learning programme. These include gaining top management support; conducting workshops that carefully explain what action learning is and is not; allocating roles of team members and facilitators; establishing milestones; and sustaining an implementation strategy. Marquardt suggests there are a number of common pitfalls that need to be avoided in undertaking an action learning approach. By noting these you increase your chances of ensuring true discovery occurs and not just action.

Some of the pitfalls to watch include:

- the area to be studied is unimportant or uninspiring, abstract or poorly defined;
- the terms of reference are driven by political forces outside of the group and commitment of the team members is lacking;
- the task at hand is beyond the authority or scope of the team or there is little or no way of applying the learning to the workplace;
- the mix of the group is unbalanced or unrepresentative;
- the organisation fails to provide resources, equipment, information, time and facilities to undertake the process;
- the desire to support innovation and better thinking is quickly replaced with rejection of ideas and protection of the status quo;
- the process becomes sluggish because of unmatched or unreasonable expectations;
- the team members are untrained in handling learning or group dynamics;
- the workplace is craving an instant solution, resolution or quick fix;
- the facilitator or mentor guiding the process is poorly skilled.

IDENTIFYING LEARNER MOTIVATION

Unless there is self-motivation, workplace learning and business performance will suffer. In the past I have paid dearly for selecting the wrong person to do a job or project. As a consequence, my team and organisation suffered from a substandard outcome.

One of the major things I have learnt in this area is the importance of spending time and effort identifying the motivational fit between the person and the needs of each job or project. Let us assume you have a person who enjoys doing highly technical and independent projects. Imagine that a new team-leader job arises. What do you do? It is quite likely if this employee is placed in this vacancy, he or she will in time become stressed and dissatisfied. In this scenario, it would probably be better to find another person who finds team leadership motivating and enjoyable. Assuming you make this decision and you hire another individual, will it necessarily produce the best result? Well, the answer is that we do not know. Why? Quite simply, having a desire to learn and use important skills does not immediately mean that someone is competent. To overcome this dilemma, references and diagnostic tools can be used to determine whether an applicant has the track record and the competency required. Even then, the selected applicant will need excellent feedback, freedom to enhance capabilities, quality mentoring and agreed goals to reach his or her true potential.

Given this scenario, it is clear that selecting the correct people to perform long-term or short-term assignments can at times be quite complex. However, if the right questions are asked and non-discriminatory practices are followed, there is a reasonable chance of locating the best person for each on-the-job learning challenge. What is required are flexibility, creativity and excellent listening skills.

Using one-to-one discussions with employees

To assist in the process of identifying suitable learners, the guidelines described below, which use structured one-to-one discussions with individuals as a vehicle for facilitating empowered personal growth, can be adopted.

The fundamental goal behind these guidelines is finding and inspiring people to meet the ever-changing demands of the workplace. In undertaking this process be wary of assuming that a good learner will automatically meet your needs. What is more important is that the individual is motivated to learn and perform within agreed responsibilities.

These guidelines are separated into two sections. The first section focuses on preparation, while the second provides practical tips on holding an actual one-to-one discussion. The second section also contains a narrative case study to highlight how an actual one-to-one discussion could unfold.

Preparation

The following guidelines will help you to prepare for your one-on-one discussion.

The individual should be approached regarding the desire to hold a one-to-one discussion. After establishing rapport, the purpose of the one-to-one discussion needs to be spelt out. For example:

> The goal of this one-to-one process is to explore your learning motivation. At the end of the process, I hope that both you and I will be better placed to determine how projects can be allocated that will increase your job satisfaction. However, it must be stressed, there are no guarantees.
>
> During the one-to-one discussion you control what you say and do, the process is totally voluntary. What is shared will be kept strictly confidential, unless there is agreement to do otherwise. It may also be necessary to hold a series of follow-up one-to-one discussions to complete the process.

If the person agrees to participate, both parties need to allocate a minimum of one hour to hold their initial one-to-one discussion. The individual is then asked to perform some preparation for the first one-to-one discussion. Preparation is as follows:

> Write down three activities that you have done in the past that at the time you found very motivating. There is no restriction on where you choose these activities from. These experiences can be drawn from either a work or non-work situation. For example, it is possible that some of your best experiences may have occurred during your past employment or in childhood. What is important is that the experience was exceptionally motivating.

When issuing this preparatory work, it is important to deal with any anxiety up front. Be careful not to make any unwarranted assumptions about gender, cultural background or disability.

Holding the one-to-one discussion

The following tips will assist you during the one-to-one discussion:

- After establishing rapport, ask the individual to start by telling one of his or her three stories. Ensure the story is specific (for example, completing last year's business plan) rather than a long-term protracted experience (for example, completing a two-year course of study).
- Remember that non-work examples of motivating experiences are fine. For example, a single parent re-entering the workforce after a five-year break may have undertaken very interesting non-paid work while being out of full-time employment.
- Actively listen by probing with active verbs or phrases. By focusing and probing using a key phrase or active verb, you and the employee will be able to identify the learning motivation and payoff faster and more efficiently. For example, if a person said during a discussion, 'I loved building my garden furniture', a suitable probe would be 'What do you mean by build?'
- While listening, take time to summarise and paraphrase your observations. Avoid jumping to conclusions; it is important to check assumptions.
- Explore the employee's pleasure. In terms of learning motivation, it is more important to identify 'how they learnt', 'what part they played' and 'what they did', rather than exploring 'why' he or she did something. Avoid asking 'why' questions; they are not relevant.
- As the person talks, write down the active verbs he or she uses. Make special note of active verbs that radiate the greatest pleasure. You will find this is when the person becomes more positively animated.

- If a tangent develops, say thank you and return him or her to the story and to what part he or she played in it.
- After approximately 20 minutes, or when exploration of the first story is exhausted, move on to the other two stories, repeating the same process. Remember, you are only interested in what the learner did and nobody else.
- Having finished the three stories, go over the active words together. Look for any pattern in the actions expressed, especially where the individual became animated or excited. Celebrate the good feeling by asking the individual to talk about how he or she feels.
- Seek confirmation between yourself and the individual on key themes listed. Jointly explore the implications of this information for workplace learning requirements.
- Make it your business to ensure that you are both clear about the KRAs of the job or project to be performed. It is important that both parties spend time developing a common understanding of essential and desirable competencies required before any plan of action is agreed.
- Agree on a plan of action or follow-up meeting.

Final thoughts on conducting the one-to-one

Holding learning motivation one-to-one discussions is very rewarding and good fun. This is not surprising given that we are asking people to share what motivates them. Apart from the wealth of information that can be gained from such an exercise, it can dramatically help learner confidence by identifying transferable and or portable skills.

Although this discussion has been explored within the context of a one-to-one exercise, this process can also be used effectively in small groups during action learning, career planning, management development and life-skills management seminars. To assist in making sense of the potential two-way conversation in a one-to-one discussion, the following case study describes a possible exchange between an employee and a manager of a civil engineering office.

Case study: Learning to motivate

Pre-work is undertaken as recommended. The two parties then meet at the one-to-one meeting. Both parties are very keen to participate and are looking forward to the process.

The following extracts of the conversation show how the skills of probing and clarification are performed to explore learner motivation:

Manager: Which story do you wish to start with?
Employee: I'll start with the 'blueprint' story.

Manager: What do mean by the 'blueprint' story? [probing]

Employee: Well, you remember last December when you were sick for two days, I organised the blueprint for the new cultural centre. I got a big buzz out of that.

Manager: What gave you a big buzz out of it? [probing]

Employee: I loved the chance to supervise the team to get the job done.

Manager: Which aspect of supervision did you enjoy the most? [probing]

Employee: Leading the team meeting.

Manager: Let me get this clear. It was not so much that you were doing a blueprint for the office, but it was 'leading the meeting' that gave you a big buzz. Is that correct? [clarifying, summarising and paraphrasing]

Employee: Yes, that is correct.

Manager: I also assume that a big buzz came when you completed the task. [testing understanding]

Employee: No, not really. It was just getting everyone together, at short notice, and gaining their support. I enjoy the coaching part.

Now the manager would explore the coaching angle by using the probing, clarifying, summarising, paraphrasing and testing skills. This would be done until the avenue of coaching is exhausted or a new avenue is exposed.

STRETCHING THE COMFORT ZONE

Since becoming interested in workplace learning, I have spent significant time in Australia and overseas expanding my understanding of how individuals can improve their learning. Many of the lessons learnt from these experiences have already been shared. Two notable areas of discovery have been the areas of understanding 'job fit' and mental diversity. However, on reflection, a turning point in my career was the attendance at the Center for Creative Leadership in Greensbro, North Carolina. The premise behind much of the research from the Center for Creative Leadership was that outstanding personal growth comes from diverse developmental experiences, particularly those that stretch people outside their comfort zones. That is, the larger the number of diverse developmental experiences, the greater the potential for personal growth and capacity to cope with the new or different. Being in the comfort zone for protracted periods is not seen as beneficial to personal growth and workplace learning.

The process of stretching needs to be undertaken with sensitivity and consultation. Stretching just for its own sake can be quite destructive, particularly without adequate 'back-up' support and coaching. Simply putting a person in a new task or asking them to do a project does not guarantee anything, unless the learner motivation of the employee and the KRAs of the business are jointly examined.

Like most individuals, I have met many people who have lacked versatility and stretching in their careers. In many cases, these people have had their career managed for them for many years. They have been travelling on the 'organisational career bus' through life. Unfortunately, when change comes, it often arrives with a vengeance. The process of restructuring and retrenchment would be a very clear example of this painful process. There, overnight, people's lives and sense of meaning can be destroyed. The most saddening part is that the restructuring process often results in a debate about profit rather than helping people rebuild their lives with confidence and hope.

The following three strategies are particularly useful in supporting the positive stretch of people's comfort zones. These strategies are:

- allocating work assignments based on development needs;
- 'flagging' early warning signs;
- using a time-based approach to develop learning within career paths.

Allocating work assignments based on development needs

Personal growth can be enhanced by examining past developmental experiences and allocating work projects that produce different and more powerful learning outcomes. One of the best references in this field of study is *The Lessons of Experience* by McCall, Lombardo and Morrison (1988). They identified that different developmental assignments generate quite distinctive learning outcomes. Although concentrating on executive leadership as a focus, this framework can be easily adapted to other occupations. Table 16.1 provides a summary of the seven developmental areas. In each case the learning outcome is highlighted.

Taking these seven categories and comparing them to the developmental history of a person, it is possible to weigh up the potential benefits of a proposed on-the-job assignment. Assuming that all parties understand the seven areas described, it is then possible to develop a plan to leverage the impact of discovery and personal growth.

Table 16.1 Developmental assignments and learning outcomes

Developmental assignment	Learning outcome
Early work experiences	Helps the transition to work and shows people how to behave at work. This helps provide self-awareness.
First supervisor experience	Creates a situation where a person is responsible for other people. This is quite different from pure technical and procedural work.
Leading project/task force	Requires giving up being a technical or functional expert, and leading a team where understanding and facilitating other people's points of view is required.
Switching roles within an organisation(s)	Assists a broader understanding of line and staff responsibilities. A wonderful exposure to changes in corporate culture and mindsets.
Starting from scratch on a major project	Provides practice in resolving a project's KRAs from the very beginning. Includes the development of competencies in building a team, dealing with tough situations and being an effective leader.
Fix-it/turn-around jobs	Being tough and persuasive.
Leaps in scope	Making more influential and more strategic decisions. Relying on others to get your actions implemented.

Source: Adapted from *The Lessons of Experience* (1988) M. McCall Jr, L. Lombardo and A. Morrison, Lexington Books, Massachusetts, p 61.

'Flagging' early warning signs

Another useful way to maintain personal growth is to notice and watch behaviours that can derail one's career. In this regard, Daniel Goleman (1998) identified that recent research by the Center for Creative Leadership has found that rigidity and poor relationships have become emerging themes in poor performance. Goleman goes on to say that this finding is added proof that emotional intelligence is a far more reliable indicator of career success than traditional measures such as IQ and technical know-how.

Such a listing of potential derailments can act as an 'early warning signal' by giving a framework to improve performance before the negative consequences of the adverse behaviour begin to emerge. The 'early warning signals' include:

- being unable to resolve poor interpersonal relationships;
- failure to mould, nurture and coach others;
- inability to build and lead a team;
- being out of touch with change;
- neglecting adequate follow-through of actions;
- being overly dependent on too few mentors;
- being unwilling or unable to resolve conflict.

Using a time-based approach to develop learning within career paths

The final perspective in helping on-the-job learning is to view development as a time-based cycle. An excellent reference source is the book by Dalton and Thompson entitled *Novations Strategies for Career Management* (1986), in which they suggest that employees travel through four stages during a career life cycle. The four stages in order of evolution are:

- *Stage 1: Apprentice,* where an individual follows directions and learns the basics.
- *Stage 2: Colleague,* where the individual shifts to becoming a supportive and independent contributor to the organisation; this normally means that the individual can perform his or her normal tasks unaided.
- *Stage 3: Mentor,* where an individual assumes responsibility for others and starts to provide positive coaching.
- *Stage 4: Sponsor,* where an individual actively contributes to the shaping of the organisation by exercising power, influence and experience to get things done.

Having an awareness of various stages of development, people are better placed to improve the quality of workplace learning assignments by examining and studying key challenges and the time required to progress through all four stages.

One of the best examples I have observed in applying this framework was with salespeople within the Sydney operation of Merck, Sharp and Dohme. As part of its comprehensive approach to workplace learning, the company was able to improve personal growth and reduce staff turnover by examining the development life cycle of the career path of its salespeople. From a study of past exit interview information it was identified that most of the staff turnover had occurred during the transition between the first two stages of the cycle: the apprentice and the colleague. This period coincided with the employee being on the road for the first time, and selling. As a result of this feedback, Merck, Sharp and Dohme incorporated developmental activities into stage 1 and stage 2 to help people through this especially critical period. The company implemented a programme where key mentors and sponsors provided support to employees undergoing this transition. As a result of this action, both personal growth and turnover improved. The Merck, Sharp and Dohme example highlights how easily time-based development models can be applied. Irrespective of the type of industry, personal growth can be improved by studying the hurdles being experienced during the life cycle of a career path.

Exercise 16.1 provides some assistance in applying the time-based approach to a career path in your organisation.

Exercise 16.1: Determining a career path development life cycle

This exercise contains two parts:

- Part 1 helps to identify high-priority career paths for further study.

- Part 2 explores the development challenges within the nominated high-priority career path.

Part 1: Why this career path?

1. Describe a key career path within your organisation:

   _____

   _____

   _____

2. What business reasons necessitate the studying of the development cycle of this career path?

   _____

   _____

   _____

   _____

---

3. Brainstorm ways in which data can be collected regarding this career path:

_____

_____

_____

_____

_____

_____

Part 2: Key research questions

4. Describe the factors that are either contributing to or hindering the personal growth within this nominated career path.

_____

_____

_____

_____

_____

5. Using the following diagram as a guide, consider the average length of time it takes to progress through each of the four stages of the career path.

Career path life cycle

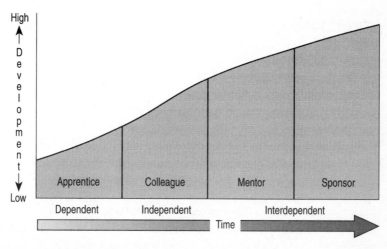

Stage	Length of time
Apprentice	_____
Colleague	_____
Mentor	_____
Sponsor	_____

Now consider the key challenges and support required for each stage of the cycle:

Stage	Length of time
Apprentice	_____
Colleague	_____
Mentor	_____
Sponsor	_____

Now consider the changes required to improve personal growth and business contribution within this career path:

_____

_____

_____

_____

EFFECTIVELY USING LEARNING RESOURCES

This chapter would be incomplete without acknowledging the wealth of on-the-job learning resources that can be commonly found within any modern workplace.

Already, in earlier chapters, a large number of resources have been discussed. These include business plans, performance management discussion, benchmarking studies, core competency statements, help-desks, knowledge maps, team meetings, celebrations of learning and tapping into both the internal and external network.

Given that most organisations have at their disposal many learning options, the question then becomes: How well are these resources being used? I have found an hour spent on this question can be an excellent investment of time for the individual, team and organisation.

Exercise 16.2 explores how on-the-job learning resources can be better utilised.

Exercise 16.2: Raising the quality of on-the-job learning resources

1. List the current learning resources available to the people in your organisation.

_____

_____

_____

_____

2. Describe the three learning resources that are of most importance to your workplace.

_____

_____

_____

3. How effectively are these three resources currently being used?

_____

_____

_____

_____

4. What can be done to improve the effectiveness of these three resources?

_____

_____

_____

_____

---

5. List any learning resources that you currently don't have, and that you believe should be developed as a matter of priority:

_____

_____

_____

_____

6. What business or people needs should be highlighted for these new resources to be introduced into the workplace as quickly as possible?

_____

_____

_____

_____

SUMMARY

Transforming workplace learning is contingent upon assessing the motivations of individuals, and then using smart processes such as action learning to facilitate understanding and personal growth. There are many ways of perfecting on-the-job learning, including promoting, stretching and balancing, observing early warning signals, examining the life cycle of career paths, and improving the quality of learning resources.

17

Getting Results From Training

I am no longer teaching subjects I barely focused on 10 years ago,
I am teaching all about how to manage oneself.

Peter Drucker

KEY PRINCIPLES

■ Having access to e-learning does not guarantee that learning takes place.
■ Training must help people with the tensions of modern living.
■ Using learning contracts helps training application and transfer.
■ Constantly update your portfolio of training products and services.
■ Engage the 'whole brain' in design, delivery and assessment.

TAKING A BROADER VIEW

It was not long ago that a discussion on getting results from training would centre around the qualities of an outstanding upfront presenter. Although still covered in this chapter, the role of presenter forms only part of the modern training equation. Today's training roles are far more diverse, and include coach, performance consultant, resource adviser, knowledge catalyst, multimedia designer and Web-based delivery specialist, to name just a few. It is therefore important to discuss training in a much broader context.

To help achieve coverage, this chapter will explore issues including fostering lifelong learning, transfer of learning and the emerging issues pertaining to e-learning. It would be useful to begin with some basic principles for all forms of training:

1. Training must be stimulating, engaging and memorable. You are competing for people's attention span and if the training is dull or useless they will quickly tune out and learn nothing, or go somewhere else if the training does not address their needs. We need to be firmly focused on the experiences of the learner and the actions they will generate. Just because an individual taps into the Internet or intranet does not mean learning takes place.

2. Training must help people with the tensions of modern living. It needs to instil confidence and hope as well as technical delivery and facts. It needs to understand the emotional and physical demands of fatigue, helplessness and powerlessness if it wishes to help implement a positive plan for action. Training must support the notions of lifelong learning.

3. Training should not always be seen as 'bells and whistles' entertainment but should be about providing greater choice on how the learner can enhance his or her capability. People are increasingly becoming 'free agents' of their own learning and they need smart strategies to move forward.

4. Training needs to reach for higher levels of insight. We need to help people to restructure the brain/mind connections in order to have greater access to their personal resourcefulness. This includes confronting issues such as dealing with our egos, our self-doubts and our moods, confronting enduring struggle, managing our aspirations and accepting responsibility.

5. Training requires a 'drip-feed' approach to learning. The term, coined by Australian stress management consultant John Townsend, reflects the need to manage the ongoing relationship with learning by reinforcing vital messages of learning. Whether it is an e-mail newsletter (an ezine), or a team leader reminding a team of the benefits of a new project, having a drip-feed approach ensures a common language and continuity of the training effort.

6. Trainers need to concentrate on the competency outcomes of learning. This is particularly important given that more and more of the training delivery has now shifted to people who do not see themselves as professional trainers. As a consequence, practical and user-friendly advice must be provided to those who help others learn. We need to remove the struggle of becoming an outstanding trainer.

FOSTERING LIFELONG LEARNING

Implicit in *Learning Unlimited* is that people need a wide range of coping and learning strategies to reach their full potential. Unless people can learn how to learn, they will have difficulty meeting the challenges of the future. People need to be reminded of their resourcefulness and unlimited capacity to make a difference. Processes must be established to encourage individuals to build their confidence and a sense of personal control. People must understand that meaningful learning occurs in a large array of both formal and informal settings, from corporate video to lunch-time chat. The nature of your business does not really matter; taking the time to discover, invent or unveil new learning without having to wait is vitally important.

Helping people to learn requires skilful questioning and personal inquiry. Depending on the need for training, sowing a seed of 'learning how to learn' can be incorporated into any training design, by helping learners to:

- remind themselves that they can overcome challenges;
- stretch their boundaries and reach a new level of competence;
- identify their own unique learning and motivational needs;
- link their personal learning goals with business plans;
- discover how to use the current learning processes, knowledge management repositories and networks to learn 'smarter';
- identify those thoughts and moods that hinder and stimulate discovery;
- memorise and recall more effectively;
- use models, theories and lessons learnt to help assist their personal growth;
- celebrate successful application.

Using learning contracts

The 'crème de la crème' of strategies for getting results from training and supporting lifelong learning is using 'learning contracts'. In helping people set learning goals and then develop a plan of action, you are making the process active and that can lead to greater skill, insight and knowledge. According to the late Malcolm Knowles in his book *Using Learning Contracts* (1986), the learning contract process includes the following four steps:

- *Step 1: Diagnosing learning needs.* This involves the learner in identifying the gap between where he or she is now and where he or she needs to be (the 'learning gap'). To achieve this, the individual will require coaching and resource information support to take ownership for his or her learning challenge. An excellent resource for this step is a competency statement.

- *Step 2: Specifying learning objectives.* The learner makes a statement of the desired learning goal, which specifies his or her knowledge, skills and attitudes intention. The learning objective is then agreed in consultation with the responsible trainer or manager.
- *Step 3: Detailing learning resources and strategies.* The learner defines how he or she is going to undertake the learning contract and which training strategies and resources he or she plans to use.
- *Step 4: Evidence of accomplishment.* This asks the learner to describe how he or she will know when the learning contract is completed. It includes an 'evidence guide' and a completion date. The participant needs to demonstrate how he or she expects to achieve the learning contract, which is then written and signed.

The following case example shows how a standard of excellence for the core competency of time management can be written into a measurable learning contract.

Example: Developing the competency of time management

Establishing a standard of excellence is the first step.

Standard of excellence
Let us assume that a team of line managers identified a 'standard of excellence' in time management as:
- a proven ability to discuss and set priorities on a daily basis;
- scheduling priorities and KRAs within business objectives.

Learning contract options
Given this standard of excellence there are numerous ways in which an employee can demonstrate learning. Examples include:
- completing a two-week 'time log' and then identifying and developing five strategies to reduce time wasting;
- listing new and/or major activities that have been implemented as a result of saving time;
- performing a range of 'special projects' that require strict scheduling within a limited time frame;
- leading team discussions that review time constraints in line with business requirements;
- summarising the knowledge gained from a time management book, multimedia program or search on the World Wide Web;

- receiving coaching and learning contract advice from a mentor who exhibits a proven track record of meeting all of the standards of excellence required in time management;
- keeping a clear and up-to-date diary;
- showing a learning journal that exhibits a moment-by-moment account of time management, discoveries achieved and actions implemented.

TRANSFERRING LEARNING TO THE JOB

Part and parcel of getting results from training courses is to have instructional design and learning methods that transfer learning to the job as efficiently as possible. To do this successfully, training design, delivery and assessment need to mirror real-life situations and needs. This covers the entire range of training methods, whether it is formal face-to-face presentations, outdoor education or self-teach packages. Having then decided on training as the best means of aiding performance, careful design needs to be incorporated to assist application and learning transfer. The following 20 principles go hand in hand with discussions in earlier chapters on knowledge creation and on-the-job learning.

---

20 practical tips for transferring learning to the job

Design
1. Make sure 'core competencies' that are developed are realistic, challenging and assessible. Prior learning must be recognised.
2. Ensure that the customer of the training has ongoing responsibility for the process from design to assessment.
3. Ensure that training design, delivery and assessment reflect and demonstrate the values and beliefs required for the KRAs to be performed on the job.
4. Check that the programme design provides realistic learning expectations. When people are being stretched, there should be adequate time to brief and support them. The programme should have an inbuilt flexibility allowing people to learn where they need to and not be bored doing wasted exercises.
5. The more opportunities to practise, perfect and teach competencies the better. Make sure access is available to those who need the training.

---

6. Run a pilot training programme and iron out any problems before wholesale implementation and marketing. Learning must be seen as worthy behaviour and it should be shown that successful skill development is rewarded or reinforced.

7. Carefully select doers for the first pilot. It is important that you have some champions to market successes as soon as possible.

8. Incorporate language and jargon that is understood by the learners.

9. Use pre-work and learning contracts to set the tone by building mature, responsible and self-directed learners as well as cementing important discoveries in long-term memory.

Delivery

10. The behaviours or roles to be performed back on the job should be made clear up front in the training.

11. Vary the pace of training delivery to match the needs of the participants. Expand thinking and learning resourcefulness by encouraging experimentation, reflection and sharing.

12. Build the self-esteem of participants by creating a supportive and nurturing learning environment. Incorporate early success so that confidence can easily and quickly be built.

13. When appropriate, use a range of learning methods. Schedule frequent 'time outs' for reflection and action planning during the training.

Post-course implementation

14. Set up a 'support network' between the learners to assist on-the-job sharing and exchange. Intranets and e-mails are great tools here.

15. Schedule review sessions and processes to discuss and celebrate learning and then use this opportunity to advance the standard of competency still higher.

16. Provide participants with self-study packages, learning contracts, practical tips and tool kits that can assist their on-the-job learning.

17. Ensure the manager/mentor/team leader of each learner is actively involved in the training process and in 'on-the-job' learning contract discussions.

18. Provide supplementary skill-development training to help the people who are performing the coaching and mentoring role.

19. Contact the learners several months after the training, asking them to demonstrate how they applied their learning.
20. Issue a training course newsletter highlighting results and send it to all past and current participants, coaches, mentors and key decision makers.

IDENTIFYING HIGH-LEVERAGE TRAINING OPTIONS

Before choosing which training method to deploy you will need to validate that your product or service is going to address your need. Often the answer lies in a non-training solution such as different systems or procedures. *Creating Training Miracles* (Rylatt and Lohan, 1995) recommended that people ask the following questions prior to formulating training strategy:

■ In 12 months' time, if the training was perfectly successful, what would be happening? If I was to visit you then, what would I see, hear or feel, which was different to now?
■ Which milestones will you need to complete for a perfect outcome to occur?
■ What are the key competencies that need to be addressed for your goal to be achieved?
■ Which non-training issues will need to be resolved before a successful outcome is achieved?
■ How do you see your role (client) and our role (trainer) in making this training a success?
■ How will you measure success?

Given you have decided that training is necessary you can then go about offering the right portfolio that best supports the needs of the learning customer. For example, if an organisation is currently reviewing five training options, how does it decide which programmes should continue? This resource management question is fundamental to the success of any training operation. Training initiatives must be focused and targeted to the business, political and people needs of the workplace.

The training portfolio matrix in Figure 17.1 will help you to review and update your training services and products portfolio on a regular basis. This matrix can easily be adapted to a number of non-training disciplines including project management, performance management and strategic planning. Having done this will enable you to decide not only what method is to be used but also which resources will be allocated to it.

As shown in Figure 17.1, the quality and suitability of the training, learning, and knowledge management products and services can be examined by exploring two variables: meaningful political support (reflected on the horizontal axis) and business impact (reflected on the vertical axis). 'Meaningful political support' represents the level of visible support received from key decision makers and stakeholders. 'Business impact' describes the amount of demonstrated performance improvement that is being produced by the product or service under question. Clearly, if either of these variables is unknown, further research needs to be undertaken prior to trying to commence any resource management review.

Assuming that a planning team has some sense of the level of 'political support' and 'business impact' for the range of products and services under review, the process of resource management review can continue. To do this, classify each service and product into the four broad categories shown in Figure 17.1: wooden spooners; bread and butters; proven performers; and rising stars. After gaining agreement on categorisation, the team then shifts its attention to required action.

The four categories on the portfolio matrix can be interpreted as follows:

■ *Wooden spooners* (commonly referred to as also-rans) have low political support/low business impact. Irrespective of how few resources have been allocated to a product or service classified as a

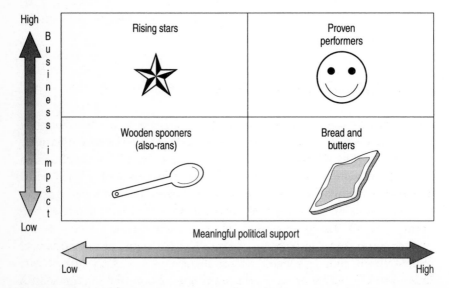

Figure 17.1 The training portfolio matrix

'wooden spooner', the workplace learning and business process would benefit if the resources were used elsewhere. Ongoing investment in a 'wooden spooner' should be viewed as a waste of time and money.

■ *Bread and butters* have high political support/low business impact. They are interesting because they attract continuous support from key decision makers but may not be generating business results. In many cases 'bread and butters' are the 'life-blood' of training, because you are able to get early runs on the board and from there you are more able to negotiate a better option.

■ *Proven performers* have high political support/high business impact. Not surprisingly these programmes often attract the best resourcing and the greatest support. However, 'proven performers' can also be quite expensive and eat away at resources very quickly. If this is the case the training providers should seek to 'piggyback' on this high popularity and ask for more support and resources or seek to reposition the material into another delivery method such as self-teach packages. It is very easy to fall into a false sense of security with the label of 'proven performer'. 'Proven performers' can appear on the surface to be quite successful, but in reality are nothing like it.

■ *Rising stars* have low political support/high business impact. They are the high-potential areas of the training portfolio. Although not currently attracting high levels of political support they do have enormous capacity to become a 'proven performer' in the longer term. Locating 'rising stars' is an important role of change agents and employees. When found, it is important to profile the 'rising star' by packaging the right evidence and communicating its proof to the stakeholders concerned.

BEING AN OUTSTANDING TRAINER

Although much has been said to highlight the other roles of training, at the end of the day having a good instructor or presenter certainly helps your chances of getting results.

For many years I thought that truly great trainers were analytical, clear and expressive until I realised that all I was seeing was a 'mirror image' of my own training style. During a Wilson Learning International programme in 1987 my approach to training and human interaction changed forever. Since that day, I have become acutely sensitive to the wonder of many training styles. I began to appreciate the importance of being structured, procedural and trusting, while being a little less preoccupied with the 'bells and whistles' side of training. As a consequence, I began a journey of experimenting with the domain of 'intellectual and behavioural versatility'.

'Intellectual and behavioural versatility' can be defined as the capacity to discuss a range of ideas and concepts, while also being able to adapt one's training style to the learning needs of others. In my opinion the gift of a great trainer is the ability to employ different approaches to help learners build links between their own experience and what is required. Involving learners in well-considered activities that are accelerative, experiential and practical dramatically increases your chances of the training being enjoyable and useful to them.

An excellent model for explaining intellectual and behavioural versatility is the Herrmann brain dominance model already explained in Chapter 5. Herrmann provides one of a number of perspectives that can aid our understanding of mental diversity. Figure 17.2 shows teaching and learning considerations using his whole brain concept.

As can be seen, Herrmann suggests that each quadrant of the brain has quite different teaching and learning needs. Sections A and B represent the left side of the brain and Sections C and D represent the right side of the brain. Each output requires quite different design, delivery and assessment.

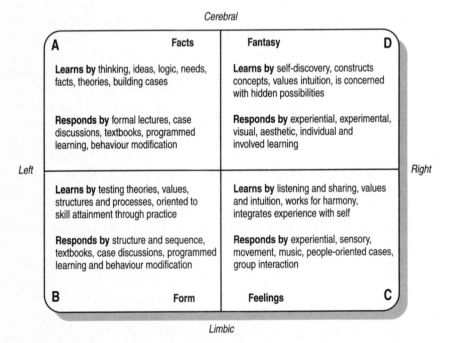

Source: *The Whole Brain Book*, © 1996 McGraw-Hill, reprinted with the permission of the author, Ned Herrmann, of the Ned Herrmann Group.

Figure 17.2 Whole brain teaching and learning considerations

The Herrmann model has given me very clear evidence of my own personal journey as a learner and trainer. Traditionally, I had been someone who loved 'facts', 'feelings' and 'fantasy', but avoided 'form'. This meant that when I trained in the past, I often frustrated learners who wanted me to be more linear and structured in my approach.

In recent times, I have increased my use of 'form' skills to supplement my natural preference for 'facts', 'fantasy' and 'feelings'. Taking the lessons of this model one step further, it is important for all forms of training to design, deliver and assess using all of the four quadrants of teaching and learning considerations. This translates into 'whole brain' learning and teaching. For me, this is the best safeguard of guaranteeing 'intellectual and behavioural versatility' while ensuring improved results in training.

There are, of course, hundreds of competencies that make up a great trainer other than 'intellectual and behavioural versatility', particularly as the training role can be played out in such a wide range of situations, including team facilitation, upfront delivery or as part of a multimedia or e-learning design. In this regard the trainer needs to discover where his or her great joy and fulfilment is and develop career plans to engage this motivation and desire in the future.

In the role of an upfront presenter I have attended many courses and read many books to help develop my skills. Some fields of knowledge include: drama, acting, comedy, psychodrama, NLP, outdoor learning and generative learning. For me, exposure to accelerative learning has been most useful. Accelerative learning can be defined as a powerful, stress-free technique that uses whole brain thinking and multisensory presentation to enable people to learn more efficiently. Accelerative learning is not a package. It is a process where a large array of skills and techniques can be used. Each time you design a new accelerative lesson plan, you need a new mix of skills. The strength ultimately comes from having well-structured lesson plans. One key tip is that you should aim to surprise people with process and not content. The power of accelerative learning comes from its capacity to enable increased learning with less conscious effort. Absorption of the information is helped along at the subconscious level. This is done by carefully using aids such as music, positive suggestion, relaxation, role playing and emotional attachment. For more information on accelerative learning see my earlier publication, *Creating Training Miracles* (1995, with Lohan).

TRAINING AND E-LEARNING

Already in *Learning Unlimited,* notably in Chapter 12 on digital technology advice and Chapter 15 on building learning communities, assistance has been provided on how to reap greater learning benefits from the computer age. One of the issues emerging from that discussion is that e-learning needs to be 100 per cent clear about its intention and outcomes if it wishes to be successful, particularly given that the ongoing merging of interactive distance learning, intranet-based training and e-learning technologies has meant literally thousands of different types of features, distinctions and capabilities are now being produced. Confusion and uncertainty on how to learn by digital means are rife.

To help get results from training using e-learning here are a number of important considerations.

Dealing with computer phobia

Throughout *Learning Unlimited* there has been great emphasis placed on the benefits and acceptance of digital technology. Little attempt has been made to expose the truth that many people are computer phobic. They are either mistrustful of computers or are downright afraid of them. Reasons range from a paralysing fear of change through to a clash of values over their use. Whatever the underlying cause, the trainer needs to confront these fears and concerns with sensitivity. Otherwise the computer will just gather dust.

Further advice includes:

- Make sure the reasons computers and their applications are being used are made clear, be it improving access, better performance, competitive advantage or higher job satisfaction.
- Design applications and uses that people can personally relate to, early involvement and success are critical, and of course plenty of fun will not be amiss.
- Stress that the computer is nothing mysterious (As my home Web page designer Peter Routtier-Wone says, 'the computer is nothing more than a cranked up telephone'.).
- Remember that it is often the struggling learner who benefits the most from computers, because tools make life easier, not harder.
- Once implementation begins, availability of computers must be guaranteed.
- Hand-me-down computers are not good enough.
- Give early opportunities for people to find people, resources and opportunities to apply their learning.
- Where possible, use the latest advances in software.
- Allow time and space for people to learn in a non-threatening environment, and if possible allow them to learn away from their desks.

Finally, it is worth noting that additional perspectives on overcoming computer phobia can be found in earlier chapters, such as Chapter 2 on leadership, Chapter 5 on helping the wounded learner and in Appendix 2 on the intelligent implementation of a digital infrastructure.

Keep an eye on learning object design

One of the exciting features of modern instructional design has been advances giving e-learners more choice on where and how they learn. This 'learning object' design has shifted the approach from past procedural approaches where you had to learn in sequence, to a new approach in which you can jump to areas of most interest. As discussed at the end of Chapter 12, advances in the language that creates multimedia will make the process of self-directed learning far more efficient in the future. The days of 'wait and see' are almost gone and that is good for the trainer and the learner.

Focused authoring systems

As Internet delivery gradually replaces CD delivery, focused authoring systems will enable trainers everywhere to use outstanding presentation software templates. Like an electronic version of a beautifully presented lesson plan, all the designer in the future will need to do is fill in the content gaps. Advances in software such as Powerpoint at the next level will provide trainers and educators with a platform for Web-based, stimulating and very interactive learning. As a result, authoring systems will make the delivery look, feel and sound good, while being easily adapted to any content you may wish to deliver or cover. All that will be required will be a strong partnership between the trainer and the Web authoring providers.

Helping the e-learner choose

Finally, given the exponential growth of e-learning, it is imperative that individuals be given some coaching on how to choose the best option for their needs. The e-learner needs to have sound criteria to separate the 'wheat from the chaff'. Learners need to be helped to shop around and to decide which instructional pathway they wish to travel and what time they are prepared to invest. Learners need to be given guidance on how to make decisions on the quality and suitability of training. Criteria include cost, length of training, competency structure, interactivity, flexibility in when the programme can be undertaken, software and hardware requirements, backup support, instructor expertise, trainer availability, feedback on learning undertaken and course guarantee.

In making this choice, the good news for the e-learner is that most Web-based and multimedia learning resources offer free demonstrations and course samples. The options can vary from pure text to highly interactive video multimedia packages. Feedback and assessment methodology can also vary from direct discussions with a subject expert to online tests. Many e-learning programs have a range of backups including online libraries, networking capabilities, bulletin boards and live chat facilities.

Web sites on e-learning

To kick start
The Masie Center Technology and Learning Think Tank
http://www.masie.com
This site also provides an outstanding service on the latest in e-learning. Make sure you join the online newsletter TECHLEARN TRENDS.

Finding online training providers
Listing the best and most cost-effective e-learning is a huge task. There is no simple answer. The marketplace is massive and is changing every minute. My suggestion is to do a search on Dogpile at http://www.dogpile.com/. Then enter key words FREE ON-LINE LEARNING and see what happens. Modify your search as desired.

You may also wish to visit the Workplace learning helpdesk for any of my recent discoveries at
http://www.excelhrd.aust.com/world.htm.

SUMMARY

Training is a vital mechanism to stimulate improved learning in the workplace. The future will see a significant increase in the volume of interest in e-learning, though traditional 'face-to-face' learning will still hold its place as an important part of the discovery and innovation cycle. The challenge for organisations is to continue improving results in both areas.

Irrespective of what mode of training is being used, workplace learning has entered a time where customers or learners have greater control of what and when they learn. As a consequence, training must seek to grab and hold people's attention in order to have impact and appeal.

18

Promoting Mentoring And Coaching

> As the next millennium begins, leaders will have to be made because
> not enough have been born.
>
> Peter Goldrick

KEY PRINCIPLES

- Mentoring and coaching are vital to growth and learning.
- Workplace mentoring programmes must be voluntary.
- Reward excellent coaches and mentors.
- Coaching is a high-leverage transformation process.
- Everyone must understand his or her role within the workplace learning process.

TAKING AN ACTIVE APPROACH

It does not really matter what form of business you are involved in, or what status of employment you enjoy. The skill of searching for people to provide new perspectives is fundamental to personal growth. Whether it is a person engaging a consultant to help build team leadership skills, finding a friend to shed some optimism on a difficult situation, or finding someone who can constructively balance parenting skills with work demands, workplace learning always requires plenty of good coaching and mentoring. This is not surprising given that rapid change redefines our boundaries, accountabilities and capabilities on a regular basis. One only needs to reflect on the demands placed on us to remain healthy and sane in the modern workplace to realise that individuals have much to self-manage to remain productive and marketable. In my third book, *Navigating the Frenzied World of Work* (1997), I discussed the importance of having an integrated life management strategy in order to stay ahead of the pack. Added to this is a long list of other areas where people may seek help during their working life. To name a few: financial planning, health strategy, career transition, image consulting, relationship counselling and juggling family and work pressures. Putting all this together, it is very easy to see why we need fellow-travellers to help us on our journey.

The difference between coaching and mentoring is often more pedantic than actual. However, the word 'coach' in this book is being used to describe someone who performs the role of training, inspiring and moti-vating others. Coaching is seen as fundamental to the role of people management. Mentoring is slightly less directive and structured. For example, in a sporting team you may have a number of mentors who offer you different advice, information and friendship in addition to what the coach says. In normal conversation the words 'role model' could describe a coach or mentor, but they are more typically used of a person in a mentoring role.

Jargon aside, the common difficulty in this field is an apparent absence of role models, mentors and coaches. There may be a corporate black hole of skills in the areas desired. A business may wish to develop good people managers but find no people who can role model the desired behaviours within the existing workplace. As a consequence, outside assistance will be required to address the imbalance.

This chapter provides practical tips on how to get the best value out of both mentoring and coaching processes, while recognising that at times they could be happening simultaneously. The discussion begins by exploring the power of mentoring as an agent of change.

MENTORING AS AN AGENT OF CHANGE

Think about the people who have influenced you in your life. Who were they? Did you know them personally or were they heroes or heroines you never actually met? What effect did they have on your present values and beliefs? What qualities or traits made these people special? What sort of support, advice or encouragement did they give you? Was their advice always correct (or in hindsight correct), or were their 'words of wisdom' not so great after all? All these questions can help us clarify the value and impact that 'mentors' have on our lives.

Mentors have had a major impact on my life. In childhood there was a number that I vividly remember. My Sunday School teacher Mrs Carne taught me about moral standing and kindness at the tender age of eight.

My brother Dennis stressed the importance of mental toughness while I was playing table tennis as a temperamental 13-year-old. My school friend Mark Fahey impressed on me the need for friendship while I was confronting the difficult age of 15 and the thrill and excitement of watching Shane Gould winning three Olympic gold swimming medals in Munich in 1972.

During my last year of high school, I actively sought the help of a number of mentors to help me choose a career. This advice led to a largely unsuccessful clerical and accountancy career that lasted seven years. At 25, I made a career change to training after much help and guidance from a university colleague called Luke. Having become a full-time consultant when I was 29, my mentoring needs changed. Instead of looking for a career change, I shifted my attention to developing and maintaining my professional expertise while sustaining my health and balance with my family and marital commitments.

The reason for sharing my personal story is to highlight how my life has been shaped by the power of mentoring. My guess is that you have a similar story to tell. In your life, there has been a long list of people who have helped you become what you are today. Taking this observation one step further, we can also safely assume that we have been mentors to others at various stages of their lives. As a result, all of us have already experienced mentoring from both 'sides of the fence', both as mentor and protégé.

So what does this discussion have to do with transforming workplace learning? The answer is everything. Mentoring is a natural phenomenon that is occurring every day of our lives and as a result it directly or indirectly affects the quality of learning and performance in the workplace. It is essential that mentoring be talked about and undertaken in an open and helpful way. To do this, it is desirable that people develop an excellent understanding of mentoring as a positive contributor to personal growth and workplace learning.

The qualities of a good mentor

The *Concise Oxford Dictionary* defines a mentor as an 'experienced and trusted adviser'. This definition captures the spirit of successful mentoring by allowing coaching, counselling and training to be legitimately covered under the 'mentor' heading. In addition, this definition allows mentoring to be seen as a natural part of all learning and discovery. In many ways mentoring should be viewed as a state of mind and not a structured process.

So what makes someone an 'experienced and trusted adviser'? David Clutterbuck, in his book *Everyone Needs a Mentor* (1985), uses a mnemonic to summarise the desired qualities. He states that a good mentor has the ability to:

- Manage the mentoring relationship.
- Encourage the protégé.
- Nurture the protégé.
- Teach the protégé.
- Offer mutual respect.
- Respond to the protégé's needs.

In addition to these qualities, a mentor must:

- be interested in developing his or her potential and that of others;
- be an excellent listener;
- be able to share experience, knowledge and observations;
- demonstrate what is expected of others;
- encourage the expansion of thinking and application;
- have an extensive network of resources and contacts;
- have a track record of successful mentoring relationships.

Protégés, on the other hand, need to:

- value the time and experience of the mentor;
- listen carefully;
- express dilemmas, feelings and emotions;
- undertake self-examination and review;
- ask good questions;
- always be willing to expand his or her potential.

As in all partnerships, the mentor and protégé must foster openness, trust and mutual respect.

What, then, are the workplace benefits that can be expected from mentoring for both the organisation and the individual? Some of the common outcomes include:

- clarification of the mission and goals of the organisation;
- development of competencies;
- increased productivity, cost effectiveness and innovation, by improving communication and mutual understanding;
- improved capacity to resolve work/life challenges;
- support of career development and knowledge management;
- promotion of the sharing of experience and networking from a range of people;
- increased confidence and fulfilment of both the mentor and the protégé.

Implementing a workplace mentoring programme

It is quite mysterious that organisations debate the value of having an open and consultative mentoring and coaching programme within their workplace. In fact, like workplace learning, mentoring is already happening. Some of it is very effective. On the other hand, some of it is quite destructive and discriminatory. Organisations, therefore, have a choice: to promote positive mentoring and coaching or let poor practices go unabated and unchecked, leaving people underutilised.

Remembering that mentoring occurs through workplace boundaries and beyond, the question then becomes: What can be done to make mentoring as effective as possible? To assist in the process of implementation, the following 15 guidelines are recommended:

1. Top management must visibly support the policy and make themselves personally available to be mentors and protégés.
2. The mentoring programme should be totally supportive and interactive with all other workplace learning and knowledge management processes. When starting the programme, begin small, trialling a pilot before implementing it on a large scale.
3. Mentoring should never be a forced relationship where one person is directed to mentor another. A better strategy is to train and familiarise both the protégé and potential mentor with the skills required and let the process happen naturally and voluntarily. Use intranets and the World Wide Web as a clearing house to help people find contacts and mentoring advice as required.
4. Do not assume that a mentor has to be a top-down relationship. Some of the best mentoring relationships are within the broader learning community.
5. Do not assume that protégés and mentors are trained. Always provide guidelines, resources and training as required. Orientate all parties before the process begins.
6. Mentors should obtain fulfilment and self-esteem out of the process and should not feel pressured to perform their role. Mentors should be prepared to develop their own skills in the mentoring process. Mentors should never seek unwarranted favours from the protégé. It would surprise many people that often the mentor learns and benefits more during the process than the protégé.
7. Set up a support group for mentors to share their insights from the process. When these meetings are held, mentors must keep confidential the discussions with protégés. Set specific objectives and use e-mail to keep close contact between meetings.

8. Protégés should not see mentoring as a signal to neglect their core job and waste other people's time. They should not break trust with mentors by sharing the outcomes of their discussions with others.
9. Protégés should avoid targeting only high achievers as mentors. Often the best mentors are people who do not want rapid promotion and are more willing to share quality information and experience.
10. Mentoring programmes should never be used as a substitute for holding performance management discussions.
11. Both the mentor and the protégé should be able to cease a mentoring relationship at any time.
12. Over-reliance on one mentor is never recommended. It can lead to cloning and this can cause political difficulty and embarrassment if the relationship sours or if the mentor moves on to another job. A better strategy is to encourage people to seek out and use a wide range of mentors. Limit the duration to 18 months, which encourages people to move on and establish new networks and contacts.
13. People who provide excellent mentoring should be honoured and praised for their efforts.
14. Ensure that excellent mentors are not flooded by a multitude of protégés. It is quite common to see well-meaning 'mentors' becoming quickly 'burnt out' from never-ending 'one-to-one' discussions.
15. Continuously evaluate the process. This can be done by identifying examples and testimonials about people who have improved their performance and learning output through being either a mentor or a protégé.

TRANSFORMING PEOPLE BY COACHING

Improving the skill of on-the-job coaching provides organisations with the best opportunity to develop workplace learning or business potential. Coaching is one human activity that can have a daily transformative effect on the productivity, morale and learning of individuals and teams.

Yet, in many workplaces, leaders often ignore the role of coaching entirely and concentrate more on getting the task done, without investing the time to develop the long-term capability and potential of its people. Part of the reason for this is that individuals are rarely rewarded for or trained to do the role of coaching properly.

Given the perceived importance of coaching, what does it take to be a good coach? To help address this question, two issues are discussed in the remainder of the chapter:

■ What makes a good workplace learning coach?
■ How do you hold a 'one-to-one' career coaching session?

What makes a good workplace learning coach?

To be a successful coach, a person needs to believe that another person will benefit from his or her help. In addition, the individual performing the 'coaching' role must be motivated to do the role well. Making people accountable for coaching under performance management may help, but it may not solve the problem as some people are not motivated to coach.

The qualities of coaching that support workplace learning are quite diverse. Performance criteria include:

- linking workplace learning to business and individual needs;
- stimulating team and individual learning and creativity;
- setting clear parameters and guidelines for high-quality discovery;
- actively communicating with employees and key contributors to the business;
- finding a mentor who is a leading coach in an area of development;
- empowering others to be learners;
- celebrating team and individual learning achievements.

How do you hold a one-to-one coaching session?

Let us begin by making it very clear that the purpose of holding a one-to-one coaching discussion is not about being a professional counsellor, a miracle worker or making guarantees. It is about being supportive, available and empathetic. Most of all it is about acting as a 'mirror' and 'sounding board' to help another person to explore his or her own issues rather than always offering your own. Holding one-to-one coaching sessions can be quite a fulfilling process as it expands our confidence and enjoyment while helping others.

Miller and Rollnick in their book *Motivational Interviewing: Preparing people to change addictive behaviour* (1991) highlight that the style and attitude of the coach can have a dramatic effect on people's motivation, particularly when 'accurate empathy' is displayed by the coach. This means helping people to clarify their own experience and ambivalence, so that they can develop their own meaning and action. Fundamental to outstanding coaching is understanding that people's readiness or eagerness to change and compete will fluctuate. What is particularly important in coaching is having checks and balances to ensure constant review over time.

In undertaking the role of holding one-to-one coaching we need to decide how often to sit down and discuss someone's workplace learning and career needs. Although this will vary depending on the nature of the relationship, a six-monthly discussion could be a good starting point. In saying this, irrespective of the timing, it is essential that an ongoing process of review be undertaken between formal discussions to ensure positive progress.

Appendix 3 provides a comprehensive listing of the points to be remembered in conducting a one-to-one coaching session. Many of the skills reflected in Appendix 3 are also reinforced in the discussion on identifying learner motivation in Chapter 16.

To further assist in undertaking a one-to-one coaching session, Appendix 4 lists powerful questions that can be used to improve the quality of discussion.

OVERCOMING COMMON CHALLENGES

Even after applying all of the practical tips contained within this book, there are going to be extra challenges that will need further action if mentoring and coaching are to be successful. There are at least four common challenges that often frustrate and stonewall coaching and mentoring discussions. These challenges are listed below with some suggested actions and considerations to help remove their impact.

An individual fails to implement an agreed action plan

- Check the individual's understanding of his or her role in the coaching and mentoring process.
- Find out if there is another factor blocking the individual's action.
- Apply the 'Empowerment of Change model of $(D + V + K) \times B'$ discussed in the Introduction.
- Ask the individual whether he or she finds action planning stressful or boring.

The individual rejects possible learning options prematurely

- Find out which beliefs or evidence are causing the individual to dismiss options so quickly.
- Does he or she have skills that can be transferred to other projects, activities or career choices?
- Is he or she frightened of change (or of its perceived personal impact or impact on others)?
- Explore whether the individual views the perceived risk of change as larger than the perceived benefit.

The individual has made an unrealistic assessment of options or talents

- Find out where the person gained his or her evidence for the assessment.
- Often a mentor or coach may be the problem, so keep an open mind.

The individual has too many options or cannot make a decision

- Find out whether the person is expecting too much and is seeking a perfect answer.
- Ask the person to develop criteria to assess the suitability of available options.
- Is the person 'paralysed' by the thought that the outcome could be worse than the current situation?

SUMMARY

Mentoring and coaching are two processes that have a direct impact on the quality of workplace learning. Mentoring happens naturally every day of our working lives. To gain maximum value from this process, organisations need to support the process in a flexible and voluntary way. Coaching, on the other hand, is an essential requirement of people management and should be deemed necessary in all workplaces. The modern workplace is perfectly placed to use relationship-based learning as central to surviving and thriving within change. It does not really matter who you are, but with a little endeavour a mentor, coach or role model can be found somewhere.

19

Revitalising And Expanding Your Knowledge Pool

> *When knowledge comes in the door, fear and superstition fly out of the window.*
>
> Mary Roberts Rinehart

KEY PRINCIPLES

- Expand the collective intelligence of the organisational 'business brain'.
- Targeted development must be based on business needs and not tradition.
- Employment contracts must support family life, health and personal development.
- Develop a proactive policy to keep talented learners and fellow-travellers.
- Explore flexible and enterprising practices in diversity, telecommuting and literacy.

STIMULATING THE BUSINESS BRAIN OF YOUR ORGANISATION

Like the human brain, the organisational business brain requires exercise and stimulation for it to function properly. Without smart processes and systems much of the available talent will lie dormant and wasted.

It is claimed that human beings use only about 10 per cent of their mental capacity. The quality of collective organisational 'business brain' use often appears to be much worse. Unlike the human brain, the latent capacity of the 'business brain' is further frustrated by alienating practices, poor systems and insufficient team learning. One of the exciting and inspiring messages that comes from studying workplace learning is that if the correct policies and practices are implemented, the potential for increasing the 'business brain' is unlimited. Who knows what is the brain capacity of the organisation, team and individual combined? However, whatever the answer, all organisations need to expand and revitalise their overall knowledge pool if they wish to achieve improved intellectual capital and performance.

Expanding and revitalising the knowledge pool simply means forming closer partnerships with a wider range of people from within and outside the traditional workplace. Given a more mobile, dispersed and transient workplace, it is important that a richer pool of expertise be accessed as a normal part of business activity. As discussed in Chapter 10 on benchmarking best practices, Chapter 12 on accessing digital technology and Chapter 15 on building learning communities, it is imperative that workplaces keep abreast of change and opportunities for the future by forming strategic alliances with a wide range of people including outside contractors, support services, suppliers, customers, unions and experts.

In addition to these general categories, it is also important that closer partnerships be built with people from different occupations, titles, cultural backgrounds, teams and geographic locations. Whether it is an employee from a non-English-speaking background helping to break into a new niche market in Asia or asking a new graduate to lead a continuous improvement team, the decision to gain the help of such people should be made for business reasons, and not because it sounds fashionable or trendy.

With this in mind, this final chapter in Part 2 suggests practical ways in which targeted workplace learning and common-sense strategies can be used to improve the flexibility and sustainability of people and their workplace for the future.

SUCCESSFULLY TARGETING WORKPLACE LEARNING ACTIVITIES

An important step in expanding the knowledge pool in a business is to initiate extra workplace learning assistance for key people. To do this effectively requires creative thinking, high-quality research and a preparedness to change existing approaches and strategies.

The business rationale of targeting is that extra assistance leads to improved business performance by transforming the capacity of the people. Examples of target groups that normally receive extra assistance include 'fast track' management candidates with high potential, graduates, management trainees and new employees.

Sadly, however, due to the nature of targeted development, many people are often 'left out in the cold' and forgotten. Common areas of neglect include part-time and contract employees, female employees, people from non-English-speaking backgrounds, older employees, employees with physical and mental disabilities, and employees who have reached a career plateau. In addition to these people, organisations also have a track record of neglecting employees in isolated geographic locations (that is, country as against city) and specific functional/occupational areas.

Determining who should get extra assistance

If workplaces are to confront their future with greater confidence, less emphasis needs to be placed on tradition and more emphasis on creativity and flexibility.

When deciding who should receive added assistance, the question should remain the same: What are the expected short- and long-term business benefits to be gained from devoting extra resources to these people? Alternatively, what damage will be caused if this particular group or individual continues to be neglected? Exercise 19.1 has been designed to assist the review of your organisation's history in targeting workplace learning processes and what can be done better in the future.

Exercise 19.1: Your organisational history in targeting workplace learning

1. List the target groups (that is, functional, geographical, gender, cultural and special needs) who normally receive extra assistance in workplace learning:

   Functional/occupational _____

   Geographical _____

   Gender _____

   Cultural _____

   Special needs _____

---

2. List the target groups (that is, functional, geographical, gender, cultural and special needs) who are normally not allocated extra assistance in workplace learning:

Functional/occupational _____

Geographical _____

Gender _____

Cultural _____

Special needs _____

3. What have been the rationale, assumptions and values underlying past decision making? Was it political, traditional, historical or pure business?

_____

_____

_____

_____

4. What changes need to be made to how targeted workplace learning assistance is determined? What new rhetoric needs to be created and communicated within the business to justify any change of strategy?

_____

_____

_____

_____

Avoiding the trap of over-targeting

Targeted workplace learning should never be seen as a substitute for or a 'soft option' to a general commitment to workplace learning. Any organisation that fails to invest in the whole workforce and that of the broader learning community is opening itself up to serious difficulties. An area that is often living proof of over-specialisation in workplace learning is when there is a loss of key staff. At such times organisations can become quickly embarrassed by the loss of their 'brain power', particularly when there has been a failure to capture knowledge for those remaining. In any case, the loss of knowledge can be a major problem and to overcome it requires careful planning and investment in workplace learning infrastructure.

STRATEGIES FOR REVITALISATION AND EXPANSION

As discussed in Chapters 3 and 15, industries and organisations are recognising that one of the best ways of surviving today's rapidly changing economy is to have a smaller and more flexible workforce, leaving greater latitude to form partnerships and learning alliances with fellow-travellers, either within or outside workplace boundaries. This produces a seamless, virtual and ever-changing flavour to how workplace learning needs to be carried out.

Given that workforces now operate within a 'borderless structure', people management strategies must be holistic and inclusive. It is important that all people in the organisational 'business brain' are included in development opportunities and have access to important knowledge, even when they may not even be full-time employees. The trend towards increasing access to intranets and groupware by a broader range of people is symptomatic of this commitment. Other examples are conducting training for suppliers or benchmark partners, including contractors in digital networks regarding key business challenges, or involving key stakeholders in business planning processes.

Many of the options for revitalising and maintaining the 'knowledge pool' have already been covered in earlier chapters. The key issues from earlier chapters include:

- Conduct regular staff surveys to determine feelings about personal growth and whether workplace learning processes are effective.
- Add lessons learnt and resources to the knowledge pool so that employees can continue to expand their competency level both on and off the job.
- Actively involve people in the design, delivery and evaluation of their workplace learning.
- Make sure people are appropriately informed about business performance and future career opportunities.
- Develop the skills of coaching, counselling, mentoring and partnership building.
- Stamp out practices and systems that alienate learning.
- Actively encourage the use of digital technology to promote learning and exchange.

- Provide resources and support to help people cope with life-skills management issues such as burnout, mental well-being, nutrition, finance, relationships, dual career couple conflict management, and health.
- Use special projects and action learning to stimulate cross-fertilisation and enhancement of learning.
- Acknowledge and reward individuals who make a positive difference to workplace learning.
- Always maintain good, positive and ethical relationships with past and current employees.
- Celebrate and promote your organisational achievements externally and internally as much as possible.

A VISION FOR THE FUTURE: EMERGING AREAS OF OPPORTUNITY

As depicted in Figure 19.1 and the list below, there are seven areas that are integral to the ongoing revitalisation and expansion of workplace knowledge pools in the decade ahead. The seven areas are:

1. finding and keeping fellow-travellers;
2. investing in survivors' development and retention;
3. investing in the literacy needs of the workforce;

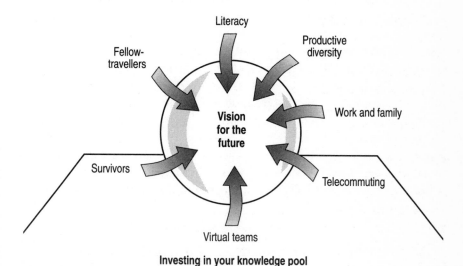

Investing in your knowledge pool

Figure 19.1 Vision for the future

4.   promoting productive diversity;
5.   helping balance work and family;
6.   acknowledging telecommuting as a legitimate employment option;
7.   effectively managing virtual work teams.

These areas are essential to the vitality and performance of workplace learning, and each is now explored.

Finding and keeping fellow-travellers

One of the interesting things about the world of work is that competitive advantage or level of expertise has as much to do with the quality of your employees as it has with the quality of coalitions, partnerships you have with people who are not on your full-time payroll. Finding and keeping fellow-travellers as part of the business brain is a vital ingredient of the workplace learning transformation process.

Sustaining relationships that are mutually beneficial and providing regular celebrations of milestones have become a natural part of business practice. People who always use other people for their own benefit and fail to return the favour can quickly lose much of their competitive advantage. The spirit of abundance, open sharing and trustworthiness is central to maintaining a knowledge pool that is healthy and progressive.

Advances in digital technology are a great help in this pursuit but so is networking over lunch. Most of all, like any good relationship, it can only be sustained with common interests, compromise and goodwill.

An emerging trend in the area of fellow-travellers is that of developing a 'corporate university' or learning portal approach to workplace learning. There, a corporation or consortium of workplaces (such as public service departments) join forces with a university or private provider to deliver vocational and higher-level qualifications such as degrees and masters' programmes, general skill development training and/or research. Not only does this provide a massive injection of intellectual capital into the business but it provides an increased chance of custom-designed solutions to needs that a business would struggle to meet by itself. Motorola, The Body Shop, Disney and McDonald's are the most notable international examples. It was estimated in 1999 that in the USA alone there are over 1,600 corporate university systems up and running and growing rapidly.

Investing in survivors' development and retention

One of the consequences of much of the restructuring in modern workplaces is an increased expectation for people to work smarter by taking on extra responsibility and workload. This on many occasions leads to a higher incidence of work-related stress and reduced morale. This is particularly the case in organisations where there has been a high level of expectation that long-term job security and internal career path were part of the employee/employer relationship. Unless managed with sensitivity many of the sought-after gains from restructuring can be lost very quickly.

Great care needs to be taken to ensure restructuring is not seen purely as a cost-cutting exercise but as providing more hope, promise and growth for the business, meaning a win for the survivors and a win for the employer. In practical terms, if the survivors feel wounded by the loss of colleagues, are anxious about job security and are expected to do more work with fewer people, leading to a difficult work life, dramatic effects on morale can be expected.

Closely associated is the need to provide a work environment that fosters hope and promise while undergoing change. It is imperative that a range of strategies is deployed to retain key knowledge and talent in the business. There is no real point investing unlimited resources in workplace learning if the turnover of key personnel is out of control. Here lies a massive challenge for the modern workforce: keeping the best people as part of the organisational business brain.

To address this challenge, employment contracts that are based on the values of mutual gain are required and family life, health and personal development cannot be sacrificed to unrealistic deadlines and workload pressures. There must be a careful balancing of the needs of all parties to ensure sustainable enterprise, creativity and excellence. With regard to remuneration, there needs to be a clear link between success for the individual and success for the employer. Retention programmes must take a prominent role in revitalising career aspirations and learning confidence. Even people on high salaries move on when things suit them.

The same effort and resources often spent on outplacement need to be allocated to those survivors who have chosen or have been selected to stay. It is imperative that those remaining feel that they are being supported in the next phase of the business challenge. One of the best ways to address this issue is to provide one-to-one coaching and workshops that enable people to review and reset their work/life goals so that they are compatible with current and anticipated constraints. The primary purpose of this support is to help people redefine success in line with future plans and core values of the business.

From a workplace learning perspective this means investing in a more holistic approach to sustainable performance. Instead of concentrating on immediate issues such as working smarter, broader and longer-term issues such as wellness, building a sense of community and 'getting a life' must be discussed and developed. Increasingly workplaces are investing in self-help in areas such as nutrition, health appraisals and stress management as a way of keeping people sane and healthy while at work, thereby reducing over-concentration on performance at the expense of mental, spiritual and physical health.

Efforts must be made to help those individuals who feel stuck or plateaued to see different opportunities to contribute to the business. Career coaching needs to be provided that expands choices and increases skills formation. When people feel unrewarded, conversations need to be held regularly to remind them of their contribution and worth and, where necessary, new goals and targets should be set.

Investing in the literacy needs of the workforce

In industries across the globe there is an ever-increasing realisation that employees often lack the literacy skills to participate effectively within a modern workforce. Traditionally, literacy can be defined as 'the ability to integrate listening, speaking, reading, writing, numeracy and critical thinking'. Having good literacy skills provides the capacity to use language appropriately, whether as a speaker, writer or reader. People suffer from inadequate literacy skills across cultures and age groups. It would be a gross oversimplification to link literacy needs only to people born in non-English-speaking countries.

The causes of poor literacy are much debated in the media, yet in many workplaces this condition is evident on a daily basis. Irrespective of the causes of inadequate literacy, the impact on the knowledge pool and the morale and potential of people is immense. Some of the common problems that result from inadequate literacy include:

- a retardation of the capacity of an organisation to innovate and introduce new technology;
- lower worker safety;
- inability of some individuals to follow or contribute to decision-making processes;
- wastage and damage;
- too much time spent communicating and clarifying messages;
- not being able to fully benefit from existing or planned workplace learning processes;
- lower awareness of innovations and changes to organisational direction, policy and structure;
- increased potential for misunderstanding of people's intentions and motives.

One of the saddest aspects of illiteracy is that often people spend considerable mental energy protecting a secret. A few years ago I met an employee in a large distribution warehouse. He had been employed there for 16 years. During that time no one in the warehouse was prepared to disclose that he could neither read nor write. Interestingly, local management knew nothing about his learning difficulty, while the supervisor (who was incidentally the employee's brother) was very non-committal about the situation. This amazing tale highlighted to me the typical story of fear and secrecy that is often attached to illiteracy.

So what can organisations do in the future, given that the trend of poor literacy is set to continue, even with massive government and industry intervention? The bottom line is that organisations have no option but to take the initiative and meet the challenge head-on. Recommended strategies include:

- acknowledging that a person confronting a literacy problem is a sign of strength rather than weakness;
- researching the levels of literacy by conducting surveys, bilingual interviews and trace analysis (trace analysis involves sending a piece of information through the workplace and then evaluating the level of pick-up, accuracy and understanding);
- coaching people to participate and develop skills;
- designing competency-based literacy programmes and packaging them in a positive way (for example, using labels such as pre-skills training or train-start as against negative images such as remedial or literacy training);
- championing people who have overcome their hurdles successfully;
- ensuring that key areas of language, literacy, numeracy and job function are worked on within the workplace learning process;
- communicating information about services such as language and information services, interpreters and translators to all staff;
- ensuring open and non-discriminatory access to all development possibilities.

As indicated, these suggestions may not solve the challenge of inadequate literacy skills, but it is clear that neither the organisation nor the individual can accept the alternative of no action. Failure to do anything is a loss by everybody's reckoning.

In addition to the typical definition of literacy, there can also be an extension to include the 'job function'. Job function literacy refers to the level of appropriate and relevant skill that an individual needs to perform his or her job effectively. Industry experts regularly talk about the 'five-year half-cycle' of functional literacy. That is, 50 per cent of a person's tasks currently being performed will be redundant in five years' time. For example, studies by Robert Kelly of Carnegie-Mellon University (Goleman, 1998) found that in the 10 years between 1986 and 1997, the percentage of knowledge stored in employees' minds that helped them to do their job had decreased from 75 per cent to 20 per cent. Similarly, a 1999 Drake Management Consulting study of 500 Australian senior managers found that only 24 per cent of Australian businesses had staff with the critical skills and capabilities to guarantee organisational competitiveness.

Promoting productive diversity

As organisations seek to improve their productivity and performance, neglecting the richness of multiculturalism can lead to serious neglect of a very important business asset. Leading organisations recognise that valuing and utilising people from different cultural backgrounds is a proactive way of revitalising and expanding the knowledge pool.

The benefits of productive diversity are numerous. They include:

- building an intimate knowledge of overseas and local niche markets;
- expanding language fluency in local and export markets;
- helping the organisation to pioneer benchmarking and business networking in non-traditional overseas and local markets;
- providing better utilisation of the experiences, talents and values vital to customer service and accelerated innovation;
- reducing the pressures of local agents in overseas locations;
- helping to develop a global mindset in business planning and operations;
- promoting a cosmopolitan, flexible and understanding image in the international and local business community.

If an organisation wishes to make better use of productive diversity in the workplace it needs to examine productive diversity in relation to skills assessment, decision making and workplace learning, each of which is examined below. In most cases the suggestions discussed under the above heading, 'Investing in the literacy needs of the workforce', are also relevant to this discussion on productive diversity.

Skills assessment

- The organisation must do a realistic audit of skills, experiences and the languages spoken by the workforce.
- Identify and then put to use the language groups found.

Decision making

■ Adequate information on business challenges and employment conditions must be communicated in all relevant languages (for example, signage and planning documents).

■ Ensure the commitment to productive diversity forms a formal part of the strategic plan and policy.

■ Create an organisational value statement, stressing the importance of productive diversity.

■ People must be held accountable for not demonstrating cross-cultural sensitivity.

■ All people need to be given the decision-making power and skills to participate fully in continuous improvement, customer service and marketing activities.

■ Bilingual workers can be used to translate at team meetings. People should be given training on how to participate at such meetings.

Workplace learning

■ Workplace learning should use simple communication, be culturally sensitive and competency based. Programmes should clearly separate the difference between skill and language difficulties.

■ Cultural awareness coaching needs to be made available.

■ People need to be given opportunities to apply and use their skills irrespective of their cultural background.

■ Bridging training programmes should be provided to help individuals deal with literacy and language challenges.

■ All internal and external language resources and workplace learning services should be made known and available.

■ Establish a mentoring programme based on the norms of language and culture.

Helping balance work and family

Helping employees to balance the extra demands of work and family is becoming an increasingly integral strategy to revitalising and expanding the knowledge pool of the future.

In modern society, where the traditional definition of the family is being broadened to include dual-career couples, homosexual couples, single parents, and extended and blended families, workplaces are required to be more sensitive to the demands of modern family life, as well as issues such as care of the elderly and children. Most people realise that the juggling of the coexistence between work and family is not easy and requires both home and organisational support. It is increasingly being recognised that flexibility is the key to retaining experienced staff. There should no longer be one strict rule for everyone.

Start by doing your research

Developing a family-friendly culture involves a number of strategies. It involves a needs assessment to identify where and how such change should take place. As a general guide, the survey needs to collect data on the current and future profile of the demographics of the workforce, the degree of loyalty and commitment to the organisation, and the needs and preferences in regard to existing family support practices and policies.

Other areas of investigation include examining the causes of existing turnover and absenteeism, reviewing the quality and relevance of the current knowledge pool, and the business advantages of a family-friendly culture. Having done this homework, the organisation can then go about implementing a range of assistance programmes and undertake a best practice study that meets workforce needs and expectations. Common areas of action include: articulating workplace commitment, education and information, flexible work, and leave arrangements for child and elderly care.

Articulating workplace commitment

Having done the research, the core values of the business need to recognise that worklife-friendly programmes are integral to the corporate strategy. Resultant strategies must reward and encourage daily expression of values, behaviours and incentives that are congruent with balancing the demands of work with the broader range of personal issues and responsibilities across the life cycle.

Education and information

Nothing beats sharing on-time and quality information on work and family issues. Methods of delivery include intranet, knowledge-sharing events and resource libraries (either fixed or mobile), organisational circulars and counselling services. Possible topic areas include:

- general health information (for example, on AIDS);
- parenting skills;
- communicating with children and elderly people;
- planning maternity or family leave;
- flexible career options;
- raising teenagers;
- budgeting skills;
- life planning;
- holidays and families;

- single parenting;
- dealing with drugs;
- coping with grief or loss;
- setting goals with your partner;
- juggling work / life demands;
- time management at home;
- finding suitable care services;
- coping with physical and mental disabilities;
- confronting learning difficulties;
- coping with depression;
- telecommuting.

Flexible work and leave arrangements

The necessary response to encouraging a family-friendly culture is versatility in both work and leave arrangements. Options include flexitime, part-time work, job sharing, flexible working times based on family demands (for example, being able to take leave during school holidays or a compressed working week), career breaks, telecommuting, a 'virtual office' where an entire group of employees can work from remote sites, leave without pay, and family leave entitlements.

Child and elderly care

In the area of childcare, strategies include establishing joint venture childcare centres both on or offsite, reserving places in community-based centres, providing a nanny service, providing childcare sick leave, providing phones for personal use, and having a family day at work to explain to your children what you do.

In the area of elderly care, strategies include resource services on taxation and community-based support, and on-site care for parents or the parents-in-law of employees.

Acknowledging telecommuting as a legitimate employment option

Promoting the option of working from home or from non-regular office locations dramatically increases the chances of attracting and keeping talented people in your knowledge pool. Whether it is a team member doing project work from home or allowing a salesperson the freedom to maintain communication by e-mail and mobile phone, there are now many logistical and technological options to help maintain the very best people in your business by deploying flexible telecommuting practices.

For too long organisations have demanded that people endure a daily ritual of commuting to a central location by bus, train, plane or car in good and bad weather. In some cases most if not all the work can be handled using telecommunications technology.

Given trends affecting knowledge work and the impact of rapid technological change, telecommuting has become one of the most rapidly growing industries in the world today. For example, in the US workforce it is estimated by Cyber Dialogue, a New York-based research firm, that during 1998 there was a 41 per cent increase in telecommuting, lifting the figure to 8 per cent of the total workforce. Thousands of workplaces worldwide have successfully implemented programmes that have either improved productivity or employee morale. Speaking as an author and consultant who spends most of my preparation time at home, there is no better way to work. Without doubt, in a virtual world of the modern workplace, failure to investigate and benefit from telecommuting would be a serious neglect of the knowledge pool capability.

The person ideally suited to telecommuting

It does take special personal qualities to reap the full benefits of the telecommuting approach. A person who is telecommuting must be:

- an excellent time manager;
- self-disciplined;
- highly independent and able to cope with long periods of isolation;
- a self-starter who can constantly measure performance and output;
- prepared to take on routine tasks such as purchasing stationery and taking numerous enquiries and messages by various forms of technology including mobile phone, e-mail and videoconferencing;
- prepared to join in with others for 'face-to-face' discussions and virtual team meetings as required;
- tolerant of and prepared to learn and invest in new advances in technology;
- passionate about getting exercise and social interaction on a regular basis.

The types of jobs that are ideally suited to telecommuting are those involving handling reports, data, sales and research. Occupations include: writers, salespersons, accountants, graphic artists, engineers and researchers to name a few. People with other responsibilities that involve some face-to-face work in offices may wish to schedule such activities on certain days and work elsewhere at other times. All this means greater flexibility in how people use their talents while maintaining the quality of life they desire in line with business objectives.

Reaping the pros and minimising the cons

There are a number of pros of successful telecommuting:

- It provides flexible working patterns, and helps keep people in the organisational business brain who might otherwise leave. Reasons for leaving could include childminding, dislike of commuting, a move to a more isolated geographic location, a desire for more autonomy and freedom, or a physical or mental disability.
- It expands recruitment and best practice options within a larger geographic capture area.
- It saves overheads (for example, office accommodation and unproductive time).
- It increases the chances of 24-hour customer service.
- It improves people's health, as they are less likely to be infected by viruses such as common colds that often run rampant through air-conditioned offices.
- It improves customer service, particularly when the 'nine to five' mentality is not suitable.
- It increases employee productivity by having fewer sick days, less commuting time, less office politics and more measurable and productive time.
- It helps place greater emphasis on effectiveness rather than attendance.

The cons of telecommuting are centred around two main areas:

- It takes significant effort to establish and administer the process, given that keeping the lines of communication open does take extra time and effort.
- It creates a level of anxiety and mistrust when people are unable to directly observe and control others. However, with established communication rituals and access to intranet and groupware facilities many of the disadvantages can be overcome.

Overcoming fears

Most of the difficulties of telecommuting can be handled if appropriately managed. What is essential, however, is that the process remains voluntary; as soon as it becomes mandatory it is prone to failure. Associated with this is a preparedness to review and survey the workforce and knowledge pool to ensure that the best telecommuting options are being accessed.

Like most of the strategies discussed throughout this book, implementing telecommuting should follow the principles of excellent project, change and performance management.

Effectively managing virtual work teams

As mentioned on numerous occasions, virtual work teams are becoming a major phenomenon of modern workplace learning.

Clearly, having team members located in different time zones and places provides many challenges. Given the quality and cost effectiveness of modern digital technology this trend is set to continue. Gone are the days when teams were located only in one area or proximity. As was discussed in Chapter 12, advances in technology such as desktop conferencing, application sharing, networks and groupware mean that where you live and when you sleep are increasingly less of an issue in teamwork. Of course there are times when you should be physically together but more often than not you can do much of the knowledge work apart.

Not surprisingly, virtual teams are having a major impact on how work and learning is being done. To manage such a process, people need to be sophisticated in how they co-ordinate the team effort. Appointed team leaders or project managers need to overcommunicate key values and messages and invest more and more time in coaching their team on how to link their activities to business objectives. Supplementing this must be an ongoing commitment to strengthen the team performance through active sharing and knowledge creation. There must be a desire to review not only what is being done but also what is being learnt. Fundamental to the process is building a solid, trusting relationship within the team as quickly as possible, even though team members may never physically meet (as with a study team connected by the Internet).

SUMMARY

This final chapter of Part 2 has addressed a number of strategies to revitalise and maintain a knowledge pool in your organisation both now and in the future. To meet this challenge organisations must be prepared to rethink their allocation and composition of business, human resource and workplace learning strategies.

As organisations confront the dawn of a new millennium, there are seven areas that need priority action. These are finding fellow-travellers, investing in survivors' development and retention programmes, investing in literacy enhancement, promoting productive diversity, helping balance the demands of work and family, acknowledging telecommuting, and, finally, effectively managing virtual work teams.

PART 3

Moving To Action

Having explored the abundance of unlimited learning opportunities it is now time to move on to the final consideration: action planning. It is here that the real learning begins, taking the lessons learnt in the previous chapters and applying them to reality.

In moving to action it is easy to become overwhelmed by the enormity of the task, particularly when we are dealing with an ever-evolving and continuously changing workplace. However, with calm reflection and the sharing of wisdom, your understanding and that of others will evolve to another level of insight that will open new doors and reveal new choices.

At times, you may feel vulnerable and at other times you may feel confident. Whatever your mood and reaction, never lose sight of the difference you are trying to make. Even in the most difficult of circumstances it is your sense of mission that will help you prevail. So with excellent diagnosis, a commitment to overcoming obstacles, courage, persistence and celebration, new frontiers will be discovered.

Learn the skill of pursuing a few key goals, rather than trying to do too much. It is far more important to invest energy in building a shared understanding of why learning is important than building hundreds of programmes and initiatives. Secure a better future with promise and hope.

Chapter 20 will help you resolve the many challenges associated with transforming learning in the workplace by providing you with a smorgasbord of activities to guide you into action.

20

A Smorgasbord Of
Action-planning Activities

> *You will learn and grow according to the nature and consequences of your action.*
>
> Robert Anthony

INTRODUCTION

This chapter of action-planning activities has been structured into three exercises, each containing a series of practical questions and activities. These are:

- *Exercise 20.1: Identifying your business needs.* This exercise will help identify your priorities for workplace learning. It explores both business and people issues.
- *Exercise 20.2: Reviewing* Learning Unlimited. This exercise will help you revise the key points from both Parts 1 and 2 that are relevant to your situation.
- *Exercise 20.3: Drafting a written action plan.* As the name suggests, this exercise provides a series of planning activities that will stimulate the development of a plan of action.

HOW TO USE THE ACTIVITIES

When doing the exercises in this final chapter, do not feel constrained by the questions. If you feel that other questions or issues are more important, work with those first. These exercises should only be seen as a guide. Each workplace, business or learning community is different and often the basic principles will need to be adapted to meet contingencies.

If at any time you would like to contact me please do so by e-mailing me on arylatt@oze-mail.com.au or by visiting my Workplace Learning Help Desk at http://www.excelhrd.aust.com/. Good luck!

Alastair Rylatt

Exercise 20.1: Identifying your business needs

1. What is the mission or purpose of your organisation?

_____

_____

_____

2. What are the key themes of the mission or purpose?

_____

_____

_____

3. List the three major business/people issues currently confronting your workplace.

_____

_____

_____

4. List the three major business/people issues that you anticipate will be confronting your workplace in 12 months' time.

_____

_____

_____

5. Which of the business/people issues identified in the two questions above are best handled by non-workplace learning strategies?

_____

_____

_____

---

6. Which of the business/people issues identified can workplace learning help the most? Why?

_____

_____

_____

_____

_____

_____

7. For each of the business/people issues identified, what would you see, hear or feel if these issues were addressed perfectly?

_____

_____

_____

_____

_____

8. Given your answer to the last question, how could you prove or document that better learning would lead to improved workplace performance and knowledge capability?

_____

_____

_____

_____

_____

_____

_____

Exercise 20.2: Reviewing *Learning Unlimited*

The following questions are designed to help you revise the key points made in *Learning Unlimited*. Remember to use the questions as a prompt. If you believe another question is more appropriate, work with that first.

Introduction

1. Identify one area of personal, team or organisational change that needs significant improvement. Consider this need, in terms of the transformation model ($T = (D + V + K) \times B$) and make a list of a few starting points on how positive transformation can be made.

_____

_____

_____

_____

Part 1: Developing a true commitment to change
Chapter 1: New mindsets for workplace learning

1. Of the new mindsets discussed in Chapter 1, which ones are most integral to your organisation's future?

_____

_____

_____

_____

2. If these new mindsets are not genuinely accepted by your organisation, how could you go about educating your key stakeholders about them?

_____

_____

_____

_____

Chapter 2: Leadership and the learning agenda
1. List your strengths as a change agent.

_____

_____

_____

2. How would your key customers rate your skills as a change agent?

_____

_____

_____

3. What are your priority areas of improvement as a change agent?

_____

_____

_____

Chapter 3: Meeting the demands of change
1. Which workforce and career trends are currently having the biggest impact on your organisation?

_____

_____

_____

2. Describe the impact of these trends on your people and business.

_____

_____

_____

Chapter 4: Championing knowledge work
1. How would you rate your personal and workplace capacity to create new ground and to reflect on past wisdom?

_____

_____

2. Using Exercise 4.1 as a guide, how would you develop or enhance your reflective wisdom?

_____

_____

_____

3. How would you rate the performance of your workplace with regard to Quality or Business Excellence standards?

_____

_____

_____

_____

_____

_____

Chapter 5: Helping the wounded learner

1. Which policies, practices or strategies help wounded learners in your workplace?

_____

_____

_____

2. Which practices or behaviours inhibit employees from dealing with their learning challenges?

_____

_____

_____

Part 2: Proven implementation strategies

Chapter 6: Identifying and evaluating business requirements

1. What is the most practical and readily acceptable way to quantify business improvement for workplace learning and knowledge sharing in your organisation?

_____

_____

_____

_____

Chapter 7: Gaining and maintaining political support

1. Who are the stakeholders and fellow-travellers who hold the key to the success of workplace learning in your business?

_____

_____

_____

2. Which business or political issues will gain the greatest support or endorsement from these people at this time?

_____

_____

_____

_____

3. How could you go about gaining visible political endorsement?

_____

_____

_____

_____

Chapter 8: Empowering ownership for learning

1. What current policies, practices and attitudes encourage involvement in workplace learning?

_____

_____

_____

_____

2. What current policies, practices and attitudes detract from involvement in workplace learning?

_____

_____

_____

_____

3. List ways in which involvement in workplace learning could be improved in your organisation:

_____

_____

_____

_____

Chapter 9: Stamping out practices that alienate learning

1. Describe ways in which greater trust or sharing could be fostered in your business.

_____

_____

_____

_____

2. List past events, folklore, regular rituals, symbols or policies that provide concrete evidence of your organisation's current level of commitment to learning.

_____

_____

_____

_____

_____

_____

3. How would you rate the quality of alignment between business, human resource and workplace learning systems in your organisation?

_____

_____

_____

4. Of the 20 knowledge-creation and stimulation activites listed, which would be of most immediate value to your business?

_____

_____

_____

Chapter 10: Benchmarking best practices
1. Given your current business needs, what are the most pressing areas for best practices study?

_____

_____

_____

_____

2. What would be the 'terms of reference' of such a benchmarking study?

_____

_____

_____

_____

3. Who should be on the benchmarking study team?

_____

_____

_____

_____

Chapter 11: Stimulating competency-based learning
1. How would you go about determining the competencies needed to meet your upcoming business requirements?

_____

_____

_____

_____

2. Of the examples listed in 'Ingredient 5: Evidence Guide', which three methods seem to be the most flexible and useful to assess competency-based learning in your business?

_____

_____

_____

Chapter 12: Accessing digital technology
1. Which digital technologies could most benefit workplace learning processes in your workplace?

_____

_____

_____

_____

_____

_____

2. Using Appendix 2, 'Intelligent implementation of a digital infrastructure', as a guide, what would be your first five steps to improve knowledge management within the next six months?

_____

_____

_____

_____

_____

3. What resources do you have that can help you begin this journey?

_____

_____

_____

Chapter 13: Embracing team learning
1. Describe a team that you believe has the capacity to dramatically improve its learning at this time.

_____

_____

_____

2. What changes need to be made to improve team learning within your organisation and your learning community?

_____

_____

_____

_____

_____

Chapter 14: Celebrating learning

1. What milestones or learning celebrations need to be better organised to help acknowledge the outcomes of successful work-place learning?

_____

_____

_____

_____

2. How can storytelling and metaphors be used to improve the quality of workplace learning in your organisation?

_____

_____

_____

_____

Chapter 15: Building learning communities

1. Using the 10 principles listed in 'Sparking human spirit', what could you and your business do differently to foster a greater sense of community?

_____

_____

_____

_____

2. What are your current strengths and areas of improvement in how you create and sustain learning relationships in your life?

_____

_____

_____

_____

Chapter 16: Perfecting on-the-job learning
1. What can be done to improve the level of understanding of learner motivation in your organisation?

_____

_____

_____

2. Which learning resources hold the key to the transformation of discovery and personal growth within your organisation?

_____

_____

_____

3. How could action learning be better utilised in your business or learning community?

_____

_____

_____

_____

Chapter 17: Getting results from training
1. How could the delivery and availability of learning be improved to make it easier?

_____

_____

2. What training products and services are your 'rising stars'?

_____

_____

_____

_____

3. In your organisation, what could be done to improve the transfer of learning? (See discussion on '20 practical tips for transferring learning to the job'.)

_____

_____

_____

_____

_____

4. What are your current strengths as a trainer?

_____

_____

_____

_____

_____

5. What areas of e-learning are you most curious about or need further development in?

_____

_____

Chapter 18: Promoting mentoring and coaching
1. How is positive mentoring supported in your workplace?

_____

_____

_____

_____

2. Describe the best coaches in your business or learning community. What makes them so special?

_____

_____

_____

_____

3. What are the barriers to effective coaching and mentoring in your workplace, and what can be done to overcome these obstacles?

_____

_____

_____

_____

_____

Chapter 19: Revitalising and expanding your knowledge pool
1. Which target groups in your organisation need greater assistance?

_____

_____

_____

_____

_____

2. Which strategies are required to revitalise, expand or retain the 'knowledge pool' of your organisation?

_____

_____

_____

_____

_____

_____

3. What impact is the increased incidence of virtual teams and telecommuting having on your organisation and industry?

_____

_____

_____

_____

_____

_____

_____

_____

_____

Exercise 20.3: Drafting a written action plan

To assist in the development of a measurable action plan, the following activities have been designed to help you achieve your goals.

1. Define a KRA that you wish to achieve in the area of workplace implementation. (To help you develop some initial ideas for your workplace learning process, use the following map to explore and build on your initial ideas.)

Your workplace learning map

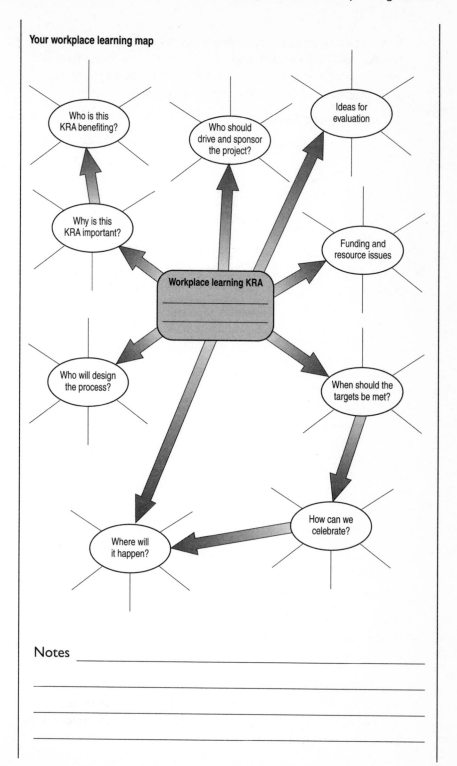

Who is this
KRA benefiting?

Who should
drive and sponsor
the project?

Ideas for
evaluation

Why is this
KRA important?

Funding and
resource issues

Workplace learning KRA

Who will design
the process?

When should the
targets be met?

Where will
it happen?

How can we
celebrate?

Notes _____

_____

_____

_____

271

2. Given your analysis from activity 1, write down the issues that you feel will need action over the next year. In doing so write each issue against one of the symbols listed below (for example, the symbol L could mean develop a marketing plan).

Symbol	Issue
L	
*	
$	
@	
#	
0	
+	
<	
>	
⬭	
Y	
=	
/	
\	
∧	
~	
9	
?	
☐	

Having listed your ideas against the symbols, plot the symbols representing your issues on the priority matrix below. (If you need more symbols just invent some.)

Priority matrix

		Less than 1 month	Between 1 and 3 months	Between 3 and 6 months	Between 6 and 12 months
Potential impact on the success of the project	HIGH				
	MODERATE				
	LOW				

Level of urgency
(when this issue should be actioned and completed)

3. Now complete your action worksheet on the next page. After you have developed your action plan, ensure that you take time during implementation to celebrate success when it occurs. Be prepared to amend your plans as new contingencies arise. It is important to approach decision making with a spirit of discovery rather than an expectation of perfection.

ACTION WORKSHEET

Describe the outcome I will achieve	How will I initiate and maintain it? (Be specific)	Starting date	Completion date	What challenges will I need to confront?
1.				
	List the resources I will need to achieve the desired outcome:			
2.				
	List the resources I will need to achieve the desired outcome:			

How committed am I to achieving these goals?

No _____ Total
commitment   commitment

What can I do to increase my commitment level? _____

APPENDIX I

The Benefits Of Competency-based Learning

The following listing summarises the range of benefits derived from competency-based learning.

Benefits to individuals/employees

- encourages clarification of current competency;
- allows a clearer picture of career path options and the transferability of skills;
- stimulates lifelong learning and goal setting;
- supplies a structure to review learning options;
- provides a benchmark for personal growth;
- creates a common language for workplace learning, performance management and career development activities;
- provides a visible signature of an organisation's commitment to learning.

Benefits to workplaces/industries

- supplies accurate mapping for workforce competency level;
- identifies high-priority workplace learning needs;
- enables comparison with industry and world best practices;
- provides a better structure to promote workplace growth and achievement;
- enables a clearer method to evaluate the suitability of talent;
- provides a structure to improve human resource systems, business planning and continuous improvement processes;
- increases the measurement of prior learning;
- promotes greater opportunity for cross-training and multiskilling;
- provides a common language;

- provides improved portability of people across and between the industry;
- inspires greater confidence that the industry is meeting the right standards;
- sets the foundation for improved international performance.

Benefits to national economy

- improves skills formation which leads to enhanced international competitiveness;
- encourages new international investment;
- provides more efficient and relevant vocational education and training;
- provides a nationally consistent assessment of workplace learning;
- helps maintain consistency between providers and competency frameworks;
- pioneers a national framework to develop accreditation of learning providers and assessors;
- enhances equity and fairness.

APPENDIX 2

Intelligent Implementation Of A Digital Infrastructure

The following notes form a checklist for implementing a digital infrastructure or platform within an organisation to support workplace learning and knowledge management.

Developing a clear vision

- Start by communicating the reasons for the implementation. Common reasons include: coping with change, meeting business demands, process management, staying closer to the customer and overcoming brain drain.
- Ensure you have a clear understanding of why you desire digital technology in your business. Talk about how digital technology changes relationships and corporate culture. Carefully describe how people are expected to behave differently, particularly the shift to a more open, seamless, collaborative and sharing culture.
- Set aside a minimum of three years to bring about large-scale change. Ninety per cent of the change is to do with beliefs and attitudes; implementing digital technology requires you to behave differently in the way you relate to one another. If people can't do that, it won't succeed. The first year they may think you are mad. The second year they start to see the returns, and in the third year you will get the payoff. The dilemma is that no one can wait three years.
- The long-term success of implementation will be determined by ongoing system reviews, proactive management and thinking, clear accountability, consistent skill development and the sharing of knowledge.

Establishing the digital infrastructure

- Develop a measurable financial plan. If you spend more than one-third of your money on the technology, it is an IT project, not an knowledge management project.
- Begin your development from existing resources systems, libraries and databases. Do not feel you have to shelve everything.
- Ensure you have realistic ideas about which processes, networks and tools you wish to use. Identify a clear purpose to a possible structure and organise the tools, processes, storage and systems. Benchmark the best technology options, learn how to use the technology in a cost-effective and enterprising way. Closely weigh up the opportunity costs of all purchases and lease arrangements. Review business impact on a regular basis.
- Develop a common infrastructure of computers, tools and applications. Design smartly by getting the best value out of the networks and set up common standards and protocols.
- Seek out systems that are learner-friendly and inspire curiosity, confidence and measurable results. Place greater emphasis on desire, appetite and attention span rather than on access.
- Assess the current state of awareness and educate people in the fundamentals. Be prepared for significant marketing, promotion and education.
- Work in partnership with others, form joint projects on design, delivery, support and evaluation.
- Allocate dedicated roles for knowledge creation and sharing. Make it mandatory that everyone communicates with the key people who affect their job.
- Use project teams to build and maintain the infrastructure.

Codification and storage

- Getting the best knowledge out of digital technology requires an intelligent human to structure the data in the first place, interpret the data into an identified pattern and make the decisions to take action. Take your time to carefully consider data size, access and data type.
- Build key repositories of knowledge aligned to the corporate vision. Train people on how to input lessons learnt into the archive.
- Set and enforce standards, methods and practices. Coach people on how fast and sophisticated you need to be at a particular point in time. Do not produce a highly interactive multimedia package when an e-mail will do.

- Discover and tap into informal networks of knowledge within the business. Make it your business to find knowledge-sharing champions.
- Determine your stand on access security (inside and outside), and where possible adopt a 24-hours-a-day, seven-days-a-week, inclusive approach.

Filtering and upkeep

Remember knowledge can become information if there is too much, it is unmanageable or poorly filtered. Appoint key people to maintain and review the databank. All knowledge must be reviewed for usefulness and appropriateness.

Key questions to consider in the filtering and upkeeping of knowledge include:

- Is the current knowledge good enough?
- Where do we need more content, or more people to create and share vital knowledge?
- Where do we need to develop people faster or share things more quickly?
- Is the right knowledge getting to the right seeker?
- What navigational support is required?
- Which messages should the leaders be giving?

Each year, ask yourself whether you spend a smaller percentage of resources on keeping systems running or a greater percentage on new business solutions.

The value of storytelling cannot be underestimated; a convincing narrative delivered with elegance and passion can make all the difference.

Coaching

- Digital technology has a polarising effect. It often frightens or confuses people, so do not ignore the human psychology.
- Early success and familiarisation is the key. Accept that digital technology will not suit everyone and at best people will need plenty of time, coaching, customer support and training to use the options available.
- Coach people in how best to use and benefit from the technology. Choice of the right tool can lead to a desire to contribute. Use internal and external mentors and consultants to support the change.

Rewarding contribution

- Start with a pilot scheme on a small scale. Accomplish something first, then trumpet what has been achieved. Don't publish a success until you have done something worthwhile.
- Contributions must be rewarded in financial and non-financial ways.

Celebrating success

- Ensure that learners and the organisation take time to celebrate their achievements in using the technologies.
- Develop the science of continuous improvement of the processes from design right through to monitoring improvement and wastage.

APPENDIX 3

Tips For The One-to-one Coaching Session

The key issues to be remembered by a coach during a one-to-one session are:

- Set aside at least an hour of uninterrupted discussion.
- Treat each person as you would like to be treated – with respect and dignity.
- Ensure that both parties are clear about the expectations for the discussion.
- Probe for understanding, and listen for the key words and phrases.
- Ensure that both parties accept their role in promoting workplace learning, career development and business enhancement.
- Encourage self-assessment and discovery.
- Paraphrase and test understanding during the discussion.
- Help the individual to recognise the difference between fact and opinion.
- Let the learner do most of the talking.
- Accept the learner's comments and emotions with empathy.
- Recommend resources where appropriate.
- Ensure total confidentiality.
- Finish in a positive way, ensuring an action or strategy has been agreed.
- Always give the individual the right to agree or disagree.
- Recognise that the person may choose not to share some personal information with you.

Above all else, be kind to yourself and recognise that the repertoire of skills required to conduct a coaching session takes time to develop.

APPENDIX 4

Powerful Questions For One-to-one Coaching Sessions

To improve the impact of discussion, it is recommended that the following discussion sheet be handed out to each individual prior to the meeting. Alternatively, you may wish to customise the discussion sheet to meet your own unique needs.

Give the person at least a week to prepare his or her thoughts. Depending on their issues and concerns, each individual should be encouraged to answer as many of the questions on the discussion sheet as possible.

Discussion sheet

Clarifying the session's purpose and agenda

What goals do you have for your discussion?

_____

_____

_____

_____

The current situation

What do you find particularly interesting in your current job?

_____

_____

_____

_____

What would you like to do less of?

_____

_____

_____

_____

What different learning opportunities or competencies would you like to develop in your current job?

_____

_____

_____

_____

Linking business and individual needs

What do you see as the challenges confronting the workplace at the moment?

_____

_____

_____

_____

Which skills do you have that best enable you to meet these challenges?

_____

_____

_____

_____

What competencies do you feel need to be developed within the next 12 months?

_____

_____

_____

What support or resources do you feel you need to develop these skills?

_____

_____

_____

_____

Interpretation of future plans

What future goals have you established?

_____

_____

_____

_____

How did you identify and research these goals?

_____

_____

_____

_____

What are the advantages and disadvantages of your future plans?

_____

_____

_____

_____

Do you see any link between your future plans and your current responsibilities?

_____

_____

_____

What resources and experiences do you need to help achieve your goals?

_____

_____

_____

_____

How do you plan to keep yourself moving towards your goals?

_____

_____

_____

How confident are you of achieving your goals?

_____

_____

Session summary

What do you feel are the key messages to come out of this discussion?

_____

_____

_____

_____

What do you see as being your next action?

_____

_____

_____

Which resources will you be seeking?

_____

_____

_____

_____

When should we meet again to review your progress?

_____

_____

_____

_____

Further notes

Bibliography

Abernathy, D *et al* (1999) 'Trendz', *Training and Development*, November.

Abernathy, D (1999a) 'Internet2: The next generation', *Training and Development*, February.

Abernathy, D (1999b) 'What's ahead for online learning', *Training and Development*, May.

Abernathy, D (1999c) 'An intranet renaissance', *Training and Development*, August.

Abernathy, D (1999d) 'WWW. Online. Learning', *Training and Development*, September.

Australian Committee for Training and Curriculum ACTRAC (renamed Australian Training Products Limited) (1995) *Workplace Training Category 2 – Certificate IV: Participant workbook and overhead transparencies*, ACTRAC, Melbourne.

American Society for Training and Development (ASTD) (1999) *1999 Measurement Kit: Tools for benchmarking and continuous improvement*, ASTD, Alexandria, Virginia.

ASTD (1986) 'Career guidance discussions: A resource for managers', Info-Line Series, ASTD, Alexandria, Virginia.

Argyris, C (1982) 'The executive mind and double loop learning', *Organizational Dynamics*, August, pp 5–22.

Argyris, C (1993) *Knowledge for Action: A guide to overcoming barriers to organizational change*, Jossey-Bass, San Francisco.

Australian Human Resource Institute (1999) 'War for talented workers hots up', *HR Monthly*, October, pp 30–31.

Australian National Training Authority (1998) *Frontline Focus – Implementing the frontline management initiative*, Prentice Hall, Sydney.

Australian Quality Council Limited (1999) *2000 Australian Quality Awards for Business Excellence*, Australian Quality Council Limited, Sydney.

Barton, T (1999) 'Harnessing online learning', *Training and Development*, September, pp 28–33.

Beck, M (1992) 'Learning organisations: How to create them', *Industrial and Commerical Training*, **21** (3) Spring, pp 21–28.

Beckhard, R and Harris, R T (1977) *Organizational Transitions: Managing complex change*, Addison Wesley, Reading.

Bell, C R (1996) *Managers as Mentors: Building partnerships for learning*, Berrett-Koehler, San Francisco.

Bellman, G (1992) *Getting Things Done when You are not in Charge*, Berrett-Koehler, San Francisco.

Bishop, K (1999) 'Execs Inc', *Sydney Morning Herald*, 24 April, Employment Supplement.

Bolles, R N (1998) *The 1999 What Colour Is Your Parachute*, Ten Speed Press, Berkley, California.

Camp, R (1989) *Benchmarking*, ASQC Quality Press, Milwaukee.

Cartell, A (1999) 'Learning to learn – voyage of discovery for all involved', *Training and Development in Australia*, August.

Caudron, S (1999) 'Now what', *Training and Development*, September.

Chattell, A (1998) *Creating Value in the Digital Era*, Macmillian Business, Basingstoke.

Chang, R Y (1994) *Success through Teamwork*, Richard Chang Associates Inc., Publications Division, Irvine.

Clanon, J (1999) 'Organizational transformation from the inside out: Reinventing the MIT Center for Organizational Learning', *The Learning Organization*, MCB University Press, **6**, (4), pp 147–56.

Clutterbuck, D (1985) *Everyone Needs a Mentor*, Institute of Personnel Management, Bugbrooke.

Confessore, G and Confessore, S (1992) *Guideposts to Self Directed Learning*, Organisational Design and Development, Pennsylvania.

Cox, E and Leonard, H (1991) *From Ummm ... to Aha! Recognising women's skills*, Women's Research and Employment Initiatives Program, Australian Government Publishing Service, Canberra.

Csikszentmihalyi, M (1997) *Finding Flow: The psychology of engagement with everyday life*, Basic Books, New York.

Dalmau, T, Dick, B and Boas, P (1989) *Getting to Change*, Interchange Publishers, Kenmore.

Dalton, G W and Thompson, P H (1986) *Novations Strategies for Career Management*, Scott, Foresman & Company, London.

Davenport, T H and Prusak, L (1998) *Working Knowledge: How organizations manage what they know*, Harvard Business School Press, Boston.

de Geus, A (1997) *The Living Company*, Nicholas Brealey, London.

De Lacy, A (1999) 'Understanding the knowledge worker', *HR Monthly*, February.

Derr, B (1986) *Managing the New Careerists*, Jossey-Bass, San Francisco.

Dick, B (1999) *Values in Action*, 2nd edn, Interchange Publishers, Chapel Hill.

Digh, P (1999) 'Mentoring is about developing people', *Training and Development in Australia*, October, pp 6–7.

Donovan, G (1998) *The Customer and the Performance Power of Self Managed Teams*, Wellness Australia – Workplace Global Network, Subiaco.

Dryden, G and Vos, J (1997) *The Learning Revolution*, 2nd edn, The Learning Web, Auckland.

Duarte, D L and Synder, N T (1999) *Mastering Virtual Teams*, Jossey-Bass, San Francisco.

Dunphy, D and Stace, D (1991) *Under New Management*, McGraw-Hill, Sydney.

Ethnic Affairs Commission of NSW – Human Rights and Equal Opportunity Commission (1993), *Retrenched Workers-Rights Projects*, The Marketing and Public Affairs Division of the Ethnic Affairs Commission of NSW, Sydney.

Evans, C R (1994) *Marketing Channels*, Prentice Hall, New Jersey.

Evans, T (1999) 'The gospel of the learning organisation', *HR Monthly*, May, pp 14–19.

Fetteroll, E C, Hoffherr, G D and Morgan, J W (1993) *Growing Teams*, Goal/QPC, Methuen, Mass.

Field, L (1990) *Skilling Australia*, Longman Cheshire, Melbourne.

Fisher, K and Fisher, M D (1998) *The Distributed Mind*, AMACOM, New York.

Fitz-enz, J (1993) *Benchmarking Staff Performance*, Jossey-Bass, San Francisco.

Fletcher, S (1997) *Designing Competence Based Training*, 2nd edn, Kogan Page, London.

Freeman, J (1998) 'Get a life,' *Sydney Morning Herald*, 30 May, Employment Supplement.

Fulmer, R M, Gibbs, P and Keys, J B (1998) 'The second generation learning organizations: New tools for sustaining competitive advantage', *Organizational Dynamics*, Autumn.

Gardner, H (1983) *Frames of Mind*, Basic Books, New York.

Gardner, H (1991) *Seven Ways of Knowing*, 2nd edn, Skylight Publishing, Illinois.

Gardner, H (1994) *Seven Ways of Learning*, Zepher, Tucson.

Garrick, J (1998) *Informal Learning in the Workplace: Unmasking human resource development*, Routledge, London.

Gates, B (1999) *Business @ the Speed of Thought*, Viking, Melbourne.

Gittins, R (1999) 'When downsizing backfires on the bosses,' *Sydney Morning Herald*, 6 October, p 21.

Goleman, D (1998) *Working with Emotional Intelligence*, Bloomsbury, London.

Goleman, D (1995) *Emotional Intelligence*, Bloomsbury, London.

Gore, A (1998) *You Can Be Happy*, Prentice Hall, Sydney.

Gray, M, Hodson, N and Gordon, G (1993) *Teleworking Explained*, John Wiley & Sons, Chichester.

Grinder, M (1991) *Righting the Educational Conveyor Belt,* 2nd edn, Metamorphous Press, Oregon.

Harper, B and Harper, A (1992) *Skill Building for Self Directed Team Members,* MW Corporation, NY.

Harper, B and Harper, A (1994) *Team Barriers,* MW Corporation, NY.

Harvard Business School, (1998) 'Creating a system to manage knowledge', Harvard Business School Publishing, Boston.

Heermann, B (1997) *Building Team Spirit,* McGraw-Hill, NY.

Henry, J E and Hartzler, M (1998) *Tools for Virtual Teams,* ASQ Quality Press, Milwaukee, Wisconsin.

Herrmann, N (1990) *The Creative Brain,* Brain Books, North Carolina.

Herrmann, N (1996) *The Whole Brain Business Book,* McGraw-Hill, New York.

Hesselbein, F, Goldsmith, M and Beckard, R (1997) *Organization of the Future,* Jossey-Bass, San Francisco.

Honey, P (1998) *101 Ways to Develop Your People, Without Really Trying,* Peter Honey Publications, Berkshire.

Honey, P and Mumford, A (1986) 'Learning Styles Questionnaire, organisational design and development', *HRD Quarterly,* Pennsylvania.

Houston, J (1997) *A Passion for the Possible: A guide to realizing your true potential,* Harper, San Francisco.

Imai, M (1986) *Kaizen: The Key to Japan's Competitive Success,* Random House, New York.

Jaffe, D and Scott, C (1989) *Self Renewal: A workbook for achieving high performance and health in a high stress environment,* Simon & Schuster, New York.

James, J (1996) *Thinking in the Future Tense,* Touchstone, New York.

Jeffers, S (1998) *Feel the Fear and Beyond,* Rider, London.

Jensen, E (1988) *Superteaching,* Turning Point, California.

Jensen, E (1994) *The Learning Brain,* Turning Point, California.

Kaye, B (1985) *A Guide for Career Development Practitioners: Up is not the only way,* University Associates, San Diego.

Kaye, B and Jacobson, B (1999) 'True tales and tall tales: The power of organizational story telling', *Training and Development,* March.

Kanter, R M (1989a) 'Becoming PALS: Pooling, allying and linking across companies', *Academy of Management Executive,* **3,** (3), pp 183–93.

Kanter, R M (1989b) *When Giants Learn to Dance,* Simon & Schuster, London.

Kaplan, R S and Norton, D P (1996) *The Balanced Scorecard,* Harvard Business School Press, Boston.

Kelly, K P (1994) *Team Decision-making Techniques,* Richard Chang Associates Inc., Publication Division, Irvine, California.

Kirkpatrick, D (1993) *Supervisory Training and Development,* AMACOM, New York.

Knowdell, R (1992) 'Career planning and development: It's like a vehicle', *Career Planning and Adult Development Network Newsletter*, November.

Knowles, M (1986) *Using Learning Contracts*, Jossey-Bass, San Francisco.

Knox, A (1986) *Helping Adults Learn*, Jossey-Bass, San Francisco.

Kolb, D, Rubin, I and McIntyre, J (1979) *Organizational Psychology*, 3rd edn, Prentice Hall, New Jersey.

Kotter, J P (1986) *Leading Change*, Harvard Business School Press, Boston.

Lacey, K (1999) 'Building bridges – Making mentoring happen', *Training and Development in Australia*, October, pp 8–10.

Lazear, D (1991) *Seven Ways of Knowing*, 2nd edn, Skylight Publishing Inc, Illinois.

Lazear, D (1994) *Seven Ways of Learning*, Zepher, Tucson, Arizona.

Lei, D, Slocum, J W A and Pitts, R A (1999) 'Designing organizations for competitive advantage: The power of unlearning and learning', *Organizational Dynamics*, Winter.

Leibowitz, J and Beckman, T (1998) *Knowledge Organizations*, St Lucie Press, Boca Raton.

Leibowitz, Z, Farren, C and Kaye, B (1986) *Designing Career Development Systems*, Jossey-Bass, San Francisco.

Leonard, D (1998) *Wellsprings of Knowledge*, Harvard Business School Press, Boston.

Limerick, D, Cunnington, B and Crowther, F (1998) *Managing the New Organisation (Collaboration and sustainability in the post-corporate world)*, 2nd edn, Woodslane, Sydney.

Linder-Pelz, S (1993) *Mid-life Moves*, Allen & Unwin, Sydney.

Lundin, W and Lundin, K (1993) *The Healing Manager*, Berrett-Koehler, San Francisco.

Lynch, R and Werner, T (1992) *Continuous Teams and Tools Improvements*, QualTeam Inc., Atlanta.

McCall, M Jr, Lombardo, L and Morrison, A (1988) *The Lessons of Experience*, Lexington Books, Massachussetts.

McCann, D (1988) *How to Influence Others at Work*, Heinemann Professional Publishing, Oxford.

McGill, M E, Slocum, J W Jr and Lei, D (1992) 'Management practices in learning organizations', *Organizational Dynamics*, Summer, pp 5–17.

McLagan, P A (1989) *Models for HRD Practice*, ASTD, Alexandria, Virginia.

Mager, R F (1975) *Preparing Instructional Objectives*, 2nd edn, Pitman Learning, California.

Mathews, P (1996) *Workplace Learning: Developing an holistic model*, Working Paper No. 5/96, Charles Sturt University, Wagga Wagga.

Margerison, C and McCann, D (1990) *Team Management*, Mercury Books, London.

Marquardt, M (1999) *Action Learning in Action*, Davies-Black Publishing, Palo Alto, California.

Marquardt, M and Kearsley, G (1999) *Technology-based Learning*, St Lucie Press, Boca Raton.

Marquardt, M and Reynolds, A (1994) *Global Learning Organization*, Irwin Professional Publishing, New York.

Maybury-Lewis, D (1992) *Millennium: Tribal wisdom and the modern world*, Viking, New York.

Mellander, K (1993) *The Power of Learning: Fostering employee growth*, ASTD, Alexandria, Virginia.

Michaels, B and McCarty, E (1992) *Solving the Work/Family Puzzle*, Business One Urwin, Homewood, Illinois.

Miller, A and Mattson, R (1977) *The Truth About You*, Fleming Revell, Old Tappon, NJ.

Miller, W R and Rollnick, S (1991) *Motivational Interviewing: Preparing people to change addictive behaviour*, Guildford Press, New York.

Mohrmann, S A, Cohen, S G and Mohrman, A M (1995) *Designing Team-based Organizations*, Jossey-Bass, San Francisco.

Morgan, M (1993) *Creating Workforce Innovation: Turning individual creativity into organisation innovation*, Woodslane, Sydney.

Morrisey, G L, Below, P J and Acomb, B L (1988) *The Executive Guide to Operational Planning*, Jossey-Bass, San Francisco.

Morrison, A and White, R (1992) *Breaking the Glass Ceiling*, 2nd edn, Addison Wesley, New York.

Mumford, A (1997) *Action Learning At Work*, Gower, Aldershot.

Murray, M and Owen, M A (1991) *Beyond the Myths and Magic of Mentoring*, Jossey-Bass, San Francisco.

Noer, D (1993) *Healing the Wounds*, Jossey-Bass, San Francisco.

Noone, L (1993) '5 proven methods for improving employee performance on the job: A special report', *Training Australia*, Sydney.

Norington, B (1999) 'Steggles settles mother's work case,' *Sydney Morning Herald*, 14 August, p 5.

Office for Multicultural Affairs (OMA) (1993) *Australian Business and Cultural Diversity*, Australian Government Publishing Service, Canberra.

OMA (1994) *Best Practice in Managing a Culturally Diverse Workplace – A manager's manual*, Australian Government Publishing Service, Canberra.

Ohmae, K (1990) *The Borderless World*, HarperCollins, New York.

Owen, H (1992) *Open Space Technology*, Abbott Publishing, Maryland.

Phillips-Jones, L (1996a) *The Mentor's Guide*, Coalition of Counseling Centers, Grass Valley, CA.

Phillips-Jones, L (1996b) *The Mentee's Guide*, Coalition of Counseling Centers, Grass Valley, CA.

Popcorn, F and Marigold, L (1996) *Clicking: 16 trends to future fit your life, your work and your business*, Harper Collins, New York.

Richards, C (1999) 'Coles-Myer starts its own university', *Sydney Morning Herald*, 14 April, p 2.

Robbins, H and Finley, M (1995) *Why Teams Don't Work*, Pacesetter Books, Princeton.

Rolfe-Flett, A (1996) *Tailor Made Mentoring for Organisations*, Synergetic Management Pty Limited, Kincumber South.

Rose, C and Nicholl, M J (1997) *Accelerated Learning for the 21st Century*, Delacorte Press, New York.

Rosenbach, W E (1999) 'Mentoring: A gateway to leader development' *Training and Development in Australia*, October, pp 2–5.

Rylatt, A D (1993) 'Australian career development', in *Organizational Career Development*, eds T Gutteridge, Z Leibowitz & J Shore, pp 57–77, Jossey-Bass, San Francisco.

Rylatt, A D (1997) *Navigating the Frenzied World of Work: The complete survival guide*, Woodslane, Sydney.

Rylatt, A D (1998a) 'Building community in our workplace', *People and Performance*, New Zealand Association for Training and Development, October.

Rylatt, A D (1998b) 'Creating and sustaining learning communities', *Training and Development in Australia*, **25**, (6), pp 17–18.

Rylatt, A D (1999a) 'Why do our Titanic ideas get sunk?', *HR Monthly*, Australian Human Resource Institute, July, pp 30–33.

Rylatt, A D (1999b) 'Creating high quality knowledge work,' *Training and Development in Australia*, August, pp 9 –10.

Rylatt, A D (1999c) 'Workplace learning: A new box and dice', *People and Performance*, New Zealand Association for Training and Development, **6**, (5), pp. 25–27.

Rylatt, A D and Lohan, K (1995) *Creating Training Miracles*, Prentice Hall Australia, Sydney.

Scatena, D (1999) 'Three-letter world', *Daily Telegraph*, 4 December, p 36.

Scholtes, P (1988) *The Team Handbook*, Joiner, Madison.

Scott Peck, M (1980) *The Road Less Travelled*, Touchstone, New York.

Seibert, K W (1999) 'Reflection in action: Tools for cultivating on-the-job learning conditions', in *Organizational Dynamics*, Winter, pp 54–65.

Seligman, M (1991) *Learned Optimism*, Random House, Milsons Point.

Senge, P M (1990) *The Fifth Discipline*, Doubleday Currency, New York.

Senge, P M (1994) *The Fifth Discipline Field Book*, Bantam Doubleday Dell, New York.

Senge, P M (ed) (1999) *The Dance of Change*, Nicholas Brealey, London.

Slywotzky, A J and Morrison, D J (1998) *The Profit Zone: How strategic business design will lead you to tomorrow's profits*, Allen & Unwin, Sydney.

Spendolini, M J (1992) *The Benchmarking Book*, AMACOM, New York.

Stevens, P (1990) *Career Transitions*, The Centre for Worklife Counselling, Sydney.

Sveiby, K E (1997) *The New Organizational Wealth*, Berrett-Koehler, San Francisco, CA.

Swiss, D J and Walker, J P (1993) *Women and the Work/Family Dilemma*, John Wiley & Sons, New York.

Tapscott, D, Lowy, A and Ticoll, D (1998) *Blueprint to the Digital Economy*, McGraw-Hill, New York.

Theobold, R (1997) *Reworking Success: New communities at the millennium*, New Society Publishers, Gabriola Island.

Tkal, L (series ed) (1994) *Technology Survey Report: Educational technologies 1994*, Open Training and Education Network, NSW Department of School Education, TAFE, Sydney.

Tomasko, R (1993) *Re-thinking the Corporation*, AMACOM, NY.

Vocational Employment, Education and Training Advisory Committee (VEETAC), 'Assessment of performance under competency based training: Adminstration of competency based training', VEETAC, Sydney.

Wang, Charles B (1997) *Techno Vision II*, McGraw-Hill, New York.

Watkins, K E and Marsick, V J (1993) *Sculpting the Learning Organization*, Jossey-Bass, San Francisco.

Watson, G (1992) *The Benchmarking Workbook: Adapting best practices for performance improvement*, Productivity Press, Cambridge.

Wheatley, M J and Kellner-Rogers, M (1996) *A Simpler Way*, Berrett-Koehler, San Francisco.

Wilson, E (1999) 'Perfect harmony', *Sydney Morning Herald*, IT Supplement, 6 April.

Work and Family Unit of the Department of Industrial Relations (WFUDIR) (1994) *The Workplace Guide to Work and Family*, Australian Government Publishing Service, Canberra.

WFUDIR (1998a) *Newsletter No. 17*, Department of Employment, Workplace Relations and Small Business, 17 August, Canberra.

WFUDIR (1998b) *Newsletter No. 18*, Department of Employment, Workplace Relations and Small Business, 18 December, Canberra.

Yost, E B and Corbishley, M A (1987) *Career Counselling: A psychological approach*, Jossey-Bass, San Francisco.

Young, C (1989) *Balancing Families and Work*, Women's Research and Employment Initiatives Program, Australian Government Publishing Service, Canberra.

Index